ANCIENT PHILOSOPHY

Editions
Commentaries
Critical Works

Edited by
LEONARDO TARAN
Columbia University

A Garland Series

RICHARD ROBINSON

PLATO'S EARLIER DIALECTIC

GARLAND PUBLISHING, INC.
NEW YORK & LONDON
1980

For a complete list of the titles in this series,
see the final pages of this volume.

The volumes in this series are printed on acid-free,
250-year-life paper.

Bibliographical note:
This facsimile has been made from a copy in
the Yale University Library (B398.L8.R63.1962)

Library of Congress Cataloging in Publication Data

Robinson, Richard.
Plato's earlier dialectic.

(Ancient philosophy)
Reprint of the 2d ed., 1953, published at the
Clarendon Press, Oxford.
Includes index.
1. Plato. 2. Dialectic. I. Title. II. Series.
[B398.D5R63 1980] 184 78-66583
ISBN 0-8240-9588-X

Printed in the United States of America

PLATO'S
EARLIER DIALECTIC

λέγε οὖν τίς ὁ τρόπος τῆς τοῦ διαλέγεσθαι δυνάμεως,
καὶ κατὰ ποῖα δὴ εἴδη διέστηκεν,
καὶ τίνες αὖ ὁδοί

PLATO'S
EARLIER DIALECTIC

BY

RICHARD ROBINSON
FELLOW OF ORIEL COLLEGE, OXFORD

SECOND EDITION

OXFORD
AT THE CLARENDON PRESS

Oxford University Press, Amen House, London E.C.4

GLASGOW   NEW YORK   TORONTO   MELBOURNE   WELLINGTON
BOMBAY   CALCUTTA   MADRAS   KARACHI   LAHORE   DACCA
CAPE TOWN   SALISBURY   NAIROBI   IBADAN   ACCRA
KUALA LUMPUR   HONG KONG

SECOND EDITION 1953
REPRINTED LITHOGRAPHICALLY IN GREAT BRITAIN
AT THE UNIVERSITY PRESS, OXFORD
FROM CORRECTED SHEETS OF THE SECOND EDITION
1962

PREFACE

THIS book is called *Plato's Earlier Dialectic*, and not simply *Plato's Dialectic*, because it contains no examination of the theory of synthesis and division prominent in certain late dialogues, namely the *Phaedrus*, *Sophist*, *Statesman*, and *Philebus*. It is concerned only with the presentation of elenchus and definition in the early dialogues, and the theory of hypothetical method in the middle dialogues.

I assume that we can roughly divide the dialogues into three periods, early, middle, and late. By the 'middle dialogues' I mean mainly those which Sir David Ross in *Plato's Theory of Ideas* takes to have been written between Plato's first and second visits to Syracuse, except that I put the *Phaedrus* into the late period, and I regard the *Meno* as on the line between the early and middle dialogues. My middle dialogues are therefore ?*Meno*, *Cratylus*, *Banquet*, *Phaedo*, *Republic*, *Parmenides*, and *Theaetetus*.

Each of the three temporal groups has characters of its own in several respects. In respect of method, the outstanding features of the early period are the Socratic elenchus and the Socratic definition. The notion of dialectic is not characteristic of the early period, but is found in both the middle and the late. Prominent in the middle period is the notion of hypothesis, and in the later period the notions of synthesis and division. This is not to say that no trace of elenchus occurs after the *Meno*, or that no trace of division occurs before the *Phaedrus*, or any such sweeping and simple statement that would be overthrown by a single instance to the contrary. What is meant is a matter of degrees or percentages or emphasis. The presence of just one elenchus in the middle dialogues, and the presence of fifty of them there, would equally overthrow the statement that elenchus was peculiar to the early dialogues; but they would not equally affect the statement that elenchus is prominent in the early and not in the middle or late dialogues.

The first edition of this book was published by the Cornell University Press in 1941; it consisted of 500 copies, and is now exhausted. I am grateful to two members of the staff of the Cornell Press at that time, namely, Stanley Schaefer and

Woodford Patterson, for their kindness and efficiency. They were not able to get me a Greek type suitable for use along with Roman type; but in other respects they made a beautiful book.

Owing to the war I sent no review-copy to the continent of Europe, and I believe no notice has yet been taken of the book there. Reviews were published in U.S.A. and England, some of which are very searching and valuable, and have caused me to make considerable alterations in my text.

Where I still maintain views rejected by my critics, the cause is often a deep difference of view between them and me on the general nature of the progress of human thinking. My guiding assumption about the history of human thought is 'evolutionist'. That is, I assume that each element of our thought has come into existence at some period of our history, so that at some previous period none of our ancestors possessed it. My critics, however, and especially the more philologically inclined among them, tend rather to what is sometimes called 'creationism'. Such and such a truth, they tend to think, must have been obvious since man was man. At any rate in philosophy and logic they think the truth has already been definitively ascertained to a greater extent than I do. Logic tends to seem to them a selfevident and eternally evident science; and they are not impressed by the controversies and doubts and difficulties that have arisen among expert mathematicians and logicians in the last sixty years.

This view, that logical truths are obvious and always have been obvious, entails that anyone who at any time in the past denied or disregarded any of these truths must have been stupid. Hence, when I say that Plato held a view in logic disagreeing with a view prevailing today, my creationist critics take me as saying that Plato was stupid. Thus Professor Wild wrote of 'agreeing with . . . Robinson that Plato was a very bad logician' (*Philosophy and Phenomenological Research* II 546). But I did not say that Plato was a very bad logician, and I hold that he was a very great logician. Greatness in science consists mainly in leaving the subject much more advanced than when you entered it. It does not consist mainly in holding the same views as a majority of men will hold at a later date, or even in holding true views.

When my critic combines the creationist assumption about man's understanding of logic with the view that to make an intellectual mistake is a moral crime, he assumes that I am 'accusing' Plato and ascribing 'guilt' to him. (Cornford in *Mind* for 1942, pp. 386, 388.)

The book incorporates many valuable suggestions from Sir David Ross, my teacher in ancient and modern philosophy, from Professor James Hutton of Cornell University, and from Professor Glenn R. Morrow of the University of Pennsylvania. Each of these scholars was kind enough to read one of the earlier drafts. This second edition incorporates many valuable criticisms by Professor Friedländer (in *Classical Philology*, 1945, p. 253) and Professor Cherniss (in the *American Journal of Philology*, 1947, p. 133), especially in the chapters on the *Meno* and the *Republic*. I have added a chapter on the *Parmenides*, originally written for this book but actually published in *Classical Philology*, 1942; I thank the University of Chicago Press for permission to reprint it. I am very grateful to Professor R. C. Cross, of the University of Aberdeen, for having at my request carefully examined and criticized all the new passages.

CONTENTS

PART I. ELENCHUS

I. INTRODUCTION: THE INTERPRETATION OF PLATO   *page* 1

II. ELENCHUS
The Elenchus in the Early Dialogues—Plato's Discussions of the Elenchus—The Personal Character of the Elenchus—Criticism of the Elenchus   7

III. DIRECT AND INDIRECT
Syllogism in the Elenchus—Direct and Indirect Elenchus—Plato's Awareness of this Distinction—Plato's Conception of the Logic of Elenchus   20

IV. EPAGOGE
Forms of Epagoge in the Dialogues—The Speakers' Conception of Epagoge—The Relation of Epagoge to Syllogism in the Dialogues—The Socratic Use of Cases—Plato's Consciousness of Epagoge—Epagoge and Definition   33

V. SOCRATIC DEFINITION
The What-is-X? Question—Critique of the What-is-X? Question   49

PART II. DIALECTIC

VI. DIALECTIC
Method—Dialectic—Question and Answer—Eristic—Who Invented Dialectic?   61

VII. HYPOTHESIS
The Notion of Hypothesis—The Use of Hypothesis   93

VIII. HYPOTHESIS IN THE *MENO*   114

IX. HYPOTHESIS IN THE *PHAEDO*
Translation of the Passage—The Metaphor of Accord in 100A—The Metaphor of Accord in 101D—Hypothesizing a Higher Hypothesis—Miscellaneous Questions   123

X. HYPOTHESIS IN THE *REPUBLIC*

A Conflict between Plato's Epistemology and His Methodology—Translation of Passages on Method in the *Republic*—Mathematics—The Unhypothesized Beginning—The Upward Path—The Synthesis-Theory of the Upward Path—Mathematical Theories of the Upward Path—The *Phaedo*-Theory of the Upward Path—The Intuition-Theory of the Upward Path—Comments   146

XI. THE LINE AND THE CAVE

The 'Cave' is not Parallel to the 'Line'—Plato's Account of the Relation between 'Cave' and 'Line'—Interpretation of 517—Conjecture (εἰκασία) and the Mathematicals—A General View of the 'Line'—Mathematics   180

XII. ANALOGY

Plato's Use of Hypothetical Method—Plato's Use of Analogy and Imagery—Plato's Discussions of Analogy and Imagery—Plato on Images and Imitation   202

XIII. HYPOTHESIS IN THE *PARMENIDES*

The first part is against Forms—The first part is against Plato's own Forms—Plato thought the arguments serious—Plato never answered the arguments—The second part does not state a doctrine—The second part does not state a method—The dialogue provides mental exercise—Cornford's interpretation combines incompatibles—Translation of the passages on method—Hypothetical method in the *Parmenides*   223

INDEX   281

Part I. Elenchus

I

INTRODUCTION: THE
INTERPRETATION OF PLATO

CORNFORD said that the second part of the *Parmenides* 'is avowedly a preliminary exercise in the study of ambiguities' (*Plato and Parmenides* 130). The student, however, will search the *Parmenides* in vain for any place where Plato 'avows' such a purpose, because the whole dialogue contains no word that could possibly be called a synonym for 'ambiguity'.

Shorey found an 'express recognition' of 'the distinction between extension and intension' in the following passage: 'Do not be surprised if animal is said to be in man, the more in the less. For if you pause to reflect closely, you will find that animal is in man, as it were as a part' (*Classical Philology* XIX 14). Yet this passage neither names the distinction between extension and intension, nor gives a general description of it, but only refers to what we might call a case of it.

The student of Plato is constantly confronted with such baffling facts as these, with the spectacle, that is, of recognized interpreters attributing explicit statements to ancient writers on the basis of passages which say something different. In this bewildering situation it is best to reflect on the nature of interpretation, and to ask oneself what constitutes 'explicitly' making a given assertion.

There are at least five ways in which misinterpretation is very common, and the first of them is (1) *mosaic interpretation*, or the habit of laying any amount of weight on an isolated text or single sentence, without determining whether it is a passing remark or a settled part of your author's thinking, whether it is made for a special purpose or is intended to be generally valid, and so on. The mosaic interpreter, when he is favourably disposed to his author, takes any chance remark and any mention of a new aspect as an important new insight adopted with solemn self-consciousness. More often, however, the mosaic habit of mind is the weapon of the unfavourable interpreter, enabling him to convict his author of contradiction.

(2) Far more common and far more devastating is *misinterpretation by abstraction*. Your author mentions X; and X appears to you to be a case of Y; and on the strength of that you say that your author 'was well aware of Y', or even that he 'explicitly mentions Y'. Because you have abstracted Y from X, you assume that your author did so too. But such an assumption must not be made on general grounds, for no man has ever made or ever will make all the abstractions possible from any one object present to his consciousness. It often takes more than one lifetime for humanity to advance from the more concrete 'A rose cannot be both red and not red' to the more abstract 'X cannot be both Y and not-Y'; and it may take as many years again to get from the latter to some established label such as the phrase 'The Law of Contradiction'. The view that Plato 'discovered the copula' in the *Sophist* is an example of this misinterpretation. There is no word in the *Sophist* that could be translated 'copula'; but what Plato there says very easily suggests to a modern mind the more abstract notion of the 'copula'; and we assume that it suggested the same to Plato.

(3) Closely related to the above is *misinterpretation by inference*. 'Plato says *p*, and *p* implies *q*; therefore Plato meant *q*.' The conclusion does not follow; for Plato may have thought that *p* did not imply *q*; or, more probably, the suggestion that '*p* implies *q*' may never have occurred to him at all; or, most probably of all, even the proposition *q* itself may never have occurred to him. Every proposition implies an indefinite multiplicity of others; and no one ever perceives all the implications of any proposition. Even those consequences which now seem to us to follow most obviously and directly from a given proposition were often not realized by the acutest of earlier thinkers, as the history of thought shows again and again. A well-known example of this kind of misinterpretation is Adam's reading of the theory of 'mathematicals' into the *Republic*. Plato says that there is only one Idea of each kind. He also says that the units which the mathematician studies are 'equal every one to every one'. The latter statement implies that there is more than one unit among the objects of the

mathematician. Hence the two statements together imply that the objects of the mathematician are not Ideas. Hence—and this is the fallacious step—Plato held that the objects of the mathematician are not Ideas. The truth is that Plato when he wrote the *Republic* had not seen the implications, and so had not made the inferences, which seemed so obvious to Adam.

One of the most frequent and most difficult tasks of the interpreter is precisely to determine what the author thought his words implied, as opposed to what those words imply to us. No doubt 'considerations of philosophical probability' must not be disregarded, as Mr. W. F. R. Hardie has said (*A Study in Plato* 157–8); but they should be minimized, or at any rate we should give them less weight on the positive than on the negative side. Thus, if it seems an overwhelming probability to us that *p* does not imply *q*, that is fairly good evidence that Plato did not mean *q* when he said *p*. If, on the other hand, it seems an overwhelming probability to us that *p* does imply *q*, that is little or no evidence that Plato did mean *q* when he said *p*.

(4) Each of the foregoing forms of misinterpretation is frequently used for the sake of *insinuating the future*, that is to say, of reading into your author doctrines that did not become explicit until later. Such insinuation of the future is often a way of improving your author, of smoothing out his mistakes; and it is common both among those who wish to increase the prestige of an ancient writer and among those who wish to recommend a modern doctrine. The oak is in the acorn, no doubt; but we must not leave it at that. There are differences between the tree and the seed, and it is the historian's business to determine them precisely, and to indicate as well as finite words can do the infinite gradations between the former and the latter. The logic of Aristotle differs from that of Parmenides both in quality and in generality and in selfconsciousness and in abstractedness. Where between these two points does Plato's logic come? He who first says that the fourth book of Plato's *Republic* contains a statement of the Law of Contradiction does a service. He who then blankly denies this assertion does only the tiny service of making men wonder. The right second thought is to determine precisely in what respects that passage is a statement of the Law of Contradiction and in what respects not. There is a continuity and also an identity between the Law of Contradiction as it appears in

Republic IV and as it appears in *Principia Mathematica*; there is also a difference.

(5) Every human being's thought comes to an end. It comes to many ends; for not merely does he die, but also, when he dies, many lines of thought which he was pursuing are left at the latest point he reached. Moreover, a thinker's last words on a given subject may appear in one of his early works; for he may have soon lost interest in that subject. It follows, therefore, that it is possible to commit the misinterpretation of *going beyond a thinker's last word*, of ascribing to him not merely all the steps he took in a certain direction but the next step also, which in reality was first made by a subsequent generation. We should look in a thinker's books for his last word; and, having found it, we should recognize that faithful interpretation can translate it, can say how he was led to it, and say what it is not, but cannot say how he was led beyond it because he was not. Plato's famous statement that the Good is 'beyond even Being in dignity and power' is perhaps such a last word, although it occurs in a middle dialogue.

These five errors are errors only when our aim is pure interpretation. From another point of view they may be valuable devices. Many of the great advances and novelties of human thought have arrived in the form of misinterpretations of the past. Plotinus' misinterpretation of Plato is an example. Plotinus by doing what he did undoubtedly enriched human thought more than he would have done by pure interpretation. Furthermore, it is possible to see contradictions in a thinker which he did not see himself, and to detect which half of the contradiction was the new thing, or the important thing, or the thing that harmonized best with his whole thought. It is possible to disentangle a new idea from old matter, and to develop it more than its originator did. Such activities are frequently carried through by thinkers who imagine themselves to be only interpreters, and who would not do their valuable work at all unless supported by this feeling of being not inventors but prophets.

That the work of a Plotinus is more valuable than that of an interpreter need not blind us to the fact that the work of a Plotinus does hinder the purpose of an interpreter, which is to make himself and others rethink the very thoughts that were thought by someone long ago. Interpretation is not just any sort of commentary, including the revelation of the historical causes and consequences of a given thought. It is the re-creation of that thought.

'But is not the way to re-create a man's thought in yourself simply to read his writings? What need is there of any interpretation besides? No doubt, when he wrote in a language unknown to you, you will need a translator; but why anything more? So interpretation seems to be translation and nothing else.'

In a sense it is true that legitimate interpretation is only translation. But we must bear in mind that no translation succeeds perfectly in its aim of making the reader rethink the thoughts of the writer. The new medium and the new mind inevitably introduce some distortion; and the farther they are removed in time and space the greater that distortion is. Besides translation, therefore, the interpreter has the function of removing from the reader's mind certain false impressions which no translation can avoid, and of introducing into the reader's mind certain additional considerations present to the author but, owing to the distance of time and space, not now signifiable by any device of translation. The modern interpreter of Plato has the task, therefore, of elucidating Plato's meaning where we nowadays, even when reading him in Greek, are liable to get the wrong meaning or no meaning from his words, owing to the differences between us and the audience he had in mind; of restoring the impression Plato meant to give, where the passage of time has caused his words, on first reading, to give another. The interpreter must try, as Bergson put it, to restore by a long and roundabout process the single direct impression that Plato intended. Such a procedure can only be an endless approximation, as Bergson pointed out. Every section of every stream of human thinking is unique; and there is no possibility of completely identifying ourselves with Plato even for a second.

The above considerations are meant to justify the unusual severity of the canons of interpretation adopted in this book. I have tried not to attribute to Plato any inference that he does not make in so many words, or any abstraction that he does not have a name for, without giving a special reason for doing so. I have assumed that to possess a single name for an idea is a later stage than to be able to express it only in a sentence, and that, if the author neither names nor states the idea, it requires very special evidence to say he had it. Most fundamentally of all, I have assumed that there is an evolution of ideas, transcending the lives of individuals, that even the most obvious ideas were once obscure and still earlier unknown, and that this evolution, while often proceeding by sudden leaps or 'mutations', often also advanced by very gradual 'variations'. The risk of these assumptions and this procedure is an ungenerous narrowness or blindness to the range of an author's ideas. The prize, in the hope of which I have taken the risk, is a more accurate appreciation of the nuances of ideas and of the history of their realization in the great minds of our race.

II

ELENCHUS

§ 1. THE ELENCHUS IN THE EARLY DIALOGUES

THE outstanding method in Plato's earlier dialogues is the Socratic elenchus. 'Elenchus' in the wider sense means examining a person with regard to a statement he has made, by putting to him questions calling for further statements, in the hope that they will determine the meaning and the truth-value of his first statement. Most often the truth-value expected is falsehood; and so 'elenchus' in the narrower sense is a form of cross-examination or refutation. In this sense it is the most striking aspect of the behaviour of Socrates in Plato's early dialogues. He is always putting to somebody some general question, usually in the field of ethics. Having received an answer (let us call it the primary answer), he asks many more questions. These secondary questions differ from the primary one in that, whereas that was a matter of real doubt and difficulty, the answers to all these seem obvious and inescapable. Socrates usually phrases them so that the natural answer is yes; and if you say anything else you are likely to seem irrational or at least queer. In other words, they are not so much requests for information as demands for an assent that cannot very well be withheld. They often seem at first irrelevant to the primary question, and sometimes they seem to fall into two disconnected groups among themselves. But at last Socrates says: 'Come now, let us add our admissions together' (*Prt.* 332D); and the result of doing so turns out to be the contradictory of the primary answer. Propositions to which the answerer feels he must agree have entailed the falsehood of his original assertion.

Such is the Socratic elenchus, often referred to also as exetasis or scrutiny and as basanismus or assay. It is so common in the early dialogues that we may almost say that Socrates never talks to anyone without refuting him. An exception is his conversation with Cephalus in the first book of the *Republic* (the first book of the *Republic* may be regarded as an early dialogue); but there the subject is personal experience and not abstract ethics.

The sureness of the refutation gives the impression that Socrates possesses knowledge about the subject on which he refutes others. This, however, he invariably denies. 'You treat me', he says in the *Charmides* (165B), 'as if I professed to know the matters I ask about, and as if I might agree with you if I wished to. But that is not so. On the contrary, I inquire into the proposition along with you because I do not know. I will tell you whether I agree or not when I have examined it.' (Cf. *Ap.* 23A.) That is always his attitude; and in harmony therewith he always puts the primary question as a request for information and not as if he were examining a candidate. Throughout the early dialogues, whether engaged in elenchus or not, he usually declares himself ignorant of the answers to all the general ethical questions that he raises. There are some extremely confident statements in the *Apology* and the *Crito*, and in the *Euthydemus* (293B) he admits knowing many small matters; but *Meno* 98B seems to be the only place where he actually professes to know something important.

And we must now observe some other curious disclaimers. Not merely does Socrates sometimes deny by implication that it is the answerer who is refuted ('It is the logos that I chiefly examine', he says, *Prt.* 333C); at other times he even denies that it is Socrates who is doing the refuting. He speaks as if the logos were what was doing the refuting, and as if the logos were a person over whom he had no control, refuting not merely the answerer and himself but even the whole company with equal impartiality and inexorability. He denies that he resembles Daedalus, who made statues move; for the logoi run away without his agency, and he would rather they remained (*Euthyph.* 11D). His language implies that he himself did not foresee the course the argument has taken, but was led along by it blindfold; and that for all he knew the argument might have turned out a proof instead of a disproof of the original thesis. He even implies at times that there is no refutation at all, of anybody or by anybody or anything. There is only a company of persons engaged in determining the truth-value of a proposition, engaged in an impersonal elenchus in the wider sense.

This denial that he is conducting an elenchus is insincere, and constitutes what is known as the Socratic slyness or irony. The arguments could not be so workmanlike and purposeful, the results could not be so invariably negative, by divine inspiration or by mathematical probability. When we examine one of the arguments in detail, and see just what its logical structure is, we become convinced that from the very first of the secondary questions Socrates saw and intended the refutation of the primary answer. There is an elenchus in the narrower sense; and it is Socrates' own work. When he says of an answer 'Well, that is good enough' (*Grg.* 498A), he gives away the fact that, though the answerer has not admitted as much as he expected, he has admitted enough for his downfall. In reality Socrates is always doing what he does openly in *Republic* I 348-9, looking for a way to persuade the answerer that his thesis is false (348A4); and if the answerer refuses to grant him a premiss (348E) he keeps the conversation going somehow (348E–349B) until he has thought of another starting-point which the answerer will admit and which will serve to refute him. The statements that he is 'seeing whether the answer is true' are insincere. So are the earnest requests for instruction by which he obtains the primary answer. So are his occasional invitations to reciprocity in elenchus (e.g. *Grg.* 462A); he makes them only to persuade the other man to submit to questioning; and, when he is taken at his word and made the answerer, his answers soon become speeches. Insincere also is the pose of suffering from bad memory. In the *Meno* (71C) it is a way to entrap Meno into pontificating, so that he can be refuted. In the *Protagoras* (334CD) it is a way of forcing Protagoras to answer questions; and Plato makes an imprudent admirer of Socrates point out the inaccuracy (336D). Socrates seems prepared to employ any kind of deception in order to get people into this elenchus.

Plato depicts or asserts various effects as following immediately from this ironical elenchus. One of these is the bewilderment of the answerer. Though the word 'elenchus' is scarcely used in the *Meno* (apparently only 75D), the thing itself is very much there; and Plato puts the following description of its effect into the mouth of the victim.

Socrates, I heard before I met you that you never do anything but puzzle yourself and others too; and now it seems to me that you are bewitching and drugging and completely spellbinding me, so that I have become saturated with puzzlement. In fact, if I may make a little joke, you are absolutely like the broad electric ray of the sea, both in appearance and otherwise. That fish benumbs anyone who comes near and touches it, and that is what you seem to have done to me now; for

really I am numb in mind and mouth, and I do not know how to
answer you. Yet I have discoursed on virtue thousands of times and to
many people; and done it very well too, as I thought at the time. But
now I cannot even say what it is. I think it is a wise decision of yours
never to leave Athens; for, if you did such things in another city where
you were a stranger, you might be arrested as a wizard. (*Men.* 80AB.)

Plato notes also that this ironical elenchus often had the effect
of making its victims angry with Socrates and ill disposed towards
him. He makes Thrasymachus complain of what he calls 'Socrates' usual slyness' (*Rp.* I 337A). Socrates refuses to make any
contribution himself; but when any other person makes one he
pulls it to pieces. He ought to realize that questioning is easier
than answering (336C). Thrasymachus believes that Socrates
deliberately tries to make trouble in arguments (341A). However
that may be, there is no doubt that the actual result is sometimes
the conversion of a pleasant discussion into a quarrel. Even in the
Laches, where the elenchus is unusually benign in tone, its first
effect is to make two old friends quarrel. In the *Apology* Plato
makes Socrates attribute his unpopularity to the elenchus (e.g.
21CDE, 23A).

Plato also tells us that this elenchus is very amusing to the bystanders (*Sph.* 230C), especially to the young and rich (*Ap.* 23C,
cf. 33C), and that young men treat it as a game and imitate it in
and out of season (*Rp.* VII 539B). This effect would naturally
increase the anger of the victim against Socrates.

§ 2. PLATO'S DISCUSSIONS OF THE ELENCHUS

The picture which we have so far obtained of the Socrátic
elenchus is by no means a favourable one. This elenchus involved
persistent hypocrisy; it showed a negative and destructive spirit;
it caused pain to its victims; it thereby made them enemies of
Socrates; it thereby brought him to trial, according to his own
admission in Plato's *Apology*; and so it brought him to his death.

The question thus arises what Plato conceived to be the justification of the elenchus. For what end was it worth while to be so
destructive and insincere, and to incur so much enmity?

Plato certainly thought that it could be justified. He did not
regard it as a deplorable defect in Socrates' character, to be
explained by medical or psychological doctrines but not to be

justified. He held that it had a sufficient reason and was a valuable procedure, to be retained in spite of some undesirable consequences. Furthermore, he certainly held that its justification was not merely the amusement provided for the bystanders.

There are three passages in the dialogues that offer something like a general discussion of the purpose of the elenchus; and we shall examine each in turn. Let us take first a passage from Socrates' conversation with Meno's servant (*Men.* 84). The question is how to construct a square double the area of a given square. The solution is yet to come; but the elenctic part, in which Socrates disproves the servant's false suggestions, is over, and Socrates breaks off to discuss the elenchus with Meno.

Do you notice, Meno, how far he has advanced already in his recollecting? At first he falsely thought he knew which is the line belonging to the eight-foot square, and answered confidently as if he knew, and did not feel at a loss; whereas now, though he knows no more than he did before, he does at least feel at a loss, and no longer thinks he knows. —You are right.—So now he is better off about the thing he did not know?—I think that, too.—Then did we do him any harm in puzzling him and numbing him like the electric ray?—I think not.—At least it seems that we have made him more likely to find out the truth. For now he will be glad to search for it because he knows he does not know it, whereas formerly he might easily have supposed on many occasions that he was talking sense about the double square if he said that it must have a side of double length.—It seems so.—And do you think he would ever have tried to discover the truth, or to learn what he thought he knew though he did not, if he had not fallen into puzzlement and come to believe that he did not know and desired to know? —I do not think so, Socrates.—Then he was benefited by being numbed?—I think so.

Of two ignorant persons, this passage implies, the one who knows that he is ignorant is better off than the one who supposes that he knows; and that is because the one has, and the other has not, a drive within him that may in time lead him to real knowledge. The elenchus changes ignorant men from the state of falsely supposing that they know to the state of recognizing that they do not know; and this is an important step along the road to knowledge, because the recognition that we do not know at once arouses the desire to know, and thus supplies the motive that was lacking before. Philosophy begins in wonder, and the assertion here made is that elenchus supplies the wonder. Though the passage contains no such word as 'curiosity', we can say without fear of 'misinterpretation by abstraction' that Plato in writing the *Meno* believed that curiosity is essential to the acquisition of knowledge, and that elenchus is the way to arouse curiosity. Elenchus is thus a method of teaching, of instilling intellectual knowledge in other persons. It does not, however, actually increase knowledge, but only prepares the ground for it.

Another discussion of the purpose of elenchus occurs in the late *Sophist* (229E–230E), put into the mouth of another than Socrates, and showing how Plato regarded the elenchus at that time of his life.

Of education one way seems to be rougher, while the other part of it is smoother.—What are these two parts?—One is the time-honoured and traditional method which men used to adopt with their sons when they did something wrong, and still do adopt very often. It consists partly in anger and partly in a gentler sort of exhortation, and the best name for it as a whole is admonition.—Yes.—But some men appear to have reached the conclusion that all ignorance is involuntary, and that no one will ever learn anything if he thinks he is already a wise man in that respect, and that the admonitory form of education involves great labour and achieves little result.—They are right.—So they aim at the removal of this opinion by another means.—What is that?—They question a man on those matters where he thinks he is saying something although he is really saying nothing. And as he is confused they easily convict his opinions, by bringing them together and putting them side by side, and thus showing that they are contrary to each other at the same time in the same respect about the same things. When the man sees this he becomes angry with himself and gentle towards others. Thus he is relieved of great and overbearing opinions about himself, and this relief is the pleasantest of all to hear and the surest for the patient. For just as the physicians of the body believe that the body cannot benefit from the nourishment it receives until the internal hindrances are removed, so do those who perform this purification believe about the soul. She cannot profit from the knowledge offered to her, until the elenchus is applied and the man is refuted and brought to shame, thus purifying him from opinions that hinder learning and causing him to think he knows only what he does know and no more.—That is the best and most temperate state to be in.—For all these reasons, Theaetetus, we must say that elenchus is the greatest and most sovereign of the purifications; and the man who has not been subjected to it, even if he be the great king himself, must be regarded by us as suffering from the greatest impurities, and as uneducated and base in the respects in which the truly happy man ought to be purest and noblest.

Here the elenchus is explicitly subsumed under the general notion of education, and explicitly preferred to another form of education in words of the highest praise. Its nature is illustrated by a comparison with medical purging, which brings out the doctrine that elenchus is not itself the instilling of knowledge, but an essential preliminary thereto, consisting in the removal of an all but complete bar to knowledge naturally present in man. This bar is the conceit that we already know.

The third passage that contains a discussion of the purpose of the elenchus is the *Apology*, one of Plato's early works. According to this work, Socrates at his trial regarded his habit of elenchus as one of the main counts against him, and set out to justify or at least to explain it. He declared that it arose from the Delphic god's response to Chaerephon, which was that no one was wiser than Socrates. He felt that he had no wisdom; but he also felt that the god could not lie. After a long time of perplexity, it occurred to him to approach a man with a reputation for wisdom and study him at first hand. He found that the man thought he was wise but was not. Going then to many other men of repute, he always had the same experience. In one class, the men of skilful hands, there was some real wisdom; but this led to so much conceit of other, non-existent wisdom as more than outweighed it. Socrates concluded that he was really wiser than the wise because, whereas they knew nothing, he knew the single fact that he knew nothing.

But why did Socrates continue the elenchus after he had ascertained these facts to his satisfaction? Because, he tells us (23AB), he felt that the god had imposed upon him the duty of demonstrating to all men that no man is wise. Later he says that the god has told him to philosophize and to scrutinize himself and others (28E); that the purpose of his elenchus and the command of the god is to shame people into putting first things first, and that the first thing is the virtue of the soul (29DE); that he is to the Athenian people as a gadfly to a noble but sluggish horse (30E). In his speech after the determination of the penalty he calls his elenchus an examination of men's lives, for that seems to be the meaning of ἔλεγχον τοῦ βίου (39C); and describes his purpose as to put men to shame for living wrongly.

The *Apology*, like the *Meno* and the *Sophist*, regards elenchus as a way of convincing men that they are ignorant of things they thought they knew; but it places this procedure in a strongly moral and religious setting of which the other two works show little trace. It tells us that the elenchus arose out of a divine oracle, and that Socrates continued it because he felt divinely commanded to do so. It represents the ultimate aim of the elenchus not as intellectual education but as moral improvement. Its purpose is, as it is expressed at the end of the *Apology*, to make men better men, to give them more of the highest virtue of a man: and in practising it Socrates is a moral reformer.

To many persons the Socratic elenchus would seem a most unsuitable instrument for moral education. They would argue that such logic-chopping cannot be followed by most persons, does not command respect, and at best improves only the agility of the mind while leaving the character untouched. Socrates was certainly a unique reformer if he hoped to make men virtuous by logic.

Yet it is clear that Plato consciously intends to depict Socrates as consciously aiming at the moral improvement of his fellows by means of his elenchus. Looking back on the picture from the late *Sophist*, he contrasts the elenchus with another method of altering men which he calls 'admonition'. 'Admonition' includes the more ordinary methods of moral education, such as rebuke and persuasion and harangue and advice. And Plato says that the practitioners of the elenchus deliberately prefer it to 'admonition'.

This is an aspect of the paradoxical intellectualism of the practical philosophy of Plato, and apparently also of the historical Socrates. It hangs together with the proposition that virtue is knowledge. The method of the Platonic Socrates differs from those of all other moral reformers because of his unusually intellectual conception of what virtue is. He believes that you cannot really be virtuous unless you have a philosophical understanding of the definition of virtue. The practice of virtue is identical with the theory of it. The way to become courageous is to find out what courage is. Contrariwise, he who does not know the definition of virtue will not behave in a virtuous manner. When Socrates says early in the *Apology* that he demonstrated to men that they knew nothing, he means that they knew nothing about wisdom and other forms of virtue; for this is the only matter that interests him. And because you cannot be virtuous without knowing what virtue is, there is to him nothing strange or puzzling in representing as vice in his third speech what he represented as ignorance in his first. In order to make men virtuous, you must make them know what virtue is. And in order to make them know what virtue is, you must remove their false opinion that they already know. And in order to remove this false opinion, you must subject them to elenchus. That is the way in which, according to the Platonic Socrates, the elenchus comes to be the appropriate instrument for moral education.

§ 3. THE PERSONAL CHARACTER OF THE ELENCHUS

The Socratic elenchus is a very personal affair, in spite of Socrates' ironical declarations that it is an impersonal search for the truth. If the ulterior end of the elenchus is to be attained, it is essential that the answerer himself be convinced, and quite indifferent whether anyone else is. In the first place, he must believe his own primary statement; otherwise the refutation of that statement will not convict him of thinking he knew when he did not. In the second place, the answerer must be quite convinced of the logical validity of the argument; if he thinks that the contrary of his thesis does not really follow from the premisses adduced, he will again not be convicted of ignorance. Lastly, he must genuinely accept the premisses; that is the implication of *Gorgias* 471D and many other passages. The art of elenchus is to find premisses believed by the answerer and yet entailing the contrary of his thesis. Polus fails to refute Socrates because he cannot find premisses that Socrates accepts. What the ordinary man believes would entail the contrary of Socrates' thesis; but Socrates does not believe what the ordinary man believes. When the refutation is a reduction to absurdity, the conclusion must seem absurd to the answerer himself. Here again Polus fails, for he reduces Socrates' thesis to results that seem absurd to Polus and to most men, but not to Socrates. Socrates and Ctesippus fail in the same way to refute Euthydemus and Dionysodorus (*Euthd.* 294, 298).

Plato brings out the personal nature of elenchus in the *Gorgias*. That dialogue, which contains the root ἐλεγχ- over fifty times in its eighty pages, represents Socrates as contrasting his own procedure with that of the law-courts. Whereas in law-courts you have to convince a third party, namely the judges, in the Socratic elenchus you have to convince your opponent himself. Hence the witnesses who are so effective at trials are useless here. The only true witness and authority is the answerer himself; and if he does not admit the fact it is irrelevant how many others do. The result depends not on a majority of votes, but on the single vote of the answerer (471E–472C, 474A, 475E).

Possibly this aspect of the elenchus explains why Socrates sometimes seems to start the argument with premises that immediately decide the point, and then to hammer out the inference at most unnecessary length (e.g. *Grg.* 474B–479E). The whole essence of the elenchus lies in making visible to the answerer the link between certain of his actual beliefs and the contradictory of his present thesis. This link must be visible to the questioner before the process begins; and so may well be visible to the onlookers too, including ourselves.

In conscious opposition to the ideal of an argument addressed to this man personally, and really convincing him by starting from premises that he really believes, which receives its clearest statement in the *Gorgias*, Aristotle set up the ideal of the listener who has the sense to recognize the expert and accept on faith what the expert tells him are the principles of the subject. 'The learner ought to believe', he says (*S.E.* 2, 165ᵇ3).

By addressing itself always to this person here and now, elenchus takes on particularity and accidentalness, which are defects. In this respect it is inferior to the impersonal and universal and rational march of a science axiomatized according to Aristotle's prescription. Plato might urge, however, that elenchus is the means by which the irrational and accidental individual is brought to the appreciation of universal science, brought out of his individual arbitrariness into the common world of reason.

If the actual Socrates practised elenchus, how did he come to it? Did he first decide to make men virtuous, then cast about for a means of doing so, and then hit upon elenchus? That seems unlikely. More probably he practised it at first simply because it was his nature to inquire into things more deeply than other men, and to be puzzled by difficulties that had not occurred even to the experts. Only when he had been asking questions for some time would he perceive that he knew better than other men in that he knew his ignorance and they did not know theirs. And only when he had thoroughly realized this would he give up asking questions for his old reason (for he would see it to be futile), and ask them now for the new end of reforming the answerer by showing him his ignorance. And very likely the new end would never have occurred to him but for the experience that his questions did actually have that result.

§ 4. CRITICISM OF THE ELENCHUS

The following objection may be made to the method of elenchus: it only tells you *that* you are wrong, and does not also tell you *why*. Real conversion makes you no longer even want to hold your former thesis, because it shows you the reason why you held it and the inefficiency of that reason. But Socrates rarely does this; there are few parallels to that part of the *Gorgias* where, having disproved the view that Pericles and the rest were good statesmen, he goes on to show us why we thought they were. And this is why the elenchus so often misses its avowed aim, the actual convincing of the answerer (*Grg.* 513C), and why what seems to Socrates a conviction may be described by others thus: 'he was bound and gagged by you in the discussion' (*Grg.* 482E).

Plato does not take account of this objection anywhere in his writings. Yet we can indicate with confidence the sort of answer that his writings suggest, the sort of answer that he would have given if the thought had been brought to his notice. The aim of the elenchus is not to switch a man from an opinion that happens to be false to an opinion that happens to be true. It is not satisfied by any exchange of one set of opinions for another, even if the new set is true and consistent whereas the old set was false and inconsistent. The aim of the elenchus is to wake men out of their dogmatic slumbers into genuine intellectual curiosity. The conviction of one's own ignorance involves and includes some dim realization of the difference between knowledge and all opinions whether false or true. In other words, the notion of the elenchus contains a germ of the Platonic conception of knowledge as absolutely distinct from opinion. The elenchus does not directly give a man any positive knowledge; but it gives him for the first time the *idea* of real knowledge, without which he can never have any positive knowledge even if he has all the propositions that express it. It is important to separate the realization *that* you are wrong from the realization *why* you are wrong or what the truth is, in order that the mind may dwell on the question what constitutes being wrong or right.

It may be urged that the elenchus would be more successful without the irony. The insincerity of pretending not to be conducting an elenchus must surely lessen the moral effect. It is not possible to make men good by a kind of behaviour that is not itself good. Furthermore, the irony seems to be a main cause of the anger which, as Socrates declares (*Ap.* 21 E, &c.), often results from the elenchus; and if elenchus really makes people hate you, surely it is bad teaching and a bad form of intercourse in general. We can hardly suppose that after the victims' anger has cooled they admit their ignorance and start to reform their lives, for the *Apology* implies that most of them have remained angry and unconvinced to the end of their days. The beneficial shame that Alcibiades felt in the presence of Socrates (*Smp.* 216), the pleasantness and utility that Nicias found in being refuted (*La.* 188), must have come from a straightforward and unconcealed elenchus; for Socrates could not refute his intimates many times and still prevent their knowing when he was about to do so.

This objection, like the former one, is not noticed or met in the dialogues. We may conjecture, however, that Plato would have dealt with it differently at different periods of his life. While he was writing the earlier dialogues he would probably have defended the ironical form of the elenchus on the ground that it supplied a necessary shock. For it may be argued that he who announces beforehand that he is going to prove you ignorant thereby destroys his chance of doing so, because you will instantly close your mind against him. Especially is this so on matters of right and wrong and good and bad. What is required, therefore, is a drastic shock, a practical demonstration of ignorance accompanied by shame. For this purpose the victim must be drawn into a parade of knowledge, and then there must be a violent reversal of the situation, which can only be accomplished by some such mummery as Socrates practised.

At a later period of his life, however, Plato would probably have dealt with the objection by admitting it and abandoning the irony. The passage in the *Sophist* (translated above, p. 12) makes no mention of irony, and asserts that elenchus makes the 'patient' angry only with himself, but gentle towards others. The seventh

Letter requires that elenchus shall be conducted in a friendly manner (ἐν εὐμενέσιν ἐλέγχοις 344B). The elenchus which Plato came to approve was a contest in which both parties openly admitted that the questioner was trying to refute and the answerer was trying not to be refuted. It was the formal and open exercise for which Aristotle wrote rules and hints in his *Topics*.

Three things happen to the elenchus in the middle and later dialogues. First, as we have just seen, it loses its irony. Second, it is incorporated into the larger whole of dialectic, which somewhat changes its character. Though still negative and destructive in essence, it is harnessed to the car of construction. Though still moral in its purpose, the ultimate moral end recedes a great deal, and a large scientific programme occupies the middle view. Third, while often referred to and recommended, it gradually ceases to be actually depicted in the dialogues. Refutations take less of the total space. Those that do occur are less obvious in form; it is not so easy to point to the separate premises, to the manner in which each is obtained, and to the place where Socrates puts them together and draws the conclusion. They are less purely negative; there is often positive doctrine that is unnecessary to the proof. In the pure form of elenchus, moreover, there tends to be only one refutation to each thesis. For the refutation professes to be final and absolute, or 'iron and adamantine' as Socrates puts it (*Grg.* 509A); but if you add a second you seem to confess that the first was not so. In the middle dialogues, however, we do find more than one argument for the same conclusion; and this is a distinct change in character. Plato now offers a series of considerations making towards a conclusion, and it is possible to admit of any one that it is not conclusive by itself. He has given up the claim to be incontrovertible, and become in truth more persuasive. Thus elenchus changes into dialectic, the negative into the positive, pedagogy into discovery, morality into science.

III

DIRECT AND INDIRECT

§ 1. SYLLOGISM IN THE ELENCHUS

LET us now examine the reasoning that Socrates uses in his elenchus. There are all degrees of explicitness and tacitness in reasoning, so that, whatever definition we frame of the difference between reasoned and unreasoned statement, there will be some passages that our definition does not confidently classify. The dogma merges into the argument by infinite stages; and the argument, in which we are expected to infer one part of a whole from the rest, merges by infinite stages into the description of a coherent system, where each of the parts is necessitated by the rest, but the reader is not invited to infer any one of them, but rather to contemplate the connected structure as a whole. If a writer says 'A is B and therefore C is D', that is an argument. But if he says 'A is B and that is why C is D', it is not an argument; for he is assuming that we already believe that C is D, and merely inviting us to realize that it follows from A's being B. When the conclusion is stated before the premises, then, other things being equal, we more definitely have an argument than when the premises are stated before the conclusion. The more explicit arguments, as those of geometry, always tell you first what they are proposing to prove.

This state of affairs prevents us from discovering any propositions true of all the arguments of the early dialogues as such. We must therefore concentrate on the more explicit cases (excluding, for example, such passages as *Ap.* 28–35, although we should call them 'well reasoned' and systematic); and these will be for the most part passages in dialogue form where the conclusion to be proved or the proposition to be refuted is clearly indicated at the beginning, even if Socrates does pretend not to be refuting it.

Let us follow Aristotle and say that every dialectical argument is either a syllogism or an epagoge (*Topics* I 12). By 'a dialectical argument' let us mean, as Aristotle does, any argument put forward in conversation, proceeding on premises admitted by the other party, and not requiring any special knowledge. It follows that every Socratic elenchus is a dialectical argument. By a 'syllogism' let us not mean, in the narrow modern sense, an argument depending on our insight into the relation of class-inclusion; but, to translate Aristotle's own words, any 'argument in which, after certain propositions have been assumed, there necessarily results a proposition other than the assumptions because of the assumptions'. This broad sense of the term is certainly the only one Aristotle has in mind throughout the *Topics*, from which the definition comes (*Topics* I 1, 100ª25); and probably it is also the only one he has in mind even in the *Prior Analytics*, although he actually studies only class-inclusion inferences there; at any rate his definition of 'syllogism' at the beginning of that work is only verbally different from the definition in the *Topics*.

The meaning of 'epagoge' may be explained later; but first we must deal with the syllogism in the Socratic elenchus. In the dialogues themselves there are no cut-and-dried names for this operation. 'Apodeixis' and its verb occur occasionally in a broad sense that would include both syllogism and epagoge. The noun 'syllogism' does not occur until the middle dialogues (*Cra.* 412A and *Tht.* 186D). The verb 'syllogize' occurs in the *Charmides* (160D) not as something to be done towards the end of an elenchus, but as something to be done in formulating a thesis: you form the thesis by syllogizing or putting together all the relevant facts. It occurs twice in the *Gorgias* (479C and 498E). Literally it means 'add up'; and as we speak of adding up a sum, although strictly the sum is the result of adding the items, so these two passages speak of adding up the conclusion; and therewith we are near to Aristotle's broad sense. The word occurs often in the middle and later dialogues with this sense of 'infer'. The word 'analogize' is also found in the same sense (*Prt.* 332D, *Rp.* I 330E, VII 524D). Another phrase for the same thing is 'What is the consequence of our statements?' (*Euthd.* 281E). The thing itself can often be noticed in the Socratic elenchus, that is, the moment when Socrates, having obtained his premises separately, explicitly brings them together so that their joint implication becomes evident to the answerer. Here is an example.

I say, Socrates, ⟨that the rhapsode is competent to judge⟩ all parts ⟨of Homer⟩.—No you do not say all parts, Ion. Or are you so forgetful? Surely a rhapsode ought not to be a forgetful man.—What am I forgetting?—Do you not remember saying that the science of rhapsody was distinct from that of charioteering?—I do.—And did you not admit that if it were distinct it would know distinct objects?—Yes.— Then on your view the rhapsodic science and the rhapsode will *not* know everything. (*Ion* 539E.)

This moment of syllogizing is the moment when all is made clear. The purpose of the separate premisses, the way they fit together, and the fact that they entail the falsehood of his thesis, now become evident to the answerer. In the earlier stages, while the premisses are being obtained, Socrates is not concerned to reveal the tendency of his questions. Sometimes, indeed, he is deliberately trying not to reveal it, in order that the answerer may not refuse to grant him the premisses he needs. This is a trick that the *Topics* recommends; and Socrates is no doubt practising it, for example, when he obtains his premisses in a queer order (as in *Prt.* 332A–333B). Most of the arguments and fallacies and dodges described in Aristotle's *Topics* and *Sophistical Elenchi* can be exemplified from Plato's early dialogues; and Alexander of Aphrodisias often does so in his commentary on those two works of Aristotle's.

The Socratic elenchus often includes an element prior to the obtainment of the premisses but subsequent to the obtainment of the thesis or refutand. This is the elucidation and elaboration of the thesis. It serves to make the answerer's conception clearer. It gives Socrates time to think of a refutation. It often allows him to interpret the thesis in a way which the answerer accepts as an interesting extension of his idea, but which enables Socrates to refute it as he could not have done if it had been more moderately or more vaguely formulated. Where this element is absent, the reason is sometimes that the answerer has himself developed his thesis in a long speech, and sometimes that Socrates defines the thesis in another way, by deliberately taking it in a perverse sense, so that the answerer is forced to say more precisely what he means.

§ 2. DIRECT AND INDIRECT ELENCHUS

The syllogisms of the Socratic elenchus fall into many types. For some of them we can easily find names from the textbooks of logic. We can recognize here a sorites, there a dilemma, there an argument by elimination or alternative syllogism, there a hypothetical syllogism, there a categorical syllogism in the narrow sense in barbara or one of its other forms. For many more there are no obvious names; and if we tried to make them we might need dozens. But there is one great division which is interesting in itself and important for Plato's theory of hypothesis, the division between direct and indirect argument.

The distinction between direct and indirect applies both to the refutation and to the establishment of propositions. To refute a thesis indirectly is to deduce a falsehood from that thesis; in other words, to show that the thesis entails a consequence which is so repugnant to you that you would rather abandon the thesis than keep it and the consequence along with it. To establish a thesis indirectly is to deduce a falsehood from the contradictory of that thesis; in other words, to show that its contradictory is false because it entails an intolerable consequence. Reduction to absurdity is a case of indirect argument, for absurdity is one form of falsehood. Direct refutation is best defined as any refutation that is not indirect; but we can also say that it is the refutation that reaches the contradictory of the refutand without at any time or in any way assuming the refutand. Direct establishment is best defined as any establishment that is not indirect; but we can also say that it is the establishment that reaches the demonstrand without at any time or in any way assuming the contradictory of the demonstrand. The argument 'A, therefore B' is a direct establishment of B and a direct refutation of not-B. The argument 'A, therefore B; but not B, therefore not A' is an indirect establishment of not-A and an indirect refutation of A. The indirect argument can be just as valid as the direct; in Aristotle's language, it can really syllogize, and not merely seem to. And it is often more striking than the direct.

Whether an argument is direct or indirect is not always clear. This is a surprising statement when we think of the distinction in general terms, and especially when we have just finished defining it; but it is not surprising when we are reading particular arguments and trying to classify them. Perhaps we can always tell confidently whether a geometrical argument is direct or indirect; but very few arguments are as explicit and as formalized as the geometrical. Moreover, it seems that every direct argument can be converted into an indirect argument; for if we can say 'A, therefore B' it seems that we can say 'Not-B, therefore not-A; but

A, therefore B'. And if this is true we can easily believe that an argument could be so vaguely stated as not to have definitely assumed either the direct or the indirect form. The following question of principle adds to the difficulty. When we disprove 'All X is A' by pointing to an X that is not A, is that direct or indirect refutation? To make it indirect we must suppose that our thought is 'If all X were A, this X would be A; but this X is not A; therefore it is false that all X is A.' Yet in practice this would usually appear an absurdly elaborate way of putting the argument; the natural way of putting it is to say 'But this X is not A' and nothing more, that is, to express only the minor premise of the hypothetical syllogism. The question is important for the analysis of the early dialogues, because they use the negative instance very commonly. Their problem is frequently one of definition; and the most obvious way to refute a definition is to produce a case that falls under the definition but not under the definiend, or contrariwise. The best conclusion is that refutation by the negative instance is essentially indirect; but owing to its extreme simplicity and lucidity it is rarely stated in the full form. If we deny this we shall find ourselves making a wide distinction between narrowly related forms. For example, the following argument is clearly indirect: 'If all X were A, then, since P is an X, P would be A; but P is not A; therefore it is false that all X is A.' Yet it differs from the simple negative instance only in that we need an extra premise in order to see clearly that P is a negative instance of the thesis that all X is A. I have therefore classified all arguments from the negative instance as indirect.

Taking only the more distinct and more formalized arguments in these nine dialogues, *Protagoras*, *Euthyphro*, *Laches*, *Charmides*, *Lysis*, *Republic* I, *Gorgias*, *Meno*, and *Euthydemus* excluding the sophists' absurdities, I count roughly thirty-nine arguments of which thirty-one seem to be indirect. Thus about three-quarters of the arguments appear to be indirect. The fraction is greatest in *Charmides*, *Lysis*, *Euthydemus*, smallest in *Republic* I and *Protagoras*.

Every indirect argument is in outline a destructive hypothetical syllogism: 'If A, then B; but not B, therefore not A'. In this formula let us call not-A the conclusion; not-B the minor premiss; 'if A then B' the major premiss; B the falsehood and also the consequent; A the assumption and also—when the argument is a refutation—the thesis or the refutand. Now in some indirect arguments the consequent follows from the assumption immediately, but in others it does not. From the assumption that all men are immortal it follows immediately that all wicked men are immortal; but that Bonzo is immortal does not follow unless we add the extra premiss that Bonzo is a man. Indirect arguments may therefore be divided into those that require extra premisses in order to deduce the falsehood from the assumption and those that do not. Many of them require many extra premisses and a great deal of inference; when that is so the major premiss expands into a long deduction and ceases to look like a hypothetical proposition, and then we lose sight of the fact that the whole argument is in outline a hypothetical syllogism. This happens, for example, in almost any reduction to absurdity in geometry. Of the indirect arguments in the early dialogues some employ such independent premisses and others do not. At *Charmides* 170, for example, from the thesis that temperance is knowledge of knowledge only, Socrates professes to deduce without the aid of any extra premiss the unacceptable consequence that temperance, when it knows knowledge, does not know what that knowledge is knowledge of. The refutation without extra premisses is common in the *Lysis*; otherwise the arguments in that dialogue would not be so unusually short.

In one sense there is an independent premiss in every indirect refutation, namely, the minor premiss of the hypothetical syllogism. Every indirect argument is a reduction to a falsehood. There must therefore be a premiss declaring that the falsehood is a falsehood; and that is the office of the minor premiss of a destructive hypothetical syllogism. But the above distinction within indirect arguments was between those that do and those that do not add other premisses, in addition to the minor, in order to get the consequent of the major premiss out of its antecedent.

When the questioner uses independent premisses in an indirect refutation, he will naturally obtain them first, or one of them first. For the thesis is, in this case, barren of consequences until married to another proposition. Besides, this order conceals the questioner's intention and thus makes the answerer readier to grant the premiss. When no independent premiss is used, the elenchus sometimes begins with an elaboration of the thesis, and this turns imperceptibly into the deduction from the thesis of an intolerable consequence.

In an indirect elenchus the falsehood to which the refutand is shown to lead may be of any kind or sort whatever, provided that the answerer recognizes it to be a falsehood. The elenchus fails, however absurd the consequence may seem to us, if the answerer himself denies it to be wrong, as we see Socrates denying in the *Gorgias* and the brothers denying in the *Euthydemus*. Obversely, the elenchus succeeds, however dubious the falsehood of the consequence may seem to us, if it seems false to the answerer him- self. This is the only thing that can be said about the falsehood universally; but there are certain kinds of falsehood that appear more often than others because of their greater convenience or greater obviousness. In general the two most striking and most useful kinds of falsehood to which to reduce a refutand are absurdity and the contradiction of plain empirical fact. No one cares to maintain a thesis if it has been shown to lead to such a flat denial of our senses as that pigs have wings, or to such an irrationality as that the part is greater than the whole; and Socrates frequently uses both these kinds; and sometimes calls attention to an absurdity by such words as ἄτοπον and ἀδύνατον (*Chrm.* 167C). The most striking form of absurdity is contradic- tion; and this is frequently in Socrates' mind. At *Laches* 196B Laches implies that the previous argument led to a selfcontradic- tion (he is probably referring to 193DE). In *Meno* 82A Socrates fears that Meno is trying to entrap him into selfcontradiction. At his trial Socrates professed to have shown that Meletus contra- dicted himself (*Ap.* 27A). In *Gorgias* 460–1 he professes to have exposed a contradiction between one part of Gorgias' thesis and another; and in two later refutations in that dialogue he seems without claiming it to reduce a thesis to a selfcontradiction (488–9 and 498). A critic blames him for enjoying this operation (*Grg.* 461BC). In the *Phaedo* (101D) he declares that a standing part of his method of discovery is to see whether the consequences of a given hypothesis accord with each other or not. Plato's dialogues often blame the antilogicians or contradiction-mongers; and this suggests that the use of the reduction to contradiction was so common as to lead to abuse.

§ 3. PLATO'S AWARENESS OF THIS DISTINCTION

We have distinguished between direct and indirect refutations; and within indirect refutations we have distinguished those that do not use extra premisses from those that do; and within indirect refutations we have also distinguished those that reduce the thesis to a selfcontradiction from those that reduce it to another kind of falsehood. We have applied these distinctions to the refutations in the early dialogues, and found that some of the refutations are direct and others indirect, that some of the indirect refutations use no extra premisses, and that some of them reduce the thesis to a selfcontradiction. The question now arises whether Plato himself also made these distinctions and applied them to his work.

To say that Plato was as aware of these logical distinctions as we are would be a gross case of 'misinterpretation by abstraction'. Even if we examine his later as well as his earlier works, we can discover no passage in which any one of these three distinctions is stated. Far from realizing the distinctions, he had not even made all of the abstractions that they presuppose; for he has no word for 'premiss' and no word for 'indirect argument'. We have therefore only been pointing out variations that are actually present in the refutations he depicts. We have not been saying, and must not say, that he himself was aware of these variations in the abstract way in which we have described them. No one can ever be conscious of all the distinctions that could truly be made about his own writings; and there is nothing surprising or derogatory to Plato in the view that he had not made these logical distinctions.

On the other hand, to be unaware of a distinction is not necessarily to fail ever to think of either of the distincts; it is more often to think only of one of them, and to apply that one not merely where it is appropriate but also where the other would be appropriate. And this is what Plato seems to have done. Failing to distinguish direct from indirect argument, he thought of elenchus as being always indirect. Not that he explicitly said to himself that elenchus is always indirect, for he did not have the logical term 'indirect'; but that, in stating or discussing any or every elenchus, he habitually *spoke as if* the elenchus consisted in making the refutand lead to a falsehood, which is what we mean by 'indirect argument'. Failing, furthermore, to distinguish the indirect elenchus which uses no independent premiss from that which does, he thought of elenchus as never using an independent premiss. Not that he explicitly said to himself that it never does so, for he did not have the logical term 'premiss'; but that, when discussing or presenting an elenchus, he habitually *wrote as if* the falsehood followed from the refutand without the aid of any extra premiss. Failing, thirdly, to distinguish the indirect elenchus which reduces the thesis to a selfcontradiction from that which reduces it to another kind of falsehood, he habitually thought and wrote *as if* all elenchus consisted in reducing the thesis to a selfcontradiction. It simply *did not occur to him* that an elenchus might sometimes not be an indirect argument reducing a thesis to selfcontradiction without the aid of extra premisses, just as many men have lived to whom it simply never occurred that the earth might go round the sun.

We are liable to object to this interpretation of Plato for three reasons. In the first place, we can point to particular refutations in the dialogues which we should all nowadays agree to be direct. Since these direct refutations are actually there in the dialogues, written by Plato himself and staring him in the face, we feel that he cannot possibly have supposed all refutations to be indirect. In the second place, whether or not there are any direct refutations in the dialogues, the logical possibility of such a species is so obvious to us that we assume that it was obvious to Plato. We feel that a great philosopher cannot have 'overlooked' such an elementary logical point. In the third place, we feel that the proposed interpretation attributes to Plato an actual logical error too gross for him to commit, namely, the error of supposing that a proposition ever can entail its own contradictory without the aid of extra premisses. Surely, we say, there are very few theses that by themselves give rise to pairs of contradictory statements, or that of themselves contradict themselves. A few queer propositions excogitated by modern logicians may do so, such as 'The class of all classes not members of themselves is not a member of itself', but surely not any proposition examined in Plato's early dialogues.

Although the first of these objections appeals to Plato's text, all three of them rest on the belief that certain logical doctrines *must* have been obvious to Plato because they *are* so obvious to any intelligent person. This belief is destructive of any true history of human thought, and ought to be abandoned. Evidently there must have been a time when the human race, or its immediate ancestor, possessed no logical propositions at all, true or false. Nor is there any necessity that logical propositions, when they did arise, should at once be those which seem obvious to us. Nor did logical propositions in any scope and abstractness arise with Socrates or with the early Plato, but, as Stenzel has shown, with the later Plato and his pupil Aristotle (*Plato's Method of Dialectic*, translated by D.J. Allan). The history of thought cannot succeed if we assume from the beginning that some idea or other is innate and necessary to any human mind.

§ 4. PLATO'S CONCEPTION OF THE LOGIC OF ELENCHUS

A genuinely empirical approach to Plato's dialogues gives a result other than that asserted in these objections; for, while it shows that there are many direct refutations in the text, it also shows that Plato regarded these refutations as indirect reductions to a contradiction.

In the *Gorgias* the proposition, that the professor of rhetoric is not responsible for the use his pupils make of their skill, is refuted in a perfectly direct manner, by first obtaining and then syllogizing the two premisses, (1) that if the pupil does not already know the truth about justice the professor will tell him, because the orator must know this, and (2) that he who knows the truth about justice is just. Yet this direct refutation is referred to beforehand as a demonstration that some of Gorgias' statements 'do not exactly follow from or harmonize with' others (457E), and afterwards as a demonstration that Gorgias has contradicted himself (487B). The latter passage also declares that Polus contradicts himself; but each of the three refutations of Polus is direct. Here then we have a striking example of the loose way in which Plato can make Socrates use the term 'contradiction'.

The same looseness appears in later dialogues. In the second book of the *Republic* (380C) Homer's and Hesiod's tales about the gods are abruptly said to contradict themselves, after a discussion which gave no evidence of selfcontradiction. Later in this dialogue (V 457C) the logos or argument is said to agree with itself in a way which seems to imply that it might have contradicted itself. The *Theaetetus* (155B) contains a curious passage of this sort. Plato there brings forward four propositions of such a kind that, as we should put it, the first three together conflict with the fourth. His own description of the situation, however, is that the first three conflict with each other when we add the fourth to them.

This misinterpretation of direct refutations as being indirect reductions to selfcontradiction came easier to Plato because of a certain confusion, or rather because of his failure to make a certain distinction. Every elenchus makes the answerer contradict himself in one sense, namely, in the sense in which the man who changes his opinion thereby contradicts his former opinion. For the answerer agrees to the premisses of the elenchus, and he agrees that they necessitate the conclusion, and the conclusion contradicts his original opinion. But it is one thing to make the answerer see the force of an argument that contradicts his former theory, and another thing to make the theory contradict itself. Plato confuses that contradiction of a thesis which constitutes an elenchus as such with the special form of elenchus which consists in showing that the thesis contradicts itself. The fact that every successful elenchus persuades the answerer to deny his former opinion, that is, to contradict it, made it easier for Plato to assume that every elenchus achieves this result by showing that the former opinion contradicts itself.

The strongest evidence of all is the passage in the *Phaedo* (101D) where Socrates makes it an essential point of method not to discuss an hypothesis itself until you have 'considered its results to see if they accord or disaccord with each other'. This passage entails that Plato was consciously assuming, or making Socrates assume, first, that the consequences of a single thesis may contradict each other, second, that if they do so the thesis is thereby disproved, and third, that the consequences of a single thesis may contradict each other without the aid of any extra premiss. The nineteenth-century readers of Plato saw these implications clearly, and shrank from them. They could not believe that Plato would assert such things, which seemed to them logical monstrosities. Jackson and Archer-Hind accordingly proposed to expel this phrase from the text as spurious. Goodrich (*Classical Review* XVIII 8 ff.) saved the text from mutilation by going through the arguments and pointing out that in reality Plato uses extra premisses. We must understand the term 'hypothesis' in a large sense, he said, as including besides some special proposition the general body of standing propositions on which the questioner may draw for premisses. But both Goodrich and the expungers assumed that Plato's logical views were like ours in a point in which they are not. Even in mathematics, even in logic, the human race changes its opinions from age to age, although much less than in history and politics. The evidence of the unmutilated *Phaedo*-text, and of the dialogues themselves, is that Plato assumed that any thesis may without marriage give birth to quarrelling twins.

The assumption that there are no extra premisses is a natural accompaniment of the assumption that every elenchus reduces the thesis to selfcontradiction. For if additional premisses are introduced, the thesis does not contradict itself by, so to speak, its own unaided efforts. It contradicts itself only because tempted thereto by the evil demon of an extra premiss. Whatever X may be, X plus Y will always produce not-X if you choose Y judiciously.

The assumption that there are no extra premisses is made easier by the ambiguity of the phrase 'according to your logos', which Socrates frequently uses in refutations, especially in drawing the conclusion. The word 'logos' can cover every premiss and every inference in virtue of its meaning 'argument', and yet imply that there has been no extraneous premiss in virtue of its meaning 'thesis'; for in the early dialogues it often means the same as our 'proposition', and the same as 'hypothesis' means in the middle and in some of the early dialogues.

Plato's way of regarding the process of refuting a thesis comes out clearly in his *Parmenides*. Zeno there explains that his book was 'a defence of Parmenides' theory against those who try to make fun of it by showing that, if everything is one, many consequences follow that are ridiculous and contrary to the theory itself' (128CD). This sentence implies very distinctly that certain persons thought that the theory of Parmenides gave rise to consequences that contradicted itself. Nothing is said about any extra premisses that might be required to produce the contradiction. The speaker assumes that the theory by itself generates its own contradiction; and it does not occur to him that the contradiction might really be between Parmenides' theory and certain other propositions that both sides were accepting. Plato goes on to make Zeno say that his own book was an attempt to show that the opposite theory led to even more ridiculous consequences; and here too there is no suggestion that the absurdity was due to the clash of the theory with other accepted beliefs.

Later in the *Parmenides*, after the theory of Ideas has been examined, Parmenides recommends to Socrates the exercise of drawing the consequences of an hypothesis, and of its contradictory, each set of consequences to be drawn out in the fullest detail. Here again the assumption is that these consequences will follow from the hypothesis alone, and not from the hypothesis together with a standing body of other postulates (136).

The last part of the *Parmenides* consists of a long example of this mode of intellectual exercise. Here the hypotheses 'if there is a one' and 'if there is no one', are each separately made to give rise to a great many consequences. In each case these consequences are divided into those concerning the 'one' itself and those concerning the 'others', thus giving four sets of consequences. Each of these four is again divided into two violently conflicting subsets, so related to each other that, roughly speaking, each proposition in one subset is the contradictory of some proposition in its fellow subset. A vast mass of contradictions is thus produced in each of the four sets of consequences. The important point for our present purpose is that in each set this mass of contradictions is represented as flowing simply and solely from the single hypothesis with which it begins. A modern logician, analysing the deduction, would say at once that many additional premisses are introduced; but Plato does not think so. A modern logician would say also that some of the supposed 'consequences' are really definitions; but Plato does not think this either. To put it in modern terms, Plato makes Parmenides proceed as if the number of the postulates in the postulate-set for each deduction were one and only one. Here, then, is overwhelming evidence that Plato thought of refutation as the deduction of contradictions from the refutand alone, without the aid of any other premisses.

So much by way of establishing the proposition that Plato, without ever clearly envisaging the alternatives, regarded all elenchus as the deduction of a contradiction from the refutand alone, without any additional premiss.

IV

EPAGOGE

FOLLOWING Aristotle's doctrine that every dialectical argument is either a syllogism or an epagoge, we have determined the syllogism in the Socratic elenchus. We now turn to consider the part that epagoge plays therein.

By epagoge I mean an argument from one proposition, or from a set of coordinate propositions, either to another proposition superordinate to the premises as the more universal is superordinate to the less universal and the particular, or to another proposition coordinate with the premises, or first to a superordinate and thence to a coordinate proposition. 'Women are weak and therefore men are weak' is epagoge to a coordinate proposition. 'Women are weak and therefore human beings are weak' is epagoge to a superordinate. 'Women are weak and therefore human beings are weak and therefore men are weak' is epagoge first to a superordinate and thence to a coordinate. This is somewhat broader than Aristotle's definition in the *Topics* (I 12), where he simply says that 'epagoge is the approach to the universal from the particulars, for example if the best navigator is he who knows, and so with the charioteer, then universally he who knows about each thing is best'. Both my definition and Aristotle's present definition differ from his account of epagoge and what he calls 'the syllogism obtained from epagoge' in the *Prior Analytics* (II 23), and resemble rather closely his account of what he calls 'paradigm' in that work (II 24).

§ I. FORMS OF EPAGOGE IN THE DIALOGUES

The simplest and shortest form of epagoge is where from one single case you directly infer another single case. Here is an example from the *Hippias Major* (284AB). 'Would not the man who is most competent to teach horsemanship receive most honour and money in Thessaly and wherever else that pursuit flourished?—Presumably.—Then will not the man who can teach the things that are most valuable towards virtue obtain most honour and money in Sparta?' More often in the dialogues we find a plurality of cases used as premisses; two and three are the commonest numbers; four and five are also frequent; anything higher is rare. Here is one from three cases to a fourth case.

Is there anyone, Meletus, who believes in the existence of human things but not in the existence of men? . . . Is there anyone who does not believe in the existence of horses but does believe in the existence of equestrian things? Or who does not believe in the existence of flautists but does believe in the existence of matters concerning flute-playing? There is not, my good man; if you do not wish to answer, I say it myself to you and to these others. But answer the next point. Is there anyone who believes in the existence of divine things but not in the existence of divinities?—There is not. (*Ap.* 27B.)

Those were inferences from a case or cases to another case, that is, from a proposition or propositions to a coordinate proposition. Also very common in the dialogues, and probably commoner, is the inference from propositions to a superordinate proposition, that is, from the cases to the universal. Here is an example from the *Protagoras* (332C) that uses three cases to infer a universal conclusion.

Now, said I, is there such a thing as beauty?—He agreed.—Is there anything opposite to it except ugliness?—No.—And what about this? Is there such a thing as goodness?—Yes.—Is there anything opposite to it except badness?—There is not.—And what about this? Is there such a thing as high pitch of voice?—He said there was.—Is there anything opposite to it except low pitch?—He said there was not.— Then, I said, does each single opposite have one and only one opposite?—He agreed.

Also common in the dialogues is the inference from cases to a universal followed by an inference from the universal to a new case. Here is an example from the *Euthyphro* (10).

Tell me, is the carried carried because someone is carrying it, or for some other reason?—For no reason but that.—And the led because someone is leading it, and the seen because someone is seeing it?— Certainly.—The truth is, then, not that someone is seeing it because it is seen, but contrariwise that it is seen because someone is seeing it; nor that someone is leading it because it is being led, but that it is being led because someone is leading it; nor that someone is carrying it because it is being carried, but that it is being carried because someone is carrying it. [He now infers the universal from these three cases.]

Is it plain what I mean, Euthyphro? I mean this, that if a thing becomes something or undergoes something, it does not become it because it is in the state of becoming it, but is in the state of becoming it because it is becoming it; and it does not undergo it because it is in the state of undergoing it, but is in the state of undergoing it because it is undergoing it. Or don't you agree?—I do.—[Now he infers the fourth case from the universal.] And that which is being loved is either becoming something or undergoing something at the hands of someone?—Certainly.—Then this too is like the previous cases. It is not loved by those who love it because it is beloved, but beloved because it is loved?

For inferring a case from coordinate cases Socrates sometimes uses the formula κατὰ τὸν αὐτὸν λόγον (e.g. *Cra.* 393C), which perhaps we might translate 'by parity of reasoning'. In such inferences the answerer may qualify his assent by saying 'if it resembles the previous cases' (*Prt.* 312A). When the inference goes to a superordinate proposition, Socrates also uses the formula 'by parity of reasoning' (*Grg.* 460B). Once he says 'Then do we put all the others, too, into the same logos?' (*Rp.* I 353CD). A remarkable passage in the *Gorgias* (496D) is thus translated by Jowett: 'Need I adduce any more instances, or would you agree that . . .?' Sometimes he uses the phrase 'all collectively' (συλλή- βδην . . . περὶ πασῶν *Chrm.* 167D, συλλήβδην δὴ ὅρα εἰ ὁμολογεῖς . . . περὶ πάντων *Grg.* 476D). Also, οὕτω καὶ περὶ πάντων (*Grg.* 467D), ἑνὶ λόγῳ (*La.* 185D), ἐν κεφαλαίῳ (*Euthd.* 281D).

§ 2. THE SPEAKERS' CONCEPTION OF EPAGOGE

In what attitude of mind do the characters make an epagoge in a Socratic elenchus? Do they think they are actually seeing the universal in the cases, thus obtaining certainty by way of intuition? Do they think they are reviewing every one of the cases, and thus obtaining certainty by complete enumeration? Do they think they are only obtaining a probable result, liable to be reversed by the discovery of a negative instance? Or do these alternatives never occur to them as distinctly as they are here put?

The answer seems to be that these alternatives do not occur to them as distinctly as here put. Even Aristotle has no full division of the senses in which we may talk about epagoge. At most he offers an account of the difference between the epagogic syllogism and the paradigm (*Prior Anal.* II 23 and 24). For the rest, he merely uses the word 'epagoge' in various senses without ever pointing to or classifying their variety. It is very probable, therefore, that Plato never distinguished between intuitively certain epagoge, enumeratively certain epagoge, and merely probable epagoge. We may try, however, to detect seeds of these conceptions in the dialogues.

Oddly enough, the most visible of these three conceptions is the one that seems to us the most useless and impracticable, epagoge by complete enumeration of the instances. The dialogues often give the impression that Socrates vaguely supposes that he has gone through all the cases. In the *Meno* (87–88), for example, where he induces the conclusion that nothing is really useful unless it is guided by wisdom, the words with which he begins the inference are these: 'Let us inquire what sort of things are useful to us, taking them individually', σκεψώμεθα δὴ καθ' ἕκαστον ἀναλαμβάνοντες ποῖά ἐστιν ἃ ἡμᾶς ὠφελεῖ. Again in the *Gorgias* (474–5) Socrates talks as if he were somehow inspecting all cases of καλόν in order to establish his conclusion that the καλόν is always either the useful or the pleasant. Even where not the shadow of an attempt is made to enumerate all the cases, the impression is often conveyed that we are supposed to have seen them all schematically or in principle, and to be drawing our conclusion on the basis of a complete review (e.g. *La.* 183C). And the frequent phrases like 'the same logos applies to the rest' often seem to be not the actual drawing of the conclusion but a skeleton review of all the unmentioned instances prior to that drawing. We at this period of human history may be overwhelmingly convinced that Socrates has in no sense reviewed all the instances; but it does not follow that Socrates and Plato, because they were no fools, would never have thought they were reviewing all the instances when they obviously were not. It was easier for them to think so because they had not clearly distinguished enumerative from intuitive epagoge, and the sense of having intuited the universal was therefore able to reinforce without conflict or detection the sense of having run through every case. How often even now, for that matter, do we bid a man run through all the so-and-so's when a moment's reflection would show us that he could not and that we do not know what the result would be if he did. Even Aristotle declared that you can tell by epagoge that there are only six kinds of fallacy dependent on language, which is an amazing statement from our point of view (*S.E.* 165ᵇ27, cf. *Topics* 103ᵇ2–6).

Another indistinction also helped to make Socrates feel that he was taking all the instances. The proposition that no Finnish titmouse has any purple colour could never be obtained by inspecting each individual tit in Finland. But suppose I know that there are only six species of tit in Finland, and infer my proposition from an examination of every species. In other words, besides the inference where we obtain the universal by inspecting every one of its particulars, there is the inference where we obtain it by inspecting every one of the subuniversals or species into which it divides according to a given principle of division. In this form the inference depends on a classification in whose correctness and exhaustiveness we should rarely feel much confidence nowadays, but which in many cases satisfied Socrates and his hearers. Thus the division of human affairs into bodily and psychical often enables him to review them all compendiously (e.g. *Chrm.* 159–60, *Men.* 88).

As to the seeds of the conception of merely probable epagoge in the dialogues, it is not easy to point to any particular passage in which it clearly appears. Aristotle in his textbook of elenchus says that the answerer ought to admit an epagoge supported by instances unless he can produce a negative instance. This entails that the conclusion is only probable, and is some slight evidence that this view is actually taken in the elenctic dialogues. That very review of all useful things in the *Meno* which is offered as an example of supposed complete enumeration (above, p. 36) is upset at the end of the dialogue by the appearance of a negative instance, a useful thing independent of knowledge; but this is very small evidence for the conception of epagoge as merely probable, since Socrates says nothing more about the logical aspect of the matter than that we now see our former statement to be false; he does not refer to the argument by which that statement was reached. There seems to be no clear case of the conception of epagoge as merely probable in the dialogues.

As to the conception of epagoge as an intuition of the universal in its cases, Aristotle once connects epagoge and intuition together, but he does not show at all clearly what their relation is (*Post. Anal.* 100ᵇ). Plato's elenctic dialogues show no trace of

entertaining such a connexion in the abstract, as they show no
trace of the abstract conception of epagoge at all; but in those
frequent passages where the conclusion is mentioned before the
cases, the purpose of the cases is often rather to aid our direct
apprehension of the conclusion than to demonstrate it indirectly.
The use of cases to infer a proposition grades imperceptibly into
the use of cases to illustrate a proposition; and between these two
points there must be an interval where the case makes the proposition directly evident. Similar is the use of an impossible
hypothetical case to make evident a truth (as in *Cra.* 432BC).

§ 3. THE RELATION OF EPAGOGE TO SYLLOGISM IN THE DIALOGUES

Let us now consider how epagoge is correlated with syllogism
in the Socratic elenchus. For this purpose we must observe that
in some arguments there is only one inference or movement of
thought; you have one set of premisses; you make one step from
them to the conclusion; and that is all. In others the premisses
have themselves been inferred, by a previous movement of
thought, from earlier premisses. Naming these two kinds simple
and complex arguments, we see that a complex argument may
be partly syllogism and partly epagoge. Within a complex argument, let us give the names 'last step' and 'main step' to the step
which comes last in time and immediately precedes the conclusion; and let us call the previous steps 'previous steps' and 'preliminary steps'. In a simple elenchus, then, the main step is the
only step; but in a complex elenchus the main step is preceded
by others which establish one or more of the premisses for the
main step.

The Socratic elenchus is nearly always a syllogism. More in
detail, the simple refutations are nearly always syllogisms; and
in the complex refutations the last and main step is nearly always
a syllogism. The probable cause of this is that an answerer is very
unlikely to grant premisses from which the contradictory of his
thesis could be obtained by epagoge. In epagoge the premisses
even when taken separately are so closely allied to the conclusion
that we can hardly help seeing that they go together. We might
think, indeed, that there could *never* be a refutation by epagoge,
arguing that, if the refutand is that no A is B, nobody will grant

that this A is B, or if he does the argument is over at once, without any need of our persisting until we have induced the universal that all A is B. But that is going too far. The answerer may admit that this A is B in another form, as that this X is Y, and be gradually brought to see that X is A and Y is B. And refutation by epagoge is fairly easy when the epagoge goes not from subordinate to superordinate but from coordinate to coordinate; for the coordinates may be so named that their affinity is hidden at first. In these and other ways it is possible for an elenchus to be primarily an epagoge; but it is rare in the dialogues, and I can point to very few cases. The first of these is a refutation in the *Cratylus* (387D–390E), which seems to consist almost entirely of the step-by-step epagoge of a very elaborate contrary to the thesis. The procedure is mostly from case to parallel case. Out of six steps only two go up to the universal in order to deduce thence the required case. The possibility of this elenchus seems to depend partly on the fact that the epagoge does not ascend to the universal, and partly on the fact that the contrary, which is a long and complicated proposition, is induced in sections, of which the earlier do not very obviously contradict the thesis and yet vaguely support the later.

Another refutation consisting exclusively of induction occurs in the *Charmides* (167–9). The refutand is that temperance is a knowledge that is of knowledge only. Socrates argues: there is no perception that is of perception only, no desire of desire only, no wish for wish only, no love of love only, no fear of fear only, no opinion of opinion only, no greater than itself, no double itself, no more than itself, or heavier than itself or older than itself. In each of these cases it is either obviously impossible or extremely doubtful that the thing could exercise its function upon itself. Hence it seems very doubtful whether there can be knowledge of knowledge. Here, from a number of coordinate propositions, Socrates first infers the superordinate that nothing can exercise its function upon itself, and then from this superordinate or from the previous coordinates or from both he infers the new coordinate that there cannot be knowledge of knowledge. The only further cases I have noticed in which the main step is an epagoge are the two longest arguments in the *Hippias Minor*.

It thus appears that practically the only function of epagoge in the elenchus is to provide some of the premisses for a final syllogism. When an elenchus is complex, as it usually is, the main step is always a syllogism; and of the premisses for these main steps some are admitted at once by the answerer, some are syllogized, and some are obtained by epagoge. For example, in the *Meno* (87–89) Socrates syllogizes that virtue is knowledge from the two premisses that virtue is useful and that only knowledge is useful. Of these two premisses the first is itself syllogized and the second is obtained by an elaborate epagoge. The premisses of these two subordinate inferences are the starting-points of the whole elenchus and are immediately admitted by the answerer. This subservience of epagoge to syllogism is probably a direct consequence of the fact that elenchus is a purely controversial form of inference. In science as opposed to controversy things go the other way; deduction is subservient to the induction of hypotheses.

We must limit still further the function of epagoge in the elenchus. It very rarely if ever happens that all the premisses for the main step are obtained by epagoge. The only arguments that come near to doing this are two in the *Gorgias*. In the first of these (503–5), Socrates deduces that the good politician will seek to make the citizens just, from the premiss that every good technician seeks to bring order into his material, plus the premiss that order in human souls is justice. He obtains the first premiss by a regular epagoge, and the second by something approximating thereto, namely the analogy: soul/justice = body/health. In the second passage (495–6) he deduces that good and evil are not equivalent to pain and pleasure from the premisses, first that good and evil are contradictories, second that contradictories cannot belong to a thing at once, and third that pain and pleasure can belong to a thing at once. He obtains two out of the three premisses by fairly regular epagoge. I have noticed no other argument that comes as near as these to inducing all its premisses. (Possibly a correct analysis would reveal some case in the first book of the *Republic*, which is very hard to analyse and very full of epagoge.) Probably the commonest structure for a Socratic elenchus to have is a syllogism from two premisses one of which is granted immediately while the other is induced. Very common variations on this scheme are for the uninduced premiss to be briefly syllogized, or for there to be three premisses instead of two.

There appears to be no special character distinguishing the

premisses that are induced from those that are not. For example, it would not be true to say that, when one of the premisses is an ethical proposition and the other is not, the latter is established by epagoge and the former obtained either directly or by syllogism.

The number of refutations containing no epagoge at all is rather high. There are only six examples of real epagoge in the thirty pages of the *Meno*, only six in the fifty-three of the *Protagoras*, and only eight or at most ten in the eighty of the *Gorgias*. The main part of the *Lysis*, that concerned with friendship, has none at all. In the *Laches*, once the work of definition has begun, there is only one epagoge, and that not specially clear (193A–D). Even in *Republic* I, so far as that book can be analysed with confidence, only two fifths of the arguments seem to contain epagoge.

These figures are surprising. When we are reading the dialogues, epagoge seems both more frequent and more important than these findings make it. In the *Symposium* Alcibiades says that Socrates is always talking about 'pack-asses and smiths and cobblers and tanners'. In the *Gorgias* (490E) Callicles says: 'Your talk is always the same, Socrates.' 'Yes, indeed', Socrates replies, 'and always about the same things.' 'Positively', says Callicles, 'you never stop harping on cobblers and fullers and cooks and physicians, as if they were what we were talking about.' Aristotle declares that 'epagogic arguments' may be rightly assigned to Socrates, which seems to mean at least that Socrates employed them often and probably that he was the first man to employ them often and methodically. All these facts make it at first difficult to believe that the office of epagoge in the dialogues is as small as the above figures make it.

Yet there is no real contradiction. Epagoge tends to be, step for step, more obvious than syllogism, both because its premisses have a way of enduring in the memory and because there are often more of them to a single conclusion than in a syllogism. The last and main step may be a syllogism; and yet the premisses of this main step may be obtained by an epagoge whose bulk is far the greater part of the whole argument. But the chief reason for the appearance of contradiction is that epagoge, even in the broad sense defined above, is only a part of a much more pervasive feature of the early dialogues. There is no brief description that successfully conveys a general idea of this feature; but it is something like 'the use of cases' or 'analogy'. It ranges without a break from the clear use of cases in what we should naturally call epagoge to something that we should say is not a use of cases but a use of images or icons. At one end it is epagoge and at the other imagery. Adimantus in the *Republic* (VI 487E) laughs at Socrates for his frequent use of images. Let us try to get some impression of this continuum by taking a few points within it.

§ 4. THE SOCRATIC USE OF CASES

The word 'case' in what follows will mean anything regarded as falling under a universal, whether the universal is mentioned or only implied. This is a much wider and vaguer sense than the legal one in which a case is always a particular event or train of events. A case in the present sense need not be a particular. Socrates' cases are always universal except at the extreme where they become images. An image like the Cave is an individual; but when anything near epagoge is in progress the case is a universal. If induction means explicitly starting from particulars such as these data on this particular eclipse, Socrates practically never does anything of the sort. The premisses of his epagoge are already statements such as that the man who can do most good to friends and most harm to enemies in the way of health and disease is the physician (*Rp.* I 332D); and the speakers never inquire how they came to know these universals.

A line may be drawn within the continuum of the Socratic procedure from the purely inferential to the purely explanatory use of cases. When from certain cases he infers another, without ever stating their universal, the element of explanation is probably wholly absent. At the other extreme there are passages where the case is nothing but an illustration of the universal, and in no sense a recommendation. In the *Protagoras* (312D), for example, the case of the painter illustrates the case of the sophist, but does not prove anything about it. Between come the great majority of the passages in which inference and explanation are combined in various proportions. In the following passage (*La.* 189E–190A) inference faintly colours a use that is mostly explanation.

If we know that a certain thing improves a certain other thing when introduced into it, and if in addition we are able to introduce the former into the latter, it is plain that we know the former thing itself, since we could advise a man how to obtain it easiest and best. Perhaps you do not see what I mean; but this will make it clearer. If we know that sight improves eyes when introduced into them, and if in addition we are able to introduce it into eyes, it is plain that we know what sight itself is, since we could advise a man how to obtain it easiest and best.

The existence, then, of a great many passages where cases are used purely for illustration, and of a great many more where they are chiefly so used, gives us the impression of a pervasively epagogic style and yet does not enable us to swell the list of really epagogic steps of inference.

Another line that may be drawn within the continuum of the Socratic procedure is that from the point where the cases work only by their numbers to the point where a single case is enough. This distinction can be plainly observed without going beyond the examples of real epagoge. In epagoge by supposedly complete enumeration the number of the cases is essential to the result; they must all be there. But when the epagoge is conceived as a form of intuition, each case is sufficient by itself. The distinction also appears in the non-epagogic use of cases. In the analogy proper, and the image, a plurality of cases would actually be worse than one. These forms will be discussed in another context in the twelfth chapter; but, turning now to the other end of the line, we observe that there frequently appears in the Socratic dialogues what may be called the review of cases or the review of instances. In the *Gorgias* (501D), for example, Socrates explicitly proposes to run through a set of cases: 'As I put the questions, say which seem to you to be of this kind and which not.' He runs through a list of goods or usefuls both in the *Meno* (88) and in the *Euthydemus* (279). He runs through a list of καλά both in the *Gorgias* (474–5) and in the famous passage of the *Symposium*. The purpose of the review varies. Sometimes it is an epagoge by complete enumeration (e.g. *Grg.* 474–5). At other times it is an epagoge from cases to coordinate case; Socrates is leading on the answerer, as the word 'epagoge' implies, from cases that he admits to cases he would like to deny. Thus in the *Hippias Minor* (373C ff.), when Socrates is urging the principle that he who does bad willingly is better than he who does bad unwillingly, he starts with running and other physical activities, where the principle seems fairly likely, and passes by a series of carefully graduated instances to moral matters, where Hippias jibs in spite of all. At other times the review is not an inference at all but a methodical search for something wanted. Thus in the *Gorgias* (477BC), when the object is to find the greatest evil, we gather all evils into a few convenient and exhaustive classes, so that we have them all before our eyes, and are then able to see which of them is the greatest. In such cases, however, the review is never, at least in the early dialogues, a genuine search for something as yet unknown; it is never an ideal experiment to see how far a principle holds. It is always subservient to the elenchus, and as such is only one of Socrates' ironical methods of eliciting assent.

From the review that professes to be searching for something it is a very slight distance to the review that determines a case by eliminating all the others. Thus in the *Euthyphro* (7) the question is raised what are the things about which a difference of opinion leads to enmity and anger; Socrates thereupon eliminates in turn matters of number and size and weight and discovers that the answer is the just and unjust and noble and base and good and bad. In the *Laches* (193) he reaches the conclusion that courage is unwise endurance by reviewing various cases of endurance and eliminating all but the unwise. In the *Charmides* (174) he concludes that temperance is knowledge of good and evil by reviewing and eliminating other instances of knowledge.

This eliminative use of instances is largely a negative affair. An affirmative result is obtained only after many negatives. The distinction between affirmative and negative is another of the dimensions that can be discerned in the continuum of the Socratic procedure. Passages occur where the use is purely negative, where the thing in question is simply clarified by saying what is *not* an instance of it. Thus, knowing where there is a gold-mine is not an instance of useful knowledge (*Euthd.* 288E). In this way the negative instance serves to illustrate a proposition or to render it more precise.

Common in the dialogues is the elimination where everything seems to be eliminated and the company is left in perplexity. The second serious passage in the *Euthydemus* consists of such an elimination, and ends, as Crito comments, in 'much perplexity' (292E). The first refutation of the first definition of justice in *Republic* I consists in eliminating all suggested uses of justice until practically none is left and this virtue seems a valuelesss quality. An elenctic dialogue as a whole is an elimination of every plausible answer that the speakers can think of.

The negative and affirmative use of instances in numbers might be called respectively the eliminative and the accumulative use of cases. But the negative use of cases is not confined to the review or use of them in numbers. There is also the negative instance that Bacon made famous, the refutation of a universal proposition by adducing a contradictory case. This occurs either explicitly or tacitly in most of the indirect refutations, providing the minor premiss of the destructive hypothetical syllogism. The use of cases is common in this form in passages from which all its other forms are absent; it is frequent, for example, in the main part of the *Lysis*, where analogy and epagoge are not found. One special reason for its prominence in the early dialogues is that they are largely concerned with the definition of ambiguous ethical terms. The negative instance is the easy way of refuting any proposed definition of an ambiguous term; for, since the definition can only give one of its meanings, you merely have to produce a case that falls under another meaning.

These various ways of using cases, both affirmatively and negatively, both singly and in numbers, both for inference and for illustration, together give to the Socratic elenchus its vivid and concrete character. 'Knowledge drawn freshly and in our view out of particulars knoweth the way best to particulars again;' Socrates' starting-points are not really particulars, but we feel as if they were. His instantial method of arguing requires an unusual ability to range quickly over experience and call up the relevant parts of it. It is closely related to the poet's gift of metaphor, and to the analogical method of argument.

§ 5. PLATO'S CONSCIOUSNESS OF EPAGOGE

Plato shows virtually no consciousness of epagoge as a method. He has no name for it; or, rather, he uses the word but always to mean an incantation. He does not even have the verb in this sense; and a new meaning usually appears in the verbal before the nominal form. 'Epagein' in his pages is generally some kind of introducing or applying. When it means the introduction or citation of an authority to settle a question, that might seem near to Aristotle's sense. But it is a long way from citing authorities to citing instances. Moreover, it was not, apparently, along this line that the word reached its Aristotelian sense. From the *Analytics* (III 1) and other places it seems that Aristotle thought of epagoge not as bringing in an instance but as bringing on a learner to the universal conclusion. Plato speaks once of leading on a person to knowledge (ἐπάγειν, ἀνάγειν, *Plts.* 278A), a passage which will be discussed later; and he calls the conversion of the prisoners in the Cave a periagoge (*Rp.* 518DE); but that is all. Nor has he any other word that indicates this concept.

Leaving the negative evidence of his language, we draw equally blank when we try to find some consciousness of epagoge in any of his methodological observations. He twice makes others declare that Socrates is always talking about cobblers and cooks and so on; but that is not a recognition of epagoge as such. The upward path assigned to dialectic in the Divided Line is not epagoge (below, pp. 163 ff). Nor is anything to be made out of the contempt for the body and its senses expressed in the middle dialogues. This scorn is not equivalent to an unfavourable estimate of the powers of epagoge; for it is probable that, if he realized the logical nature of epagoge, he did not connect it with sensation. The premisses of Socrates' inductions are not sense-data. The connexion which Aristotle laid down between epagoge and sensation (*Anal.* III 18 and IV 19) is not necessary to epagoge in the broad sense given to it in this chapter for the purpose of describing what actually happens in the early dialogues. It seems, therefore, that Plato shows no methodological consciousness of epagoge. Apparently we must conclude that his depiction of it in the early dialogues made no impression on his own theory of method.

§ 6. EPAGOGE AND DEFINITION

When Aristotle says that one might justly ascribe to Socrates epagogic arguments and universal definition (*Metaph.* M 4), he does not mean, as Sir David Ross points out, that Socrates was the first to practise these activities. Nor, on the other hand, can he mean, surely, that Socrates gave an abstract logical account of them such as we find in Aristotle's *Organon*. Such an account would have left its traces in the Socratic writings; but we find in them, as we have just seen, no description of epagoge at all, and, as we shall see, no very abstract description of definition. Aristotle must have meant something between these two points, namely that Socrates pursued what were actually questions of definition, and used what was actually epagoge (although he did not call them so), far more persistently than any previous thinker and so persistently that abstract logical reflections on their nature almost inevitably arose soon afterwards. The reason why he does not include syllogism, although Socrates practised that even more assiduously, is probably that it had previously been forced on the world's notice by Zeno; Socrates was anticipated in his persistent syllogizing but not in his persistent epagoge.

Many readers, including Stewart and Ross, take Aristotle to be implying that the purpose of Socrates' epagoge was to obtain definitions. Aristotle does not here explicitly mention any connexion between the two things except that they might both be attributed to Socrates; nor, so far as I know, is there any passage where he indicates a special connexion between definition and epagoge (except perhaps *Post. Anal.* 97^{b}7–39). The fact that the present passage explains why Socrates wanted definitions, and does not explain why he practised epagoge, has perhaps suggested the view that he regarded epagoge as a means to definition. But the true account of this difference seems to be as follows. The passage is really about definition entirely and not about epagoge at all, because definition is closely related to the theory of Ideas, which is the subject of the chapter. Epagoge enters only in a single sentence, where Aristotle, having declared that Socrates did not practise dialectic, softens what might seem a paradox by admitting that he did practise two things very similar to dialectic, namely definition and epagoge.

This interpretation has the further advantage of removing what would otherwise be a difficult puzzle, namely, why Aristotle ascribes to Socrates only definition and epagoge when Socrates surely introduced some other things quite as much as these. The form of his sentence clearly implies that in some sense *only* definition and epagoge can be justly attributed to Socrates. Yet Socrates introduced also at least the doctrine that virtue is equivalent to the knowledge of good and evil, and, as a practical consequence of this doctrine, his characteristic moral elenchus. This minimum of originality has always been attributed to Socrates; and without it we should not know how to understand the Socratic writers. The explanation of the puzzle is that Aristotle is asking himself only what Socrates introduced *in the way of dialectic*. He answers that dialectic as such arose later than Socrates; but Socrates did introduce two activities very closely related to dialectic, namely definition and epagoge.

For these reasons it is improbable that Aristotle is here suggesting that epagoge was essentially a means to definition. But, whatever Aristotle may have thought, and whatever may be the truth about the historical Socrates, there is as a matter of fact no necessary connexion between definition and epagoge in Plato's elenctic dialogues. The most we can say is that epagoge is an item in the elenchus and definitions are prominent among the propositions against which the elenchus is directed. This implies that epagoge is a means to the destruction rather than the establishment of definitions; and even so it amounts to very little when we go into detail. The propositions that Socrates refutes are by no means always definitions; among them are that justice is better than injustice, that the rhapsode is the best interpreter of Homer, that virtue is teachable, that Socrates ought to escape, that those who become friends are like each other, that those who become friends are unlike each other, that contradiction is impossible. Furthermore, the arguments by which Socrates refutes the refutands, whether definitions or otherwise, are virtually never epagoge in their main step but always syllogism. They merely use epagoge to establish the premisses of the syllogism; and even so there is generally at least one premiss obtained without epagoge. The conclusions directly established by epagoge, that is, the premisses for the main steps, are very rarely definitions; and thus it comes about that what epagoge does directly establish in the dialogues is hardly ever a definition. Even in those rare cases where one of the premisses of the syllogism is itself a definition, such a premiss is directly admitted by the answerer at least as often as it is induced.

V

SOCRATIC DEFINITION

§ I. THE WHAT-IS-X? QUESTION

THE Socrates of Plato's dialogues is continually asking questions. Let us distinguish these into the primary question and the secondary questions. In each discussion he first proposes some important problem, usually ethical; and that is the primary question. As soon as an answer is suggested, he proceeds to examine it by means of a series of questions to the answerer; and those are the secondary questions. This chapter is concerned only with Socrates' primary questions.

These primary questions have, roughly speaking, one of two forms: either 'Is X Y?' or 'What is X?'. Examples of 'Is X Y?' are: 'Is justice better than injustice?' in the *Republic*, 'Are those who become friends like each other?' in the *Lysis*, and 'Ought Socrates to escape?' in the *Crito*. Examples of 'What is X?' are: 'What is justice?' in the *Republic*, 'What is temperance?' in the *Charmides*, and 'What is courage?' in the *Laches*. Of these two types it is the What-is-X? form that stands out and catches the attention of every student of Plato's early dialogues. This is not, apparently, because there is actually more space devoted to the discussion of What-is-X? questions than to the other type; for only three or four of the early dialogues are primarily and directly engaged in such discussion throughout their philosophical parts, namely the *Euthyphro*, the *Laches*, the *Charmides*, and the *Hippias Major*. The *Gorgias*, the *Meno*, and *Republic* I (which we may count an early dialogue) all abandon the question 'What is X?' for the question 'Is X Y?'; while the *Ion*, the *Hippias Minor*, the *Apology*, the *Crito*, and the *Protagoras*, never raise the question at all. The explicit question of the *Lysis* is not what friendship is but what its condition is, although the former question is present as a faint undercurrent, and there is perhaps some confusion between the two. The What-is-X? question therefore owes its prominence in the early dialogues not to spatial predominance but to the emphasis which Socrates puts upon it.

Socrates often expresses dissatisfaction with the answer he

E

receives to his What-is-X? question, on the ground not that it is false but that it is not the *kind* of answer he had in mind when he asked 'What is X?'. Thus in the *Theaetetus* (146), which in this respect is just like an early dialogue, Socrates, having asked 'What is knowledge?' and been told that it is geometry and shoemaking and so on, replies that he asked for one and has been given many. 'You were not asked what things there is knowledge of, nor how many sorts of knowledge there are; for our aim in asking was not to count the sorts of knowledge but to know what knowledge itself is.' He then gives an illustration of the kind of answer he wants: if he had asked 'What is clay?', he would have wanted, not a list of the various sorts of clay, but simply 'earth mixed with liquid' (147C). In this explanation there are two key phrases that Socrates uses to indicate his desire. One is the opposition between the 'one' and the 'many'; he wants the one knowledge and not the many knowledges. The other is 'what X itself is'. These phrases constantly recur when Socrates is talking about his What-is-X? question.

He explains his question at length in the *Meno* (71–77). Here also he gives examples of the sort of answer he requires: if he asked 'What is figure?', a good answer would be 'the limit of a solid' (76A). Here also he uses the opposition of the one and the many (77A): he explains that he wants not some virtue but virtue (73E), that which is the same in all the Xes (75A). The *Meno* also has two other ways which are of great importance to Socrates in explaining the nature of his question. One is the use of the word εἶδος or form; he wants, he says, 'some one identical form possessed by all the virtues, through which they are virtues, to which the answerer ought to look in explaining to the asker what virtue really is' (72C, cf. *Euthyph.* 6D). The other way of explaining the question is by means of the word οὐσία or being or essence; when he says 'What is X?' he wants the being or essence of X (72B, cf. *Euthyph.* 11A).

Socrates frequently asserts that the question What is X? is prior to certain other questions about X, in the sense that we cannot find sure answers to those other questions until we have found sure answers to this one. You cannot, he says, know what *sort* of thing X is until you know *what* X is. Thus you cannot really know whether virtue is teachable until you know what virtue is (*Men.* 71, 86DE, 100B; *Prt.* 360E), nor whether justice is a virtue until you know what justice is (*Rp.* I 354C). You must also know what X is before you can know whether it is beneficial (*Rp.* I 354C and *La.* 189E–190A), or how it is to be obtained (cf. *La.* 189E–190A and all the passages on the teachability of virtue). The most surprising of all his assertions in this line is that at the end of the *Lysis*: 'Well, said I, we have become ridiculous, Lysis and Menexenus, both I who am old and you. For as these people go away they will say that we think we are friends of each other—for I count myself among you—but we have not yet been able to discover what a friend is.' This is surprising because it seems to imply that until you know what X is you can never say whether this is a case of X. That our knowledge of X is prior to our knowledge of its cases is implied also in the *Euthyphro* (6E), where Socrates says that when Euthyphro has told him what X is he is going to use it as a paradigm or pattern to determine which things are X and which not. In fact, the impression vaguely given by the early dialogues as a whole is that Socrates thinks that there is no truth whatever about X that can be known before we know what X is. He never explicitly says so; nor, on the other hand, does he ever set any limits to the priority of this question. Prior to ascertaining what X is, he seems to think, we can form more or less probable opinions that X, whatever it may be, possesses the character Y, but can never be certain of such a thing (cf. *Tht.* 196DE).

Nor does Plato represent Socrates as seeking to answer his What-is-X? question by looking to cases or examples of X. On the contrary, as we have seen, he makes Socrates rebuke those answerers who give him some of the many Xes instead of the one X itself. Only when an answer of the desired sort is already given does anything like a case appear in the Socratic discussions; and then it is used not to establish but to refute the proposed answer.

If we look in the early dialogues for justifications of this principle, for reasons why the question What is X? must always be answered prior to any other question about X, we do not find them. On the contrary, the principle is offered as self-evident and too obvious for discussion. There is, however, something like an argument to this point in the mature *Phaedrus* (260). Imagine, says Socrates, that I were to urge you to use a horse in war, while neither of us was acquainted with horses, but I knew that you thought a horse to be that domestic animal which has the longest ears. This would be absurd. But it is like what actually happens in cities, for ignorant orators persuade ignorant cities to do bad things, both parties being under the impression that they are good things. Before you can say anything useful about horses you must know what a horse is; and before you can say anything useful about the good you must know what the good is. A twentieth-century philosopher would reply that it is a matter of experience that we can and do make useful statements about X without being able to say what X is in the way Socrates desires; and therefore the above argument must conceal some false premiss or fallacious inference.

The presentation of the What-is-X? question in Plato's early dialogues is no more abstract than I have represented it above. If we describe it, as I have so far refrained from doing, by means of such words as 'definition' and 'example', if we extract from it explicit rules and principles of definition, we pass to a stage of abstraction higher than the dialogues themselves display. We can, indeed, pick out an occasional word to be appropriately translated by 'example' or 'definition', and we can very easily formulate, from Socrates' instructions to his hearers, rules resembling those in a modern textbook; but that is only to say that each level of abstraction is near to the next! The actual picture in the dialogues is not more but less abstract than the picture here given; for Socrates does not use the letter X; he never gives the function but always one of its arguments.

Throughout the long series of his dialogues Plato continued to believe in the propriety and importance of this search for essences which he had depicted at the beginning of his writings. He can laugh at himself from time to time, and represent the demand for the 'one' instead of the 'many' as a piece of sophistical perversity (*Sph.* 239E–240A); but it remained his own demand. It is what he refers to as 'taking the logos of the essence' (*Rp.* 534B) or simply 'giving a logos'. It came to seem to him much more difficult than he had at first assumed it to be (*Letters* VII, 342–3, is one of his most despondent discussions of it); and he was thus led to spend much thought on devising methods to accomplish it. The great theory of dialectic is the theory of the method of discovering essence. Especially is this so in the *Sophist* and later dialogues, when the instrument of dialectic was division; for the purpose of division was precisely to give the definition of the essence. It is somewhat less so in the middle dialogues; for the method of hypothesis, which is the form dialectic takes there, is not so much a way of discovering essence as a way of evading the search for essence while still paying lip-service to the principle that you cannot know anything else about X until you know what X *is*. At least this seems to be the purpose of the method of hypothesis in its first appearance, which is in the *Meno*. The problem of that dialogue is whether virtue is teachable. Socrates declares that to answer we must first ascertain what virtue *is*. The attempt to ascertain this fails, however; and rather than abandon the discussion they are led to *hypothesize* a certain account of the essence of virtue and consider whether it would be teachable on this assumption (87).

Repeated failures in the effort to discover any particular essence only increased Plato's eagerness and his certainty that the essences were there. He thus came to introduce an element not found in the early dialogues at all, namely reflection on *essence in general, or the essences as a body*, as opposed to concentrating always on one particular essence; and these reflections are what is called Plato's theory of Ideas.

§ 2. CRITIQUE OF THE WHAT-IS-X? QUESTION

If we now cease to confine ourselves to something like English translations of Plato's words, and make use of modern terms and higher abstractions in order to criticize the What-is-X? question, the first thing we notice is that Socrates is looking for equivalences. He wants an answer, say 'X is AB', such that every X is AB and nothing else is AB. If given an answer, such as 'X is A', where A is not equivalent to but broader than X, he points out that other things besides X are A, and asks to have marked off the part of A that is equivalent to X (e.g. *Prt.* 312; *Grg.* 449 ff., 453C ff.).

There are, however, various sorts of equivalence or convertible proposition; and it appears that Socrates is not ready to accept any kind. In the first place, there are verbal definitions, such as '*Hund* means dog'. Socrates does not want these. He is not asking for a dictionary-definition of some word previously unknown to him. On the contrary, the X in his questions is always some word which he and his companions use every day of their lives, some word which, in unphilosophical circles, they would be said to know the meaning of perfectly well. Thus, while, in the ordinary sense, he knows what the word X means (and what it means is surely the thing X), he nevertheless does not know what the thing X is. Yet he expects the answer to his question to be itself a set of words. It seems, therefore, that his procedure implies, though he was unaware of it, that there is a word or set of words which gives or enshrines a knowledge of the thing X in some way in which the word X does not enshrine a knowledge of the thing X even for those who understand it and use it correctly. If the desired answer is 'X is AB', then, although he understands the word X just as well as the words AB, and although they both indicate the same entity, yet when he has the whole phrase 'X is AB' he knows satisfactorily what that entity is, and when he only has the word X he does not.

Any equivalent of X may serve as a means by which someone identifies X or distinguishes it from something else; but, among such equivalents, some, as we vaguely say, 'give the essence of X' and others do not. It is possible to identify X without giving its essence, by making use of other elements of reality and their relation to X. The proposition that 'virtue is the only human character which can never be misused' identifies virtue by referring to human character and misuse; and it evidently does not give its essence. It simply gives virtue a unique place in the context of reality, as two numbers give a point a unique place in a system of plane coordinates. Every statement giving X's essence serves to identify X; but not every statement serving to identify X gives its essence.

Now will Socrates be satisfied with any sort of identification, or does he insist on an identification through essence? The answer is that he has not made this distinction, and speaks sometimes one way and sometimes the other.

On the one hand, many passages suggest that all he wants is a mark that shall serve as a pattern by which to judge of any given thing whether it is an X or not. In the *Euthyphro* (6E) he describes his aim in just this way. In the *Meno* (74BC) he gives the fact that there are figures other than roundness as the reason why roundness is a bad description of figure. In the same dialogue (75B) he offers the following as an example of the kind of answer he wants: 'Figure is that which alone of all things invariably accompanies colour.' This is clearly nothing more than a designation or identification; and, though Meno objects to it, he does so on the ground not that it ought to be more than a designation but that it would not identify the thing for a person for whom the word 'figure' by itself did not already do the business. The same purpose is suggested again by Socrates' habit of illustrating his What-is-X? question by cases where X is an individual (*Men.* 71B, *Tht.* 209, *Grg.* 453C); for surely a convertible proposition about an individual cannot be more than an identification. It is suggested again by a word he often uses to describe the process of answering a What-is-it? question, namely ὁρίζειν. For this term, never losing the feel of its original connexion with boundary-stones, suggests laying down a mark to distinguish a field from the next, without in any way describing the soils or the crops in the fields so delimited. And in Plato's dialogues the translations 'distinguish' and 'determine' are suitable as often or more often than 'define'.

In many other passages, however, Socrates' purpose in asking What is X? is evidently not, or not merely, to distinguish X from everything else. It is to get at what he calls the essence or the form of X, the one in the many, that single identical something whose presence in all the many Xes is guaranteed precisely by the fact that we call them all Xes (*Men.* 74D).

There is thus a duality in Socrates' conception of the question What is X? On the one hand it is merely the search for an equivalent of X, for any description convertible therewith. On the other hand, it is the search for something felt to be narrower than this, for one special equivalent of X which is felt to be X in a more intimate way than any of the others.

There is a curious trace of this duality in the *Theaetetus*. The last ten pages of that dialogue contain a rather careful discussion of the conception of logos, and distinguish three meanings of the word. The first of these meanings is the expression of a thought in words. Now Aristotle often narrowed this meaning of logos down to the expression in words of a thought that gives a definition. Logos thus came to mean the formula of a definition, the description that gives the essence; and this is prepared by a passage in the *Republic* (534B), where Plato says that the dialectician takes the logos of the essence of each thing. In this sense, then, logos means the expression of an answer to the question What is X? The interesting point is that Plato's other two senses of logos in the *Theaetetus* appear to reflect the two ways in which Socrates regards the What-is-X? question in the early dialogues. According

to one of these senses the logos is that in which the thing differs
from all other things; here we have clearly the notion of the What-
is-X? question as the effort to differentiate and distinguish. The
notion of it as a search for essence is reflected in the other sense,
according to which the logos of X is a statement of the elements
of X; for that the essence of a thing is to be found in its elements
is a notion that always arises when the search for essence is
pushed very far.

Socrates almost invariably assumes that his term X is univocal.
He has no fear of ambiguity. Since you call all these things by one
name, he says, tell me what is the one thing you mean every time
(*Men.* 74D). 'We are accustomed to posit some one form for each
set of things to which we apply the same name' (*Rp.* 596A). There
is, however, one curious passage where his answerer tentatively
suggests that X is not the same in all the Xes, and Socrates rebuts
the suggestion with a strange and puzzling argument. It comes in
the first six pages of the *Meno*, which are the longest piece of
methodology in the early dialogues; and it will be worth our
while to quote it at length.

Do you think the health of a man is different from the health of a
woman? Or is it the same form everywhere, so long as it is health,
whether it be in a man or in anything else?—The health of a man and
the health of a woman seem to me to be the same.—And so with size
and strength? If a woman is strong, she will be strong with the same
form and the same strength? By 'the same' I mean that it makes no
difference to strength as strength whether it occurs in a man or a
woman. Or do you think it does?—No, I do not.—And will it make
any difference to virtue as virtue whether it occurs in the young or the
old, in woman or in man?—I somehow feel, Socrates, that this is not
like those others.—What? Did you not say that the virtue of a man
was to manage a city well, and of a woman to manage a household
well?—I did.—And can one manage a city or a household or anything
else well unless one manages it temperately and justly?—No, indeed.
—And if they manage justly and temperately, they will be managing
with justice and temperance?—Necessarily.—Then the man and the
woman, if they are to be good, both need the same qualities, namely
justice and temperance.—Apparently.—What about the young and
the old? Could they ever become good if they were intemperate and
unjust?—No, indeed.—They would have to be temperate and just?—
Yes.—Then all men are good in the same way; for they all become
good by obtaining the same qualities.—It seems so.—But they would

not have been good in the same way, unless their virtue were the same. —No, indeed.—Since therefore the virtue of everyone is the same, try to say, &c. (*Men.* 72–73.)

In this passage Meno's reply, 'I somehow feel, Socrates, that this is not like those others', gives expression to an inkling that virtue is not the same in all virtuous persons. This is the only occasion in the early dialogues where it is suggested that the term proposed for definition might be ambiguous. The suggestion is made to come from an answerer, and not from one of the most intelligent and attractive answerers in these dialogues. Socrates is represented as not entertaining it seriously for a moment; he regards it as a view natural to those who have not reflected but evidently false to those who have.

The argument which Socrates offers to convince Meno that virtue is the same in all cases apparently consists in pointing to an identity in all of them, an identity which he indicates by the words 'justice and temperance'. Now pointing to an identity in all the Xes does not prove that X is a univocal word unless the identity to which you point is the very thing that X means. (For example, the premiss that all tops are material objects does not prove that 'top' has only one meaning, because what 'top' means is certainly not 'material object'.) Hence Socrates' argument proves that the word 'virtue' always means the same only if the thing that he points to, and that Meno admits to be present in all cases of virtue, is the very thing that the word 'virtue' means. But, if Socrates can thus point to the very thing that 'virtue' means, and Meno can thus instantly recognize it, why are they asking what virtue is and, according to their own account, failing to find out? They seem to know already what is the one virtue in the many virtues.

Socrates is also assuming some sort of realism as opposed to nominalism, though this again is nothing that enters his head, but only one of the logical consequences of what does enter his head. He is assuming that this form or essence or one in the many is not a word in the mouth, nor a concept in the head, but something existing in the particular Xes independently of man. Earth-mixed-with-liquid, for example, is one essence really occurring in many different things, such as fuller's earth and brickmaker's clay and so on. 'In every action the holy is the same as itself, and the unholy is opposite to all the holy and like itself, and everything

that is to be unholy has some one form according to its unholiness'
(*Euthyph.* 5D). The identical character appears and reappears in
different parts of experience, irrespective of what man may think
or say.

Someone might say that, if you ask what is common to all the
virtues, and expect a verbal answer, the perfect answer is 'virtue',
and any other word or words will necessarily be wrong. The early
dialogues contain no trace of such a suggestion. Socrates' behaviour implies that there will always be some correct answer
which does not contain the word 'virtue' or a synonym. Now if
your account of the essence of X is not to contain the word X or
any synonym, it seems that it will have to consist in an explication
of the structure of X, an exhibition of X in a more extended form.
It will have to give X seen through a telescope, as it were, though
the magnification must not be too great for the whole of X to
remain in the field. Thus Socrates' behaviour further implies that
X will always have a structure that can be unfolded. It will
always be like the planet that becomes bigger in the telescope,
and not like the star that remains a point. It will never be a
simple entity having no true analysis. This implication, un-
detected in the early dialogues, had risen into Plato's consciousness to some extent when he wrote the *Theaetetus*; for he there
conceives of a man maintaining that the primary elements have
no logos, which is to say that no account can be given of their
essence (201 E); on this hypothesis the question What is X? would
have no true answer when X was a primary element.

The foregoing discussion reveals several assumptions that must
be made if Socrates' question is to be a legitimate question admitting of a true answer. First, we must assume that the word X
is univocal. Second, we must assume that the thing X has an
'essence'. Third, we must make some sort of realist assumption
about the ontological status of this 'essence'. And, fourth, we
must assume that this 'essence' is not a 'primary element' but has
a structure that can be explicated; for otherwise we must already
know what X is in asking the question in Socrates' sense.

In view of all these assumptions, and of the possibility that we
already know what X is when we raise the question, it is surprising that we are all of us so willing to ask What is X? in Socrates'
sense, and so unsuspecting of the difficulties it may lead us into.
One cause of our willingness seems to be the vagueness of the

What-is-X? form itself. For it is, perhaps, when unsupported by a context, the vaguest of all forms of question except an inarticulate grunt. It indicates less determinately than any other the sort of information the questioner wants. The most precise form is Is X Y?, since the answerer then knows that the asker wants precisely the information that X is Y or that X is not Y, whichever is true. Less precise are Where is X? and When is X?; they tell us that a time or a place is wanted, but not by reference to what we are to determine the time (whether, for example, by reference to the birth of Jesus or to a certain collision of carriages), nor how narrowly we are to define the time (for example whether to a minute or to a century). Vaguer still is Why is X?, since there is an indefinite plurality of facts that are causes or reasons or explanations of any given fact. Vaguest of all is What is X?, for it amounts only to saying 'Please make some true statement about X'. Some examples will make this clearer. Who is Abner? He is a painter. Who is Abner? He is the man who painted the portrait of Lorme in this exhibition. What is a rhombus? A thing you learn about in geometry. What is a rhombus? A plane figure. What is a rhombus? A rhomboid having two adjacent sides equal. Each of these five is a reasonable answer to a What-is-it? question; yet each is a very different kind of proposition.

The vagueness of the form of a question is usually lessened by its context. The situation in which I ask 'Who is Abner?' may show clearly that I want you to tell me some relation in which Abner stands to you and no one else does, or that I want you to tell me his business. The situation in which I ask 'What is potassium?' may show that I wish to know what the word 'potassium' means, or whether this substance is an element, or to what class of element it belongs, or what is its atomic weight. Instead of putting the question vaguely and relying on the context to make it clear, I might do better to use a more precise form. Thus for the above four cases of 'What is potassium?' I could say respectively 'What does that word mean?', 'Is potassium an element?', 'What sort of element is it?', 'What is the definition of it?'.

The explanations which Socrates gives of his question provide a context determining this vague form to mean the search for essence as above described. But it is the half-felt presence of all the other possible meanings of What is X? that prevents our seeing the pitfalls in this search for essence. Whenever a difficulty arises, we interpret the question in some other way to avoid it. For example, if the conception of essence becomes momentarily embarrassing, we take What is X? as merely a request for identification. Such an evasion is always possible, because there are several other, non-Socratic senses in which What is X? is always a proper question. One of these is 'What does the word X mean?', the request for a verbal definition. Another is 'Give a unique designation of X', the request for a mark of identification. A third seems to be, 'Make some true statement about X', for What is X? is sometimes as vague as that. The vague form What is X? is an especial temptation 'to answer questions, without first discovering precisely *what* question it is which you desire to answer' (G. E. Moore, *Principia Ethica* vii).

Another cause of our willingness to ask What is X? without restriction is that it really is a useful habit to turn to definition when in perplexity. Very often, after we have pressed an inquiry a certain distance, we cannot go farther until we use more precise terms. A What-is-X? question is then in place; and, though this is always a verbal definition, the useful habit thus acquired will, in combination with our usual failure to distinguish the senses of this question, lead to our putting it in some senses and some cases where it is not useful.

Again, it often happens that a theory is put forward in the form 'X is YZ', where this is supposed to be a convertible proposition; and that after some debate this theory is disproved. 'X is *not* YZ.' Then it is very natural to think: 'Well then, what *is* X?'. So we slide into the What-is-X? question without full consciousness of doing so. The *Republic* does not open with the question, What is justice?, but with the question, Is justice honesty and paying what one owes? (331C). Not until five pages later (336C), after this and another theory about justice have been refuted, is the question raised 'What *is* justice?'.

Lastly, we ask the What-is-X? question unrestrictedly because the following seems such a plausible argument: 'If we know what a thing is, we can surely say what it is' (*La.* 190C, cf. *Chrm.* 159A). Conversely, we feel that we do not know what a thing is unless we can give some description that is convertible with it and does more than merely identify it.

Part II. Dialectic

VI

DIALECTIC

T H E previous chapters, though ranging over the whole of Plato's work, have attempted to deal only with matters appearing first in the early dialogues. It is now time to observe what new elements arise in the middle dialogues.

The greatest single innovation of the middle dialogues is no doubt that Socrates, instead of inquiring after particular 'essences' or 'forms' as he previously did, now begins to talk about the whole body of the 'forms', and is as much concerned about the nature of a 'form' in general as he is about any particular 'form'. But what is more relevant to the subject of this book is the change from a destructive to a constructive manner. The assumption that there are 'forms' served in the early dialogues only to introduce the destruction of every proposed account of a 'form'; but now, losing some of his previous interest in defining particular 'forms', Socrates uses the general assumption as a groundwork on which to construct various positive doctrines, for example that soul is immortal.

The constructive tone of the middle and late dialogues entails the subordination and partial disappearance of the negative elenchus in them. What is now required is a method for attaining positive doctrine, not for rejecting it. Is there such a method in the middle dialogues? The attempt to answer this question makes us aware of a third important difference between the early and the middle periods, namely, that the early gives prominence to method but not to methodology, while the middle gives prominence to methodology but not to method. In other words, theories of method are more obvious in the middle, but examples of it are more obvious in the early. Actual cases of the elenchus follow one another in quick succession in the early works; but when we looked for discussions of the elenchus, we found them few and not very abstract. The middle dialogues, on the other hand, abound in abstract words and proposals concerning method, but it is by no means obvious whether these proposals are being actually followed, or whether any method is being actually followed. The *Phaedrus* is full of remarks on method; but to what extent is it itself methodically written? It evinces a keen consciousness of rhetorical and of dialectical method; but it evinces no particular consciousness of method in the composition of the non-rhetorical parts of itself. It rather seems to imply that there should not be much method in a dialogue, since it says that a dialogue must be partly play. In considering the middle dialogues from a methodological point of view, therefore, we shall be concerned more with their theory than with their practice of method.

§ I. METHOD

Plato's conception of method is closely connected with his conception of art or science, of τέχνη or ἐπιστήμη. Every art or science has its methods, and every method belongs to some art or science. The two conceptions bring out different aspects of the same whole, which may be generally described as rational selfconscious human activity pursuing by indirect means some foreseen end that cannot be attained directly. Let us examine the elements of this definition one by one.

An end or purpose is essential to both art and method. Without something to be achieved they cannot occur. 'Say then what is the manner of the power of dialectic, and what kinds it falls into, and what are its roads. For they, apparently, would lead the traveller there where he would have, as it were, rest from the road and an end of the journey' (*Rp.* 532DE).

But if the purpose can be fulfilled directly, like turning the head in a healthy man, there is again no method or art. A means as well as an end is essential to these two conceptions. And, even when the end requires a means distinct from itself, we still have only luck or instinct or skill if the man can give no account of how he does it. Method and art include the selfconsciousness that I am aiming at this end by this means.

When within this complex we distinguish art from method, what we are doing is suggested by the fact that method is, and art is not, a specialization of the notion of 'going'. The 'method' is the description of the temporal actions in their temporal sequence, by which the desired end is brought about; whereas the 'art' or 'science' is the recital of the facts and principles which prescribe those actions. 'Art' tends towards permanent knowledge, but 'method' towards changing 'procedure'. The derivation of the procedure from the knowledge is the debatable ground claimed both by 'method' and by 'art'; for the distinction between them becomes vague as soon as we bring principles and practice together. Sidgwick's 'methods of ethics', for example, are the three modes of determining what is right in detail based on three principles about human conscience in general.

The end aimed at by an art or method may be something intellectual, such as getting new ideas, testing the truth of ideas, proving and disproving propositions, and all the various mental occurrences that might be collected under the title of 'increasing knowledge'. This is the kind of method with which Plato is chiefly concerned; and I shall use the word with this restriction in future.

It follows from the distinction between means and end that the idea of method involves the idea of temporal stages, differing from each other in character as well as in date, and having a fixed order. In order to obtain the end you do something else. You necessarily do it before you obtain the end, and it is necessarily different therefrom. This is the means. And the means itself is usually divided into temporal parts in the same way. Method thus involves a continued effort, sustained through the successive stages of a long process. It is a 'diexodus' or passage right through and out (*Plts.* 277B, 279C).

The general idea of orderly progression, of doing one thing first in order to get at what you really want, is very common in the dialogues. In the *Republic*, for example, Socrates proposes that they shall study the large letters first, so that they may afterwards read off by means of them the small letters in which they are mainly interested (368). The prime question of the dialogue, What is justice?, is kept in mind throughout, and orders the whole inquiry. Here and elsewhere the leader frequently asks or tells his companions what is the next step. 'Should we be proceeding in order if we next divided the cognitive science?' (*Plts.* 259D). Since we wish to know how justice and injustice arise in a city, will it or will it not be useful to consider how the guardians of a city will be educated (*Rp.* 376C)?

The same idea is present wherever Socrates urges that one question is prior to another and must be answered first. The commonest form of this is the doctrine that we must not raise any other question about X until we have disposed of the question what X is. Other forms, however, also occur; for example, we cannot know what constitutes correctness in derived names until we know what constitutes it in primary names (*Cra.* 426A).

The idea is present also in all those processes of methodically going through a series, whether to eliminate certain members or to construct a whole by the addition of parts or for some other purpose, which are frequent in the dialogues. It is present again in those programmes of inquiry which the dialogues often sketch and sometimes perform, such as the plan for finding out what justice is (*Rp.* 368), the plan for determining whether soul is immortal (*Phd.* 78B), and the plan for constructing a natural language (*Cra.* 424).

This faith in order attains selfconscious expression in the rules for literary composition in the *Phaedrus*. Plato's advice there falls into two main parts, of which one is that you should know your subject and the other is the demand for various forms of order. First in this latter demand comes the generalized form of the rule which the early dialogues insist upon in so many particular cases: start with a definition; the What-is-X? question is prior to all other questions about X (263). Then comes the insistence that you should begin at the beginning. This is explained both metaphorically and directly. The metaphor is that 'every discourse should be like an animal, having its own proper body, not lacking head or foot but possessing both middle parts and extremities constructed fittingly to each other and to the whole' (264C). The direct explanation is that each item in a composition should follow 'by some necessity' from what went before; and Plato calls this 'logographic necessity'.

It is hard to be sure what types of composition Plato meant these rules to cover. He seems to suggest pretty clearly that not every discourse should start with a definition (263); and his primary concern throughout is persuasive oratory. Yet there is a distinct tendency towards universality in these rules. He says that '*every* discourse should be like an animal', &c. On the whole, it seems safe to take them as closely akin to the demand for order in scientific discourse and in scientific inquiry.

The alternative to orderly and systematic procedure might nowadays be said to be intuition. It is a familiar idea in our times to contrast the plodder who approaches the goal by careful planning with the genius who gets there in a stroke. This contrast seems to be entirely absent from Plato. He possesses the idea of intuition as well as that of method; but he does not contrast them in this way. He regards them not as antagonistic but as complementary. His passage on the Divided Line is, as we shall see (Chapter X), his fullest statement of both method and intuition. Intuition to him is not an easy way of shortcircuiting method; but the reward reserved precisely for the master of method. The contrast is between method crowned by intuition, on the one side, and random fruitless effort, on the other. The only alternative to orderly motion is disorderly motion; for there will be motion anyhow. Disorderly motion, accordingly, is what Plato feels himself to be getting away from in the search for method. Socrates' speeches in the *Phaedrus* were orderly; but that of Lysias was a jumble (χύδην 264B). The alternative to hypothetical method in the *Phaedo* is 'mixing everything together' (ὁμοῦ πάντα κυκῶντες 101E); and the phrase, 'I concoct haphazard some other method of my own' (*Phd.* 97B), would be a contradiction if it were not ironical.

One of the results of being methodical is that you may take a long while to reach a conclusion which seems obvious to everyone from the beginning. Such occurrences incline us sometimes to believe that method is a waste of time. Plato raises a particular case of this in the following words. 'Why then did we not answer straight away that weaving is plaiting warp and woof together, instead of going round in a circle and making many useless divisions?' (*Plts.* 283B). His long explanation (283-7) is not very clearly relevant for the most part; but the following can be said with confidence. Many persons today would defend the methodical pursuit of the obvious on the ground that the psychologically obvious is by no means necessarily true, so that this procedure provides *reasons* for a belief which previously rested only on irrational *causes*. Plato does not take this line. His argument is that the most valuable and difficult truths can be reached only by method, and to prepare for the conquest of them we must practise the method on simple things. He often offers us examples of practice in method, though it usually appears that they are not mere exercises, but, like the 'Studies' of a composer, have a value in themselves. Such are the definitions of weaving in the *Statesman* and of angling in the *Sophist*, the example of how to talk to your beloved in the *Lysis*. The whole of the second part of the *Parmenides*, three quarters of the dialogue, is introduced as an exercise in logical method.

Such exercise is necessary, he says here in the *Statesman*, because the most valuable and difficult truths can be reached only by method. To the important truths there are no short cuts; the long road round is the only road that really arrives. If we *could* find a short and smooth path to the art of persuasive oratory, we should be fools to take a long rough one (*Phdr.* 272C); but these alleged short cuts do not reach the goal; and, considering the greatness of that goal, we must not wonder at the length of the circuit (274A). 'I assure you, Glaucon, that in my opinion we shall never accurately grasp this matter by such methods as we are now using in our discussions; the path that leads to it is another and a longer one' (*Rp.* IV 435D). The dialogues themselves, however, do not often take the longer and surer way round. A casual conversation permits only inaccurate and summary methods. After laying down his plan for constructing a natural language, Socrates despairs of accomplishing it and undertakes only a makeshift (*Cra.* 425BC). What the *Republic* says about the soul and about virtues and about the good is far from accurate and complete (*Rp.* VI 504). Glaucon could not understand, and Socrates could not explain, what dialectic really is (*Rp.* VII 533A).

The opposition between the short cut and the long way round is one form of the general notion that there are alternative methods or ways to the goal, between which we have to choose. This is especially common in the *Sophist* and the *Statesman*. 'Of teaching by means of speech the one way seems to be rougher, while the other part of it is smoother' (*Sph.* 229E). 'Well, then, how should one begin such a risky argument? It seems to me, boy, that this is the road that we must take' (*Sph.* 242B). 'Now the argument seems to discern two roads stretching towards that part at which it is aiming, one quicker, because it cuts off a small from a large part, the other preserving more that division through the middle which we demanded earlier, but longer. We can proceed along whichever we wish.—What? Can we not take both?—

Not at once, you strange person; we can in turn, of course' (*Plts.* 265A, cf. 266E). Such a choice of roads is already clearly expressed in the poem of Parmenides.

So much by way of describing Plato's conception of method in general; but, before turning to the particular method which he recommended in his middle dialogues, let us consider for a minute the metaphor which he used to convey the notion of method. The root figure in μέθοδος is ὁδός, the road or journey; and Plato employs many forms of the notion of going or journeying to convey his meaning. The dialogues contain, however, no trace of the original evolution of the notion of method out of that of journeying. We do not see Plato first talking about ὁδοί or roads and then gradually crystallizing the technical word 'method'. On the contrary, 'method' means method from its first appearance in the dialogues. It is a technical term from the beginning. And the more definitely metaphorical expressions, such as 'road' and 'journeying', occur in the dialogues only subsequent to the technical term. It makes them possible, and not the other way about, for an examination of the dialogues will disclose the fact that, wherever the word 'method' is absent, there the use of any verb of going or any noun for way as a metaphor for method is almost always absent too.

It may be doubted whether Burnet was right in thinking 'method' a metaphor from *hunting* (on *Phd.* 79E), and whether Liddell and Scott are right in giving 'the *pursuit* of a nymph' as an example of its first sense. It seems more likely that the word came to have its technical meaning through Parmenides' 'way', which was not a hunt or pursuit of anything, but a pilgrimage to the presence of a goddess. The metaphor of hunting is, it is true, a common carrier of the idea of method in the dialogues of Plato; but it is usually not related to the word 'method'. For example, this word does not occur in the great hunting image in the *Republic* when they discover the definition of justice (IV 432). Only in the *Sophist* do the word 'method' and the metaphor of hunting come much into contact, and this is probably because there the aim of the method is to define a person whose contemptible nature makes it appropriate to regard him as a prey to be captured and killed.

Very likely the word μέθοδος, as opposed to ὁδός, never had a predominantly physical sense in any author. Very likely the transmutation of the 'journey' or 'search' into something purely intellectual was completed before the word μέθοδος was formed. The only evidence Liddell and Scott give for believing that its original sense was physical pursuit is νύμφης μέθοδον quoted by Suidas. This, however, seems to be a derived and not an original use of the word. The writer was enjoying the piquancy that often comes from taking physically what everyone else takes intellectually, and it pleased him to imagine the 'methodical' pursuit of a nymph. In a later chapter it will be argued that the word 'hypothesis' had a similar history; its first senses were intellectual, not architectural or physical in any way, and Plato in the Divided Line obtained a powerful effect by taking it in a physical sense which it had never had.

Burnet once suggested that the dictionary should generally be read backwards. The sense which it gives as the earliest is often the latest. He was discussing the word 'educare', of which in his opinion the sense of 'rearing' or 'growing' an animal or a plant was one of the earlier and not one of the later. It may be suggested that he should have applied this principle to the lexicon's article on μέθοδος. (*Essays and Addresses* 102.)

These considerations imply that Plato's μέθοδος should usually be translated by a word that has no vividly physical meaning. The English word 'method' itself seems often thoroughly suitable, especially in the *Republic* (435D, 533BC, 596A) and the *Laws* (638E, 965C). Also 'inquiry' (*Plts.* 260E, *Phdr.* 270C, *Sph.* 219A, *Rp.* 510BC) and 'way' (*Phdr.* 269D, *Phd.* 79E) and 'procedure' (*Phdr.* 270D, *Sph.* 265A, 235C). 'Method of procedure' seems right for τρόπος τῆς μεθόδου (*Phd.* 97B). Something like 'search' is required in *Sph.* 243D and *Plts.* 286D. 'Pursuit' goes best in *Rp.* 531C and *Sph.* 218D. The phrase μέθοδος τῶν λόγων is rich with at least four meanings: the search for definitions, the pursuit of discussion, the procedure of discussing, and methodicalness in discussion. It may be paraphrased as 'the search for definitions by the method of discussion' (*Sph.* 227A, *Plts.* 266D, *Letter II* 314D). The most puzzling of Plato's uses of the word is ἐπιστήμην τε αἴσθησιν οὐ συγχωρησόμεθα κατά γε τὴν τοῦ πάντα κινεῖσθαι μέθοδον (*Tht.* 183C). We seem compelled either to go very far from the ordinary senses, as do Ast with 'Annahme' and Cornford with 'theory' and Liddell and Scott with 'doctrine', or to paraphrase in some such way as this: 'And we shall not admit that knowledge is perception, at any rate not as the result of an inquiry proceeding on the assumption that everything is in motion.' The phrases καθ' ὁδόν and ὁδῷ, which seem to mean the same, may be translated by 'methodical(ly)' or 'systematic(ally)' or 'in order' or 'in an orderly way' (*Rp.* 435A, 533B; *Cra.* 425B).

§ 2. DIALECTIC

The particular method which Plato discusses and recommends is called by him 'the dialectical method' (ἡ διαλεκτικὴ μέθοδος *Rp.* 533C) or 'the power of conversing' (*Rp.* 511B) or 'the art concerning discussions' (ἡ περὶ τοὺς λόγους τέχνη *Phd.* 90B) or 'the procedure of discussion' (ἡ μέθοδος τῶν λόγων *Sph.* 227A). This 'dialectical method' fills him with the greatest enthusiasm from the time of the *Meno* (75D) to the end of his life; and he speaks of it usually in highly laudatory language. It is the best and noblest of all possible methods. It is the only art or science that is really awake (*Rp.* 533BC).

In his middle period Plato held emphatically that dialectic was not merely the noblest but also the most useful method. He does not, however, define clearly the realms to which its usefulness extends. Some passages seem to imply that it is useful in all study, art, and practice, of whatever sort. Thus he says that 'everything that was ever discovered concerning science became plain through this' method (*Phlb.* 16C). At any rate, Plato in his middle period evidently thought of dialectic as useful in linguistics (*Cra.* 390), mathematics (*Rp.* 510–11), rhetoric and psychology (*Phdr.* 269–73), and all ethical and political knowledge and conduct. Towards the end of his life he modified this to some extent. The *Laws* does not emphasize the importance of dialectic in the good city; and the *Philebus* seems to abandon the view that it is the most useful method, while reiterating that it is the surest and truest (58C).

What is the nature of this wonderful method? That is a hard question to answer. In the *Republic* (533A) Plato makes his speakers abandon the attempt to give an adequate account of it. In the *Philebus* he declares dialectic easy to describe (though difficult to practise); but the account he there gives (16–18) is intensely hard to interpret. He is most explicit in the *Phaedrus,* *Sophist,* and *Statesman;* and these dialogues throw light on the

Philebus. Unfortunately, if the interpretations given below are correct (162-5), the account in these four dialogues is not the same as those hinted in the *Republic* and the *Phaedo*; and anyhow there are several elements in Plato's notion of dialectic whose connexion is hard to see.

The fact is that the word 'dialectic' had a strong tendency in Plato to mean 'the ideal method, *whatever that may be*'. In so far as it was thus merely an honorific title, Plato applied it at every stage of his life to whatever seemed to him at the moment the most hopeful procedure. In the same way, he applied the abusive terms 'eristic' and 'sophistry' on every occasion to whatever seemed to him at that time the danger most to be avoided. This usage, combined with the fact that Plato did at one time considerably change his conception of the best method, has the result that the meaning of the word 'dialectic' undergoes a substantial alteration in the course of the dialogues. Thus in the *Phaedo* the 'resort to discussion', which is equivalent to dialectic, is identified with the hypothetical method. (For 100A3 ff., on hypothesis, gives the content of the 'observation by discussion' named in 100A1-2.) In the *Republic*, on the other hand, dialectic is supposed to consist solely of whatever that 'upward path' is which is there offered as superseding the hypothetical method of mathematics. In the *Philebus*, again, dialectic is represented as consisting solely of synthesis and division. Roughly speaking, the keyword for the middle dialogues is 'hypothesis'; and this we find in *Meno*, *Phaedo*, *Republic*, and *Parmenides*. The later keyword, 'division', appears in *Phaedrus*, *Sophist*, *Statesman*, *Philebus*. Besides these conceptions of hypothesis and division, which belonged to Plato's idea of dialectic for parts of its life only, there are others which belonged to it throughout.

This book attempts to develop first those elements that always belonged to 'dialectic', and then the notion of hypothesis; and that is all. A study of division on the same scale would take as many pages again. We begin, then, with such characters as belonged to dialectic throughout its life in Plato's mind.

Although dialectic can be used to advantage in many and various spheres, its subject-matter is in one sense always the same, and was so considered throughout Plato's life. It is always the search for 'what each thing is' (*Rp.* 533B). That is to say, it seeks the 'essence' of each thing (οὐσία, *Rp.* 534B), the formal and abiding element in the thing. It regards 'what neither comes into being nor passes away, but is always identically the same' (*Phlb.* 61E). Thus it presupposes that things have unchanging essences; and if anyone denies this he absolutely destroys the power of dialectic (*Prm.* 135BC).

Dialectic is the technical aspect of 'philosophy', in one of Plato's uses of that word. 'Philosophy' meant to Plato either the pursuit of moral excellence or the pursuit of intellectual excellence or both. The two notions were bound closely together by the persistence in his thinking of Socrates' belief that virtue is knowledge. In *Republic* II–IV the moral notion is uppermost; that the soldiers must be 'philosophic' means chiefly that they must have certain moral qualities (375–6). The intellectual notion, on the other hand, reigns in *Republic* V–VII. Philosophy as the love of knowledge has the same ambiguity of subject-matter as dialectic. On the one hand, it is the study of all wisdom whatever; and he who picks and chooses is expressly said to be no philosopher (*Rp.* 475, 486A). On the other hand, the philosopher rejects and despises the things of this world, the manifold changing appearances; and concentrates on those forms or essences which this world repeatedly but inadequately reflects (*Rp.* 475 ff.). This intellectual type of philosophy, directed in one sense to all existence and in another to essences only, is the activity which Plato calls 'dialectic' when he is thinking of the technique by which it advances.

Plato did not separate dialectic from philosophy as we tend to separate, say, logic or methodology from metaphysics. Dialectic was not a propaedeutic to philosophy. It was not a tool that you might or might not choose to use in philosophizing. It was philosophy itself, the very search for the essences, only considered in its methodical aspect. The method occurred only in the search, and the search only by means of the method.

Plato's dialectic is often of such a nature that to our minds it ought to be separated from philosophy. To us he often seems to be discussing neither physical nor metaphysical reality, but only the human logical apparatus of conceptions and terms. But still, in a manner very strange and unnatural to us, he regards himself as talking not logic but ontology. Thus in the *Phaedo* (96) he seems to regard the logical question, how it is that you can make two out of one both by addition and by its opposite division, as on a par with the physical question whether we think with the blood. In the *Sophist* (245E) what we should call a logical inquiry into such terms as 'being' and 'one', and a metaphysical inquiry into the merits of idealism and materialism, appear to him as merely a more and a less accurate study of 'being'; and later in the same dialogue his theory of communion or κοινωνία has to us such a strongly logical air that most interpreters represent it as a theory of the copula or of predication or the like, while yet Plato himself regards it as a theory of reality.

The separation of the method from the activity of which it is the method was begun by Aristotle when he undertook to write a handbook of dialectic. In the *Topics* dialectic became a technique that could be learnt by itself apart from the study of any reality, and was thereafter equally applicable to all studies or none. By thus isolating it from the source of its inspiration, Aristotle changed dialectic from the highest intellectual activity to a dubious game of debate. This made prominent the idea that dialectic is a training or exercise, valuable scarcely at all for its own sake, but mostly because it prepares the muscles of the intellect to undertake some other task. This idea is very recessive in Plato, although there is a good deal of talk about mental gymnastics in the *Parmenides*.

Without saying so explicitly, Plato implies, or at least tends towards the view, that the perfected dialectician would achieve certainty. That is, for example, the general suggestion of the Divided Line (*Rp.* 510–11). It is also the implication of this statement: 'Absolutely neither he nor any other genus shall ever boast itself as escaping the procedure of those who can thus pursue things individually and collectively' (*Sph.* 235C). Above all, it is implied by Plato's views that dialectic is the method of philosophy, that philosophy commands the faculty of knowledge as opposed to that of opinion, and that knowledge as opposed to opinion is infallible (*Rp.* 477E).

But Plato's view, that dialectic as such attains certainty, is liable to suggest to us certain inferences which he did not draw. In the first place, he did not conclude that any person is actually in the sure possession of a considerable portion of the truth. His view is rather that we should attain certainty if we could practise dialectic aright, but, owing to its loftiness and difficulty, we are unable to do so. From beginning to end he conceived it as a method very hard to practise, possible only for the unusually

trained and gifted few. To Descartes the right method was something plain and obvious. It was open to all men of good sense, and
practically everyone had good sense. The question why then we
need a Descartes to tell us of this method is one that he does not
seem to have much considered; but he implies that we have
become perverted to oversubtlety and wrongheadedness by the
doctors of the schools, and need a monitor to recall us to the state
of nature. To Plato, on the contrary, no one is a dialectician by
nature, and very few have the natural basis to become one. However great a man's gifts, he must also study hard and long. And
the goal, if it is ever attained, will be more divine than human.

In the second place, Plato's belief that dialectic would achieve
certainty must not mislead us into supposing that he held that
dialectic could be exhausted in a set of rules and acquired by
memorizing them. The sure and certain may be the mechanical
to us; but it was not to him. Dialectic was not a substitute for
thinking but a way of thinking. Plato never has the idea that it
would be a good thing to transfer as much as possible from the
realm of thinking to that of mechanical procedure or rule of
thumb, both in order to lessen errors and in order to have more
time and energy for other thinking. Campbell well expresses his
view in the following words:

Plato never conceived, as some modern philosophers have done,
that a new method could possibly level intellects, or become a substitute for invention. He never imagines a form of thinking as separable
from thought. His dialectic is not a dead organon, but an inspiration,
a divine gift, which may be imperfectly described in words, and by
oral teaching may be awakened and stimulated in the philosophic
nature, but cannot be once for all embodied in a book of aphorisms
or a chrestomathy. (*The Sophistes and Politicus of Plato* xi.)

The perfect dialectician's certainty would be an internal certainty
of intuition, not the external kind we feel after using an adding-
machine; and it could not be communicated to any sort of man,
but only to another perfect dialectician. 'By a method', said
Descartes, 'I understand sure and easy rules such that, if anyone
follows them exactly, he will never falsely take anything for true,
and, without any useless expenditure of mental effort, gradually
and continuously increasing his knowledge, will attain a true
apprehension of everything of which he is capable' (*Rule* IV).
That is far from the spirit of Plato.

Progress in a study or pursuit may usually be regarded either as an acquirement of knowledge or as an acquirement of skill. Plato, when he is considering progress in dialectic and philosophy, emphasizes skill against knowledge much more than the twentieth century would. Dialectic is a skill to be acquired, much more than it is a body of propositions to be learnt. Plato does not regard the philosopher's or the dialectician's work as the construction or accumulation of something external to himself, but as the alteration of his own personality in a fundamental way, as character-building. The nature of the alteration is vaguely indicated by the phrase 'becoming wise'. That is why he frequently insists on the training of the soul (e.g. ψυχῆς παίδευσις *Phdr.* 241C), and why he states that we should value 'the pursuit of the ability to divide according to forms' above the knowledge thereby obtained, and that the most important thing is to become more capable of discoveries (εὑρετικώτερος *Plts.* 286D–287A).

Dialectic is an art or τέχνη as well as a method, and Plato has a good many hints about its relations to other arts and sciences. He bases his decision that in Callipolis dialectic shall be studied after all other sciences on the statement that it is the coping-stone of them all (*Rp.* 534E). This means at least that it attains greater truth and precision than any other science—or *would* attain greater truth and precision if anyone ever succeeded in practising it aright (*Phlb.* 59C). Dialectic alone guarantees its premises, or has some hope of doing so; the other sciences merely draw necessary conclusions from uncertified premises (*Rp.* 510–11). Plato probably means further something like what Aristotle meant when he said that politics was the architectonic science; dialectic directs and disposes of all other sciences and arts. According to the *Cratylus* the lawgiver, or whoever it is that makes the words of a language, must go to the dialectician to find out if he has made them well (390CD). According to the *Euthydemus* (290C) the wise mathematician does not attempt to use his discoveries himself, but hands them over to the dialectician. (It is hard to imagine what sort of activity Plato would have classified as a dialectician's use of a mathematical discovery. In the Divided Line the dialectician operates on the mathematician's premises; but here he is supposed to do something with his conclusions. In the *Timaeus* Plato uses the theory of the regular solids to construct a physics; perhaps that is an example.) This architectonic character of dialectic is probably a consequence of its synoptic attitude to the other sciences. It seeks an insight into the community and relatedness of things, and infers how they are akin to each other (*Rp.* 531D). It tries to detect the related and the unrelated in all sciences (*Sph.* 227B).

The figure of the coping-stone may also be meant to embrace the statement that it is impossible to be a dialectician until you have mastered all of mathematics (*Rp.* 533A). But on this point the *Republic* seems inconsistent with the rest of Plato's writings, in which he takes the contrary view that it is impossible to be scientific in any field of activity until you are a dialectician. In the *Phaedrus* (269E) he says that all great sciences require *talk* or ἀδολεσχία; and the context seems to give this the more definite meaning that dialectic is a necessity in every important science or art, including rhetoric. In the *Philebus* (16C) he says roundly that 'everything that was ever discovered concerning science became plain by means of this', meaning dialectic. His view is perhaps that in every sphere it is possible to achieve something without dialectic, but in no sphere is it possible to achieve the best without dialectic, meaning by the best the greatest amount of systematization, clarity, and certainty.

§ 3. QUESTION AND ANSWER

Plato frequently distinguishes between sense and reason, using for 'sense' αἴσθησις and other terms, for 'reason' νοῦς, λογισμός, διάνοια, and so on. He regards these two faculties as capable of functioning separately; they are not necessarily complementary. This does not mean that each by itself can attain perfect knowledge, for sense by itself can attain only opinion; but that each by itself can reach some sort of cognitive goal which someone may consider satisfactory. Nor does it mean that reason often functions by itself; for Plato holds that, while reason can be used by itself, and while by far the best results are thus obtained, most men are incapable of the feat. The dialectician alone, in Plato's opinion, can use reason by itself; and he is a very rare person, who perhaps has not yet appeared on the earth. The dialectician is thus contrasted with the ordinary sensual man, immersed in the objects of the senses (*Rp.* 475–6). But that is not all. It is not merely that the dialectician takes no interest in sensibles as such, but also that he does not even use them as an aid to the study of intelligibles.

This distinguishes him from the mathematician, who is interested in intelligibles but uses sensible images as an aid (*Rp.* 510–11). It distinguishes him also from the physicist, who also is trying to get at a reality behind sensible appearances. Plato brings out this latter opposition in the *Phaedo*. What he there calls Socrates' 'second voyage' is said to consist in the method of logoi or discussions, and that is dialectic. Socrates says: 'I was afraid I might become totally blind in soul through looking at facts with my eyes and trying to grasp them with each of the senses. It seemed to me that I ought to resort to discussions, and study the truth of things in them' (*Phd.* 99E).

We who come after the empiricist–rationalist controversy are liable to take Plato here in a more precise or more recondite sense than he could have imagined. He has no notion of distinguishing the conceptual and the sensible elements in our thought with the minuteness of Kant. He could never have conceived the question: 'What would be left of our thinking if we had absolutely no sensible experience?' All he means is that dialectic, having set itself a question, never tries to obtain the answer by instituting any process of sensible observation, such as filling a pail with water and placing it in the open in order to look at the sun's reflection therein. If the question arose what colour Socrates' eyes were, it might seem natural to answer it by looking at Socrates' eyes. If the question arose why the earth stays where it is and does not fall, we again might hope to answer it by *looking*. We cannot directly look under the earth and see what is there; but by looking more carefully at what is and happens on and above the earth we might perhaps discover a clue to the information we were seeking. It is characteristic of Socrates' 'second voyage' to abandon this natural expectation, to give up looking and listening and the rest—a paradoxical renunciation which, he says here, was finally suggested to him by what he considered the complete failure of his and everybody else's lookings and listenings. The propositions adopted as premisses in the dialectical procedure are so adopted because they seem evident to the company. How and why they seem evident is never discussed, except that it is said not to be because some person has deliberately made an observation and reported what he saw. Sometimes the premisses are the result of experience. A list of 'the things that benefit us' (*ἃ ἡμᾶς ὠφελεῖ Meno* 87E) could not be made out antecedently to experience.

But this is common and inevitable human experience, which no one who enters a discussion can help bringing with him; and Plato is unconscious of it as an empirical element. What he is conscious of, and what he excludes from his method, is deliberately going to look, in other words, scientific observation.

The inward fact, that dialectic uses only the faculty of reason, has as its outward sign that the dialectician uses only words, and not also diagrams or experiments. The dialectician is the user of words, as the lyrist is the user of lyres (*Cra.* 390). He uses 'bare words', which Plato contrasts with geometry (*Tht.* 165A). All other methods use words and something else besides.

Furthermore, the dialectician's words are always arranged in the discontinuous form of conversation, as opposed to the continuous oral harangue and the written discourse. The *Protagoras* strongly deprecates long speeches; *Letter VII* and the *Phaedrus* strongly deprecate writing philosophy down. Plato was so absolutely certain, throughout his life, that the supreme method has its being only in conversation, that he could name it from this fact; 'dialectical' method means conversational method, and he represents an opponent of philosophy as calling it 'whispering with three or four boys in a corner' (*Grg.* 485D). This unshaken principle determined, of course, the form of his writings.

But what determined the principle? Why was Plato so convinced of a proposition which to us is something like a paradox? To obtain some insight into this, let us begin by surveying in more detail the sort of conversation which he held to constitute the supreme method.

As a conversation, dialectic was a social activity. It could not be furthered by the individual alone. The notion of communal inquiry or κοινὴ σκέψις is frequent in the dialogues (e.g. *Cri.* 48D, *Chrm.* 158D, *Plts.* 258C). The partners in this enterprise were not identical in function. The one led and the other followed (for essentially dialectic was a conversation between precisely two persons at a time; any third was, for the time, merely a listener). The leader questioned and the follower answered; for the conversation was always predominantly question-and-answer. The question was usually a request for judgement on a given proposition, requiring the answer yes or no. Thus Plato can designate dialectic as 'the education that will enable them to ask and answer questions most scientifically' (*Rp.* 534D, cf. *Cra.* 390C,

398DE); and, since dialectic is the study of essence, he can even designate essence as 'that of whose reality we give an account both in asking and in answering' (*Phd.* 78D), and define the Ideas as 'all those things on which we stamp the "what itself is" both in asking questions and in giving answers' (*Phd.* 75D). If no one is 'willing to answer', dialectic cannot occur (e.g. *Euthd.* 275C); except that, to some extent at least, a man can play both parts at once (e.g. *Grg.* 506C–507C).

The answerer was expected to say what he himself really thought, and nothing else. 'Be sure you do not agree with me contrary to your real opinion' (*Cri.* 49D). 'What else would anyone say?—Nothing, if that was how he thought.—Well, I do think so' (*La.* 193C). 'Answer as it seems to you' (*Men.* 83D; cf. many other places listed in E. S. Thompson's note on this). Parmenides chooses the youngest to be his answerer, because, among other reasons, 'he will be most likely to say what he thinks' (*Prm.* 137B).

On the other hand, the dialectical conversation had two other aims each of which might conflict with the answerer's saying what he really thought. In the first place, consistency was required. The answerer's opinions must agree with each other. The conflict between these two aims appears in the following passage. 'Theaetetus, can anything become greater or more except by being increased? What do you say?—If, Socrates, I give what seems to me the true answer to the present question, I shall say it cannot; but if I consider the previous question, and take care not to contradict myself, I shall say it can' (*Tht.* 154CD). When such a conflict arose between consistency and 'what I really think', consistency won the day, and the answerer had to abandon one of his opinions, whichever he chose.

The other aim which might conflict with the answerer's saying what he really thought was that there should be complete agreement between the speakers. 'These things must seem true not to you only but to me also in common with you' (*Plts.* 277A). There can be no 'agreeing to differ'. The leader's questions are usually invitations to assent to a certain proposition, and if the answerer declines to assent the leader cannot overlook the fact. He must reinstate agreement either by abandoning the proposition, or by going back and obtaining the answerer's assent by showing that the proposition follows from others to which he assents.

The answerer must always answer. He is not expected to plead ignorance (*Tht.* 187BC). Crito says: 'I cannot answer your question, Socrates; for I have no idea' (*Cri.* 50A). But in such a case it becomes the business of the questioner to bring the answerer to a judgement, by revealing to him the grounds for the proposition, by deducing it from earlier statements with which he agrees, or by developing its nature more. Once the answerer agrees with the questioner, however faintly, that proposition is accepted. Not that they fail to distinguish a mere 'perhaps' (as in *Rp.* 350B) from a hearty affirmation, but that it is essential to the method to put every suggested proposition into one of two categories, accepted or rejected. (How this procedure can harmonize with the claim of dialectic to reach certainty is another question, to which the only hint of an answer is in *Republic* 511; see Chapter X below.)

The principle that the answerer must say what he really thinks is a part of the principle that dialectic recognizes no authority. Neither party may accept a proposition from anyone else, however near or great. The only authority is what seems true to us two here and now. 'The question is not who said it, but whether it is truly said or not' (*Chrm.* 161C). 'As long as we ourselves agree about it, we can say good-bye to other men's opinions' (*Plts.* 260B, cf. *Phdr.* 275BC). 'Let us not consider him, since he is not here' (*Men.* 71D). Another man's dictum can become an authority only by his being present and persuading us of its truth. If Protagoras could get his head above ground, he would very likely persuade us otherwise; 'but we must take ourselves as we find ourselves, I think, and always say what we believe' (*Tht.* 171D, cf. *Hp. Mi.* 365CD). Plato never raised the question whether this principle conflicts with his strong belief in the value of experts, and his demand that men shall obey the expert statesman.

Such are the main theses in Plato's firm conviction that the supreme method lies in oral question-and-answer. What reasons does he offer why we should believe this strange doctrine?

The most hopeful place to look for his reasons is the *Phaedrus*, for there he urges at length that writing is much inferior to conversation. His argument is that the written word cannot teach, or give any great certainty and clarity (277D), for several reasons. It makes men forgetful, by inviting them to trust the ink instead of their memories; whereas true knowledge involves memory graven in the soul. Secondly, it cannot answer questions; 'if you ask a question, wishing to understand one of the statements, it only says some one and the same thing all the time' (275D). It therefore can neither explain anything you do not follow nor remove any objection you may have. (Similarly, the *Protagoras* complains that you cannot ask a poem what it means, 347E, cf. 329A.) Thirdly, the written word cannot choose whom to address, but inevitably speaks to anyone who reads it; this recalls the statement in *Letter VII* that, when unsuitable persons read philosophy, they either despise it or become vain through supposing they understand it when they do not; and in either event philosophy is brought into disrepute (341E).

For these reasons, he holds, written discourses cannot teach. Their proper purposes are only to remind those who know, and to provide amusement and recreation. They have no business with those who do not yet know. True teaching occurs only 'when a man takes a fitting soul and, using the dialectical art, sows and grows therein with knowledge words that can defend themselves and their grower, that are not fruitless but bear seed, from which others growing in other characters can continue this immortally, making their possessor as happy as it is possible for man to be' (*Phdr.* 276E).

These remarks by no means justify Plato's conviction that the supreme method is question-and-answer. All that they even attempt to justify is the doctrine that we can learn from a man only by talking to him, and not also by reading what he has written. They make no effort to show that the conversation must be question-and-answer as opposed to any other sort; and, even if we assume this, we still have no reason why the questions should come from the teacher and not, as might seem more useful, from the learner. Even if we assume this also, there still remains the fact that the *Phaedrus* appears to be solely concerned with methods of teaching and not also with methods of discovery. Now the supreme method is surely directed to the discovery of truth more than to its communication; and anyhow Plato quite evidently thinks of dialectic as a method of discovery at least as much as a method of teaching. The following passage surely includes, as an intentional and unmistakable part of its meaning, the implication that question-and-answer is essential to philosophic discovery: 'Hardly when each of these things is compared with the others, names and definitions, sights and perceptions, and men criticize them in question and answer with benevolent criticisms and without envy, does wisdom and intelligence about each thing flash out, straining human power to the utmost' (*Letter VII*, 344B).

On the main problem, then, namely, why question-and-answer is essential to discovery, the *Phaedrus*, which on first thoughts seems the most hopeful place to look, provides no information. Yet the problem urgently requires a solution. For can Plato really have thought that you cannot do philosophy by yourself? Surely a question-and-answer conversation such as the dialogues exemplify could not occur at all unless the leader had done a great deal of private discovery beforehand?

This problem has usually been overlooked by students of Plato's dialectic; and the reason is probably that they have taken him as meaning that question-and-answer is essential only to teaching and not also to discovery. But that is not all he means. Even if we reject the above-quoted passage on the ground that the *Seventh Letter* is spurious, it is still quite certain that from the *Meno* to the *Philebus* Plato is convinced of these two propositions: (1) that dialectic is the supreme method of discovery as well as of teaching, and (2) that dialectic has its being only in question-and-answer. Nettleship is one of the few who have tried to explain this (*Lectures on the Republic of Plato* 277–80).

There is not in Plato's writings anything like a satisfactory answer to the question 'Why is question-and-answer essential to discovery?' He says that two heads are better than one, and that if a man thinks of anything by himself he at once looks for someone to whom he can show it and with whom he can confirm it (*Prt.* 348D). He makes Socrates say that he queries instead of asserting 'in order that the discussion may proceed so as to make most clear to us what is being discussed' (*Grg.* 453C). He implies, and very likely rightly, that, however doubtful we may feel, we should have a working hypothesis rather than suspend judgement; and this confirms the rule that the answerer must always give a judgement (*Tht.* 187BC, 200E–201A). He says that if you set speech against speech you will need a third party to judge who wins the case; but if one party questions the other and secures his consent at each step, then the two of them are judges and advocates at once (*Rp.* 348AB). But such remarks seem wholly inadequate to justify his confidence that the supreme method is always question-and-answer; and there is nothing solider. In the places where Socrates is made to insist on question-and-answer, his reasons are either frivolous or undisclosed. If, for example, you knew no other dialogue than the *Protagoras*, you might almost think that Plato, while possessing literary genius including the gift of mimicry, did not understand the meaning of Socrates' art of question-and-answer; so empty and insincere is the defence of this art which he there attributes to Socrates. In the *Gorgias*, again, the demand for question-and-answer is accompanied by no reason in one place (449), and in another place by the frivolous reason that if Polus makes long speeches Socrates ought to have the liberty of going away (461E).

No doubt we can imagine for ourselves several fairly good arguments for Plato's view. For example, the passages just referred to suggest the argument that question-and-answer is the only way to keep ourselves reasoning in a straight line, to preserve geometrical or hypothetical method as opposed to stringing together a set of independent arguments or persuasions whose premisses are not properly confessed. But the moment we have formulated this we feel that it is far too strongly stated; 'the only way' must be softened to 'a useful way', and then the premiss will no longer bear the weight of Plato's conviction. Or we might argue thus. In a chain of reasoning it is necessary to see or intuit each step; if you go forward with a step unseen you have no knowledge of anything thereafter, and you have drugged your reason. The only way to ensure such an intuition is, to borrow an excellent phrase from Shorey (on *Rp.* 533AB Loeb), to check 'the stream of thought by . . . securing the understanding and assent of an intelligent interlocutor at every step'. But all such arguments, besides their main defect of being invented by us rather than found in Plato, seem to make question-and-answer at best a useful dodge, and by no means the imperative necessity suggested by Plato's regular inclusion of it in his conception of the supreme method.

It is useless to look for sufficient reasons for the Platonic doctrine that the supreme method entails question-and-answer, because there are none. The presence of this doctrine in Plato cannot be explained as a logical conclusion, but only as an historical phenomenon; and to this sort of explanation let us now turn.

Plato's view that question-and-answer is essential to good

method was due in general to the fondness of the ancient Athenians for discussion. They regarded thinking as a social affair, and interpreted thought in terms of speech. Although Plato recognized that a man may make discoveries in his study, he held that he does so by a process essentially the same as that of discussion. 'A process analogous to that of questioning others goes on in the mind of the single inquirer' (Nettleship). Thought proceeds by asking itself questions and answering them. Hence the self-evidence to Plato of the definition of thinking as the dialogue of the soul with itself; it does not occur to him to give reasons for that (*Tht.* 189E, *Sph.* 263E).

But the more special and efficacious cause of this Platonic doctrine is the following. Question-and-answer was unconditionally necessary to the Socratic elenchus. As such, it entered into the blood of Socrates' pupil Plato. Plato never became accurately aware of how much he was straining and distorting the Socratic views by the influence of his own distinct Platonic personality. In particular, he never fully appreciated the distinctness of Socrates' destructiveness from his own constructiveness. The elenchus, which is a purely destructive instrument, went forward in the mind of Plato by its own inertia into Plato's new constructive instrument of dialectic; and managed always to avoid the exposure of its own unsuitability thereto. Plato's conception of dialectic in the Divided Line is, as we shall see below, one of constructing by means of destroying or at least of attempting to destroy. Dialectic demands question-and-answer because it demands elenchus and elenchus demands question-and-answer. However, this was not a reasoned conclusion to Plato; it was an assumption carried over from his pupilage. Otherwise it could not have still commanded his absolute confidence even in his late period, when dialectic had taken the form of division and synthesis, and no longer bore the slightest resemblance to the Socratic elenchus.

We have a curious example in the *Theaetetus* of the subterfuges adopted by the notion of elenchus to maintain its home in Plato's alien mind, namely the figure of Socrates as a midwife. In this figure the elenchus accommodates itself to Plato's productive personality by pretending to be a method for bringing intellectual children to birth; but it slyly preserves its old destructiveness, not merely by producing births in others and never in Socrates, but also by assuming the power to decide whether the birth in question is 'genuine or a wind-egg' (151E). And, sure enough, every one of Theaetetus' productions turns out to be a wind-egg! The midwife figure, which occurs only in the *Theaetetus*, is a purely Platonic invention, made long after Socrates' death; and it serves the unconscious purpose of enabling the elenchus to preserve a good standing in an otherwise very un-Socratic mind.

Such a figure might conceal from its author the distance his mind had travelled since his youth; but it cannot conceal from his readers the growing incongruity in fact. All students of Plato remark how, in the *Sophist* and the *Statesman*, the pretence of question-and-answer misfits the form, which is really a continuous treatise; and how this pretence is practically abandoned in the *Timaeus* and the *Laws*. Aristotle, unencumbered by a Socratic pupilage, states clearly a view more consonant with Plato's later practice: conversation is actually *more* liable to error than solitary thought (*S.E.* 169ᵃ37 ff.); science does *not* proceed by question-and-answer (*S.E.* 172ᵃ15 and *Post. Anal.* I in general); and dialectic, which does so proceed as its name implies, is not the method of science.

§ 4. ERISTIC

Dialectic is, according to Plato, a dangerous method. It is liable to make men reject the good moral principles in which they have been bred, and take to pleasure-seeking (*Rp.* 537E–539A). When we ask him how this comes about, we find that his answer again presupposes the prominence of elenchus in dialectic. 'Boys, when they first get a taste of discussion, use it like a game, always turning it to contradiction, and imitating those who refute them by refuting others, rejoicing like puppies to worry and tear with their argument whoever is at hand. . . . And when they have refuted many and been refuted by many, they plunge quickly and violently into a rejection of all their former beliefs' (*Rp.* 539B, cf. *Phlb.* 15DE). Dialectic is dangerous because it entails refutation or elenchus, and there is a temptation to treat elenchus as an amusing game and practise it for its own sake.

Plato constantly has in mind a certain opposite of dialectic, something superficially like dialectic and yet as bad as dialectic is good, something against which the would-be dialectician must always be on guard. He has two chief names for this shadow or reverse of dialectic, antilogic and eristic. By 'eristic', or the art of quarrelling, he indicates that the aim of this procedure is to win the argument, whereas the aim of dialectic is to discover truth. By 'antilogic', or the art of contradiction, he indicates that it is a tendency to contradict, to maintain aggressively whatever position is opposite to that of one's interlocutor. In the *Meno* (75CD) the technical adjective 'dialectical' is opposed to 'eristical'; and the content there given to the opposition is that dialecticians are gentle and friendly to each other, that they try to say the truth, and that they answer by means of things of which the questioner admits a knowledge. The dialogue *Euthydemus* is mainly devoted to picturing or exaggerating the eristical temper, a childish contentiousness that cares nothing for truth and uses any and every device that gives an appearance of winning an argument. The rarity of the actual names in this dialogue—'eristical' only 272B; 'antilogical' nowhere—is due to the sustained irony by which this behaviour is pretended to be a difficult and valuable art. Whereas the appropriate picture for dialectic is the road or the search, that for eristic is the fight; and the eristics Euthydemus and Dionysodorus formerly taught military science, and also that form of fighting which goes on in courts of law (*Euthd.* 271D–272A).

The more detailed connotation of 'eristic' and 'antilogic' tends to be whatever Plato happens to think of as bad method at the moment, just as 'dialectic' is to him at every stage of his thought whatever he then considered the best method. Thus in the *Republic* (454A) antilogic is the inability to divide a thing according to its kinds, because that is the mistake the speakers have just made. In the *Phaedo*, on the other hand, where good method consists in distinguishing premises from conclusions and not doubting everything at once, antilogic accordingly consists in 'confusing everything together' (101DE). In the *Philebus* (17A) dialectic is the determination of the limit or mean that exists between the one and the unlimited many; and eristic is accordingly the failure to do this. Antilogic sometimes includes also the doctrine of the flux (*Phd.* 90C), and the power of making everything seem similar to everything as far as possible (*Phdr.* 261).

The reason why Plato constantly pillories eristic and distinguishes it from dialectic is that in truth his own dialectic very closely resembled eristic; and this in turn is because his own dialectic, though having a constructive purpose, incorporates the destructive Socratic elenchus. The Socratic elenchus looks to the ordinary observer like nothing so much as an obstinate determination to disprove whatever the other party says. Socrates himself may have been always pure in heart; but it is extremely difficult for anyone who practises the elenchus to be sure that he would still do so if there were no love of victory in him, and that he always desists as soon as the need for truth and enlightenment is satisfied. Part of Plato's antagonism to eristic is thus vigilance against an evil to which the Socratics were more liable than anyone else, against the enemy within their own gates; and eristic is the degeneration of Plato's own method, or at least of Socrates' own method, rather than the invention of outsiders. His belief that truth can only be found through argumentative conversation obliged Plato to reject energetically that sort of argumentative conversation whose aim is only to win. Other philosophers do not need to attack eristic because their method is utterly different from eristic.

Plato never admits this in so many words; but the following passages indicate the fact, and his feeling for the fact, that eristic was a vinegary dialectic. In the *Republic* he makes Socrates say that many fall into antilogic unintentionally, where the implication is that Socrates and his companions are, for this once at least, among the 'many', and that only an unusual skill can prevent question-and-answer from becoming antilogical.

Ah Glaucon, said I, noble indeed is the power of the antilogical art. —How so?—Why, I said, it seems to me that many people fall into it even unintentionally, thinking they are not quarrelling but conversing (διαλέγεσθαι), because they are unable to divide the subject according to kinds and so examine it. They pursue the merely verbal contradictory of the proposition, thus quarrelling instead of discussing (διαλέκτῳ) among themselves.—Yes, he said, that happens to many people; but does it concern us also at the present moment?—Absolutely, said I; we are unintentionally clinging to antilogic. (*Rp.* 454A).

Similarly, but less distinctly, the *Theaetetus* (164C) represents Socrates as admitting that he himself has just lapsed from 'philosophy' to 'antilogic'. In the last page of the *Euthydemus* Plato seems to be saying, as clearly as he can without abandoning the dramatic form, 'Do not make the mistake of condemning all philosophy because I have here convicted one sort of philosophy', which implies that the behaviour of the brothers *was* a sort of philosophy. In the *Sophist* (225) he defines eristic as skilled dispute, for the sake of victory, by question-and-answer, about the just and unjust themselves and the others in general; and the reference to 'the just and unjust themselves' shows how close we are to dialectic. The opening of this dialogue shows how close we are to elenchus; for, when Socrates expects the stranger to refute the company, Theodorus replies that 'that is not the stranger's way, Socrates; he is more moderate than those who care for controversies' (ἔριδας). The great energy with which the *Euthydemus* drives home the maxim, that we should encourage the will to learn and suppress the will to win, was necessary only because Plato's chosen method of philosophizing was a strong temptation to indulge the will to win.

More commonly, however, Plato implies that eristic has its being among persons quite outside the Socratic circle. Even while accusing himself thereof, Socrates refers to 'those clever men' as if he were not intimately acquainted with the protagonists of eristic (*Tht.* loc. cit.). These persons are not usually named; but in the *Phaedrus* (261D) the 'Eleatic Palamedes', which means Zeno, is said to be an antilogician, and the *Euthydemus* is a sketch of Euthydemus and Dionysodorus in this role.

Plato does not imply that there ever were any persons who accepted the title of 'eristic' or 'antilogician' as their natural and proper designation. His usage would be compatible with that belief; but it rather suggests that he regarded these two words, and thought everyone else regarded them, as terms which no one would willingly have applied to himself. They were not like 'communist', which today one man uses as abuse while another is proud of the name; but like 'blackguard', which no one gladly accepts. Nor is there any suggestion that he thought of them like the word 'Cynic', which originated as abuse but was accepted by those whom it was meant to hurt.

The question whether anybody chose to call himself an eristic cannot be answered from Plato's dialogues alone. It depends chiefly on what we make of Diogenes Laertius' statements that the Megarians came to be called eristics (II 106), and that Protagoras wrote an 'Art of Eristics' (IX 55) and 'was the father of the whole tribe of eristical disputants now so much in evidence' (IX 52, Hicks tr.). What we may be certain of is that many people, often professing to be doing something valuable, indulged in verbal fights of question-and-answer to which other people applied the word 'eristical' as a term of blame. Whether Protagoras was one of these is hard to judge. Sidgwick urged that, if he was, it is quite incredible that Plato would ever have represented him as so utterly averse to question-and-answer; and it is therefore impossible to reconcile Diogenes with Plato on this matter (*JP* IV 299). His solution is that Protagoras did not practise question-and-answer, and that his 'Art of Eristics' was how to make speeches on both sides of a case. 'The Art of Disputation which is ascribed to Sophists in the *Euthydemus* and the *Sophistes* . . . originated entirely with Socrates, and . . . he is altogether responsible for the form at least of [Plato's] second species of Sophistic' (op. cit. 298). The sceptical and destructive aim, however, of this eristical tendency, together with the logical puzzles and paradoxes which it used, came according to Sidgwick from Protagoras and Zeno.

In spite of Plato's care to keep the word 'dialectic' for a good method distinct from the prevalent 'eristic', it often came near to being confounded therewith. Isocrates was perhaps thinking of Plato when he spoke of 'those who make a business of argument' (ἔριδας *Antidosis* 258). The Megarians were called at one time 'eristics', and later 'dialecticians'. Plato's own most brilliant pupil wrote an elaborate handbook of dialectic, the *Topics*, which presents the method as something far more like what Plato would have called eristic than what he hoped dialectic to be.

§ 5. WHO INVENTED DIALECTIC?

The notion of dialectic which we find in Plato's dialogues was invented by Plato himself. Before giving reasons for this proposition we may define it a little more precisely. By 'the notion of dialectic' here it will suffice to mean 'the idea that there could be a supreme method for reaching ultimate truth (ultimate truth being truth about "essences" or "forms") which would operate solely by conversation in the form of question-and-answer'. We need not add that Plato at one time thought this method would make much use of hypothetical deduction and at another time thought it would make much use of division and synthesis. By 'invention' is not meant 'creation out of nothing' (for Plato's notion of dialectic was, like all human notions, closely allied to previous notions, and contained elements borrowed from previous thinkers); but rather that Plato slightly changed the elements he borrowed, so that they strike us as new varieties if not species, and that he combined these elements into an organic whole which gives a strong impression of novelty. If we add to what we mean by 'Plato's dialectic' the ideas of hypothesis and division, the organic whole becomes larger and still more strikingly novel, because it brings into relation more pairs of ideas that were unrelated before. The idea of 'essences' or 'forms' is the result of reflection on the Socratic question 'What is X?'. The idea of using exclusively conversational question-and-answer is the result of reflecting on the Socratic elenchus. The idea of hypothesis is very possibly in part a gift from Zeno, either directly or through Socrates, as Burnet and Taylor have suggested. The idea of division is hard to assign to any forerunner. In any case, each of these ideas is a little different in Plato from what it was in the man from whom he took it, and their combination in Plato is widely different from any combination in any previous or subsequent person. So much by way of defining the proposition that the notion of dialectic which we find in Plato's dialogues was invented by Plato himself.

Let us now consider the evidence for this proposition. Plato's dialectic presupposes Socrates in two ways in which Socrates himself was original, and hence cannot have existed in anyone's brain prior to Socrates. It presupposes both the Socratic elenchus and the Socratic 'What is X?', each of which was a new thing. Hence it must have been invented either by Socrates himself or by one of his pupils. But Socrates himself did not develop the theory of 'essences'; and· Plato does not introduce the idea of dialectic until those dialogues in which he is no longer merely reproducing his master. Dialectic appears first in the *Meno* or *Euthydemus* or *Cratylus*, and mainly in the *Phaedo* (without the name), the *Republic*, the *Phaedrus*, the *Sophist*, the *Statesman*, and the *Philebus*. Therefore dialectic was invented by one of Socrates' pupils. The obvious one is Plato.

The premisses of the above argument are, of course, (1) that the middle and late dialogues are not historical, and (2) that Socrates was original in his elenchus and his 'What is X?'. These premisses are not themselves argued in this book; but with regard to the first we may note at this point that a certain inconsistency in the presentation of dialectic in the dialogues suggests that on this matter at any rate they are unhistorical. This inconsistency is that Plato represents the dialectical method as familiar to Socrates' hearers and yet as requiring to be explained to them. Simmias assumes in the *Phaedo* (92) the hypothetical method which Socrates describes to him at length eight pages later (see below, p. 139). Glaucon and Adimantus in the *Republic* are familiar with dialectic (511C5) and question-and-answer (534D) and the 'customary method' of positing 'essences' (596A); and yet they require to have dialectic explained to them (532DE). The explanation of the inconsistency surely is that Plato wishes both to describe his new method and to represent it as practised in the Socratic circle.

Aristotle believed that the notion of dialectic was invented by Plato. He says in his *Metaphysics* that 'at that time there was not yet a dialectical power so as to be able to examine opposites even apart from essence, and whether the knowledge of opposites is the same' (*M* 4, 1078ᵇ25). The context compels us to understand the time referred to as being the time when Socrates was doing his work; if then Aristotle held dialectic to have arisen after Socrates' death, he surely held that it was created by Plato. We might try to circumvent this passage in one of two ways: we might say, in the first place, that Aristotle does not mean that no sort of dialectic existed during the life of Socrates, but only that that special sort did not exist which, as he says, enables one 'to examine opposites even apart from essence'; secondly, we might say that, even if Aristotle thought no sort of dialectic existed during the life of Socrates, it does not follow that he thought the inventor was Plato. Both these escapes seem to be stopped, however, by the parallel passage in *Metaphysics A*, for there Aristotle says simply that 'previously men did not possess dialectic' (οἱ γὰρ πρότεροι διαλεκτικῆς οὐ μετεῖχον, 987ᵇ32); and this, coming in a chapter devoted to Plato, seems conclusive about Aristotle's opinion.

From the proposition that Plato invented the notion of dialectic found in his dialogues we can distinguish the proposition that Plato invented the technical word 'dialectic'. This second proposition is probably also true. Since the word means 'the conversational method', it must have been coined by someone who made conversation an integral part of his truthseeking. There was, to the best of our belief, no such person prior to Socrates. Therefore the word was invented either by Plato or by Socrates. But which? A very complex and individual thing like Plato's *notion* of dialectic is most unlikely to have come into his mind from that of Socrates without change; but we cannot say the same of a mere *word*, which is relatively simple and lacking in character. All that ἡ διαλεκτικὴ μέθοδος immediately connotes is 'conversational method'; and, since this much is common to Socrates and Plato, either of them may have invented the term. If, however, we were to decide that Socrates invented it, then we should have to say, in view of our previous conclusion, that Plato gave to it a new connotation in which Socrates' connotation was only an element.

These conclusions about the origin of dialectic stand in opposition to the tendency of Taylor and Lee to trace Plato's dialectic back to Zeno (see H. D. P. Lee, *Zeno of Elea*, and the references therein to Taylor); and this tendency is strongly supported by the assertion of Diogenes Laertius (VIII 57, cf. IX 25) that Aristotle in his *Sophist* said that Empedocles first discovered rhetoric and Zeno dialectic.

The statement that Zeno was the discoverer of dialectic, whoever said it or did not say it, may be true in many of the many senses the word 'dialectic' has borne since Aristotle; but it is very inaccurate and misleading if we take the word either in Plato's sense or in Aristotle's. It is extremely improbable either that Zeno ever thought of the word 'dialectic' or that he ever entertained a method similar to Plato's or Aristotle's dialectic, and both these propositions are improbable for the same reason, namely that, whereas Plato and Aristotle both considered question-and-answer essential to dialectic, Zeno probably never even entertained the idea that question-and-answer was necessary to good method. One of his arguments, the millet-seed, has indeed reached us in the form of question-and-answer. But no one, so far as I know, believes that that was its original form; the rest of his extant arguments are all in continuous form; and it is most unlikely that his famous book was a dialogue. It is therefore preferable to accept the implication of Aristotle's *Metaphysics*, which is that dialectic was invented by Plato, and reject the contrary statement in his *Sophist*.

On the other hand, Aristotle's remark in the *Sophist*, though loose, is not wholly false. There is one important element common to Plato's dialectic and Aristotle's dialectic and Zeno's method, namely, the refutation of an opponent's thesis by deducing from it some intolerable consequence. This is the indirect argument, or destructive hypothetical syllogism, which we also discovered in the Socratic elenchus (above, p. 24). Undoubtedly Zeno's book was the first explicit and striking appearance of reduction to impossibility in the western world. No doubt it was reflection on this element in dialectic that led Aristotle in his dialogue to say that Zeno discovered dialectic, instead of the more accurate statement that Zeno discovered reduction to impossibility. For the moment he meant by 'dialectic' only refutation by reduction to impossibility, and he did not mean that Zeno used the word. Mr. Hinks has argued that the statement that Empedocles invented rhetoric is loose in the same way (*CQ* 1940).

VII

HYPOTHESIS

LET us now turn to that element of dialectic which is prominent only in the middle dialogues, namely hypothesis.

§ 1. THE NOTION OF HYPOTHESIS

Plato often uses the word τίθημι in the sense of 'posit' or 'lay down'. For example, there are at least seven occurrences of the simple verb in this sense in the twenty-eight pages of *Republic* I:

1. 'I lay it down (τίθημι) that this is what the possession of money is most useful for' 331A.
2-3. 'We seem to have defined (θέσθαι) friend and enemy wrongly.—How did we define (θέμενοι) them?' 334E.
4-6. 'Thrasymachus said (ἔθετο) that justice is doing what the governors say.—And he also said (ἔθετο) that justice is the advantage of the stronger. And in saying (θέμενος) both these things he', &c., 340AB.
7. 'I understand that this is how these things stand, and not as you at first posited (ἐτίθεσο)' 352D.

The same book contains at least four cases of a compound of τίθημι used to mean a special sort of positing or laying down (334E, 345B, 346B, 352D). This use is very common and familiar throughout the dialogues. It shades easily into the notion of judging, as we mean judging when we say 'I put him first': 'judging (θέντος) each of the men to be of equal value' (*Plts.* 257B). It also shades into the notion of opining; thus in the *Sophist* it seems to be a regular word for a thinker's views, and is to be translated 'hold': 'Do they hold (τιθέντες) that there is such a thing as soul?' (*Sph.* 246E).

Plato gives no analysis of the procedure referred to by this use of the word τίθημι; but what he meant, and what we all mean by 'positing', seems to be of this nature. If you posit a proposition, it thenceforward 'lies' (κεῖται), or, as we put it, 'stands'. It becomes a 'standing part' of your thoughts, as opposed to the propositions that you merely entertain or believe for a moment and then forget. It is not something known; to posit is not to know or apprehend or intuit or realize. It is, we may roughly say, something believed. But it may be believed with all degrees of confidence down to the very least; and perhaps it may be merely 'make-believed'. This is possible because positing is essentially a deliberate and reflective activity. The word does not cover beliefs which we hold without knowing how we came to hold them, or which we have never conceived ourselves not holding. It does not cover naïve unquestioning acceptance, nor the mere taking for granted that A is B, which is not thinking at all, but behaving as you would if you thought that A was B. Positing is only that kind of believing in which we deliberately and consciously adopt a proposition with the knowledge that after all it may be false. It involves all the obscurities of the part played by the will in judgement, or the intersection of will and understanding.

What is posited is always provisional and tentative. It is posited only 'until further notice'. We are aware that we may have to withdraw it and posit something else or suspend judgement.

Positing is deliberate in that it is consciously doing something which we need not do. But it is not necessarily deliberated in the sense of being preceded by a discussion of the pros and cons. That may or may not happen. When Socrates says 'Shall we then posit two sorts of persuasion?', there is good reason for such positing, because he has just pointed out the distinction (Grg. 454E). On the other hand, no recommendation whatever had been given for the proposition which in Republic 334E (quoted above) is spoken of as having been posited; it was merely 'laid down'.

That which is posited is a 'thesis'; but the word θέσις seems to carry this sense only once in Plato (Rp. 335A), though several times in Aristotle. Otherwise Plato has no noun to represent a proposition as having been posited by someone and now being a standing part of his thought.

Let us turn to the special kinds of positing that Plato represents by compounds of τίθημι. Among them are ἀνατίθεμαι, ὑποτίθεμαι, μετατίθεμαι, προτίθεμαι. Here the verb is apparently never used in the active voice.

Προτίθεμαι, diverging considerably from the simple verb, means to put forward or suggest or propound as something that might be posited, rather than actually to posit.

Ἀνατίθεμαι is to cease positing, and thus to realize a possibility inherent in the essentially provisional nature of the act of positing. Liddell and Scott call it a metaphor from taking back a move in a game of draughts. No doubt the game of draughts often occurred to Greeks when they were thinking of the word ἀνατίθεμαι in its logical sense; but that the word obtained its logical sense from its use in draughts is no more probable than that the simple verb τίθημι got its meaning of 'posit' from meaning 'make a move at draughts'. One might as well pick out a single strand in a hawser and declare that that is what holds the liner at her berth. The compounds of τίθημι in the logical sense take their meaning from that of the simple verb; and the strands that bind this meaning to the original physical sense of 'put' are multitudinous and innumerable.

Μετατίθεμαι is to cease positing one thing and posit a contrary proposition instead, to 'change your position'. It is thus more specific than ἀνατίθεμαι, which might be either positing something new or suspending judgement. If you posit (τίθεσαι) a proposition, then that proposition 'stands' (κεῖται) until you withdraw it (ἀνατίθεσαι) or replace it by another (μετατίθεσαι).

Ὑποτίθεμαι or 'hypothesize' is to posit as a preliminary. It conveys the notion of laying down a proposition as the beginning of a process of thinking, in order to work on the basis thereof. So far as the nature of this process of thinking is made explicit, it turns out to be the drawing of consequences from the proposition hypothesized, or the rejecting of propositions found to be inconsistent therewith, and thus obtaining a systematic or at least consistent body of propositions. A proposition hypothesized is thus a specially important proposition. It guides your subsequent thinking. It is the source of your system so far as you have one. It is more important to the system than most of its other constituents, and recurs more often in the course of discussion. It is a relatively permanent and solid part of thinking or discourse, for it determines the framework of the whole.

Ὑποτίθεμαι comes nearest of all the compounds to the meaning of the simple verb. It does not, like ἀνατίθεμαι, negative the original sense. It does not, like μετατίθεμαι and προτίθεμαι, add some new mark. It merely intensifies an element that was present before. For all positing is essentially positing as a preliminary to further thought, or at least as a basis to some kind of future activity. Thus when Socrates and Theaetetus 'posit' the waxen tablet, they do so for the sake of the future explanation of false opinion it may make possible (*Tht.* 191C).

It might be urged that, although τίθεμαι and ὑποτίθεμαι agree in being positing for the sake of future action, they differ in this respect: in τίθεμαι the positing is itself preceded by deduction, but not so in ὑποτίθεμαι; whereas τίθεμαι means 'posit as the conclusion of a process of reasoning', ὑποτίθεμαι means 'posit without reason, to be a reason for subsequent statements'. Plato does seem to have some slight tendency towards this usage; but it never crystallized so, partly no doubt owing to the convenience of sometimes using τίθεμαι to pick up a previous ὑποτίθεμαι. We have already seen that a proposition said to be 'posited' in the dialogues is sometimes actually reached by means of reflection and sometimes not; we must now observe that the same is true of propositions said to be 'hypothesized'. When Protagoras said that Simonides 'hypothesized that it is hard to become a good man in truth' (*Prt.* 339D), he was referring to the first sentence of Simonides' poem, which was therefore not supported by any previous reasoning. When Socrates said that 'in our argument we hypothesized that temperance is a good' (*Chrm.* 160D), he was referring to the first proposition of that argument (159C1), which had received no recommendation either before or after its enunciation. No doubt there are many such passages; and this sense of 'hypothesizing' tended to prevail as time went on, so that the Platonic *Definitions* defined hypothesis as 'undemonstrated beginning', and Aristotle defined it as a special sort of undemonstrated beginning. But in Plato's dialogues we also find many passages of an opposite nature, in which hypothesizing is preceded by reasoning just as mere positing can be preceded by reasoning. At the end of the *Protagoras* (361B) Socrates refers to Protagoras as having hypothesized that virtue is teachable; Protagoras had actually made a long speech offering several arguments to prove that this is so. In the *Republic* (437A) they decide to hypothesize a proposition after a pagelong discussion which includes a defence of it against possible objections. Therefore hypothesizing in the dialogues is not necessarily an absolute beginning of deduction. It is merely a beginning relative to some more or less separable train of thought; and, since all positing is with an eye to the future, it differs from the simple verb merely in emphasizing this aspect.

'Hypothesizing' is a common and familiar notion in the dialogues. Ast lists at least twenty-nine genuine occurrences of this sense. If we add all those places where the simple verb τίθεσθαι is used in an only slightly vaguer sense, the number of the occurrences will be multiplied several times.

Plato very rarely speaks of hypothesizing a proposition that one knows at the time to be false. His conception of hypothesizing hardly, if ever, extends to sheer make-belief. The following is about the most extreme example: 'hypothesizing that they would be willing to answer more law-abidingly than they now are' (Sph. 246D). It might seem more extreme when Parmenides speaks of 'the hypothesis that Zeno hypothesized, if it is many' (Prm. 136A), since Zeno was convinced that it is *not* many; but Zeno was arguing with persons who thought it *was* many, and the proposition is called an hypothesis from their point of view. In every elenchus the proposition which the answerer hypothesizes may be known by the questioner from the beginning to be false; if the questioner then pretends to be not refuting the answerer but joining with him in discovering the consequences of the hypothesis, he is pretending to hypothesize a proposition he knows to be false. But this is just the irony of the elenchus, a pedagogical and not a methodological device.

The preceding paragraph is about Plato's use of the verb 'hypothesizing'. It is not an assertion that he never deliberately practises what we might call hypothetical thinking. He often does. 'Even if . . . such a thing could not happen, Protarchus, what must follow from it?' (Phlb. 42E). But he does not call it 'hypothesizing'. His word for assuming what you already know or believe to be false is not ὑποτίθεσθαι but συγχωρεῖν. This comes out most clearly in the *Charmides*, which contains a great deal of deduction from premisses supposed to be false. And the opposition is neatly suggested in this passage: 'Let us consider it, if you like; let us allow (συγχωρήσαντες) that it is possible to know knowledge; and what we at first posited (ἐτιθέμεθα) temperance to be, knowing what he knows and what he does not know, let us not remove but grant (δῶμεν)' 172C. Here both the proposition 'it is possible to know knowledge' and the proposition 'temperance is knowing what he knows and what he does not know' seem to have been rendered untenable. Nevertheless, they are going to assume them in what follows. This assuming is called συγχωρεῖν. But when Socrates is referring to an earlier instant of the discussion, before these propositions had been invalidated, he uses τίθεμαι; at that stage they were not 'allowing' them but 'positing' them.

Hypothesizing is positing with a view to future action. Usually the action contemplated is thinking, and so hypothesizing is a term of logic. But several times in the dialogues the word takes a more practical meaning, in which what is posited is not so much a proposition from which consequences are to be drawn as a purpose to be fulfilled or a way of fulfilling a purpose; not a proposition, but a proposal. Thus the physician lays down (ὑπο-θέσθαι) prescriptions for the treatment of the sick (*Plts.* 295C); and Thrasymachus is said to have proposed (ὑπέθου, *Rp.* 346B) that the speakers should be strictly accurate in their choice of words. The practical and the logical senses of the verb are clearly closely allied; and there could be any number of degrees between laying down a proposal that has nothing to do with thinking and laying down a proposition for the sole purpose of deducing its consequences. Quite separate from this range of meanings are a few much more clearly physical senses of the word in the dialogues, such as 'found a city' (*Laws* 682C) and 'make subject to' (*Plts.* 308A).

Plato also uses the noun 'hypothesis', though less often than the verb 'hypothesize' and far less often than the simple verb 'posit'. In his writings this noun is always simply the noun corresponding to the verb 'hypothesize', and takes its meanings entirely therefrom. That is why it is often used as a cognate accusative after the verb. It does not, however, bear all the senses that the verb can take, for it has no physical or nearly physical sense. 'There is absolutely no evidence' that it ever meant 'basis', says Burnet (on *Euthyph.* 11C5); and he convincingly reinterprets the one passage cited by Liddell and Scott for this sense (eighth edition; this sense is abandoned in the new edition). If it had ever borne some such sense as 'physical foundation', Plato would hardly have written the phrase ἄλλην αὖ ὑπόθεσιν ὑποθέμενος ἥτις τῶν ἄνωθεν βελτίστη φαίνοιτο (*Phd.* 101D); for it would have carried the absurd suggestion of 'placing as base whatever base seemed best of those above'! In the *Republic* (511B) he writes 'making the hypotheses not beginnings but really hypotheses, like steps and sallies'; but there, because it suits his purpose, he is calling attention to something the word might have been used to mean but has not; and the phrase 'really hypotheses' is a humorous pretence. Burnet calls it 'a characteristic etymological pun, such as is often introduced by τῷ ὄντι '. E. S. Thompson has pointed out that the same kind of wordplay seems to occur in the *Euthyphro* 11C (ed. *Men.* p. 146): 'Your statements, Euthyphro, seem to be like the creations of my ancestor Daedalus. And if *I* had made them and laid them down (ἐτιθέμην), perhaps you would have twitted me that it was because of my relationship to him that my verbal creations run away and will not remain where one lays them (θῇ). But as it is they are *your* layings-down (ὑποθέσεις).'

The noun 'hypothesis' in Plato always means that which is posited as a beginning, whether a beginning of practice or of deduction. Thus it always corresponds either to the practical or to the logical sense of 'hypothesize'. It appears to carry the practical sense only four times (*Grg.* 454C, *Rp.* 550C, *Laws* 743C, 812A). In every other occurrence it means a proposition posited as a start towards a system of propositions. In later times the word also meant 'summary'; and this use is noticed in the Platonic *Definitions*, but does not occur in Plato's own dialogues.

Since the noun 'hypothesis' in Plato takes its whole meaning entirely from that use of the verb 'hypothesize' which refers to positing with a view to future action, it follows that we have already explained its meaning in explaining this meaning of the verb; and there is nothing more to be said on that matter. It is much better to study this notion in the verb than in the noun; for 'hypothesizing' is a species of thinking, whereas 'hypothesis' is not a species of proposition but any proposition in so far as it is hypothesized.

The above statements imply a view about the origin of the logical notion of hypothesis. They imply that it did not arise in any specialized or narrow domain of human thought, such as law or medicine or mathematics, but is a natural and inevitable notion that arises wherever men use any prolonged reflection, the notion of positing, which the Greeks commonly expressed by the metaphor of putting. It is true that the first appearance of the noun in the *Phaedo* (92D) is close to a mention of geometry. It is true that the first explicit introduction of a hypothetical method in Plato (*Men.* 86–87) is said to be borrowed from the mathematicians. But what the *Meno* borrows is a method of using hypothesis, not the original notion of hypothesis. It is reasonable to suppose, on the evidence of the *Meno* (we have no other), that the mathematicians of Plato's day were consciously using a certain procedure which they called hypothetical, and that Plato was imitating them when he first consciously used the procedure himself. But it is not at all likely that Plato learnt or even thought he learnt the very word and conception of hypothesis itself from the mathematicians. We must distinguish between the mere conception of hypothesizing and the conception of the use of hypothesizing as part of some orderly process aimed at the discovery of truth. We have determined the former, and we must proceed to determine the latter. But first let us dispose of the question whether there is in Plato any restriction on the kind of proposition that may be hypothesized.

It has sometimes been held that according to Plato an hypothesis was always a definition. Archer-Hind, for example, took this for granted in his edition of the *Phaedo*. It has more often been held that according to Plato an hypothesis was always a statement of existence. But neither of these views can stand without modification, because a survey of Plato's works discovers many hypotheses that are not definitions and many that are not existence-propositions and many that are neither. Among those that are not definitions are hypotheses that 'there is a beautiful itself by itself and a good and great and all the others' (*Phd.* 100B), and that 'likeness exists' and 'likeness does not exist' (*Prm.* 136B). Among those that are not existential are the hypotheses that 'piety is what all the gods love' (*Euthyph.* 9D) and that 'knowledge is perception' (*Tht.* 165D). Among those that are neither definitions nor existential are the hypothesis in *Republic* IV 437A, the geometer's hypothesis in *Meno* 87A, the hypotheses that 'temperance is noble' (*Chrm.* 160D), that 'virtue is good' (*Men.* 87D), and that 'not-being must not partake either of one or of the many' (*Sph.* 238E). The following sentence seems to imply that an hypothesis may be a statement of the cause or of anything else: 'Hypothesizing on each occasion the proposition I judge the strongest, I lay down as true whatever seems to me to harmonize therewith, both about cause and about everything else' (*Phd.* 100A). *Parmenides* 136AB may seem to suggest that an hypothesis is usually of existence or non-existence (provided that εἰ πολλά ἐστι means 'if the many exist' and not 'if it is many'); but it ends with the phrase 'whatever you may hypothesize as existing and as not existing *and as possessing any other characteristic'*. These facts indicate that to Plato an hypothesis was not necessarily or normally either an existential proposition or a definition.

The view that for Plato an hypothesis was always or normally an existential proposition has been supported by the view that in the *Posterior Analytics* (I 2, 72ª20) Aristotle defines hypothesis as a thesis asserting the existence or non-existence of a subject. This, however, appears to be a misinterpretation. Waitz's text may be translated as follows:

A premiss is either part of a proposition, in which one thing is predicated of one thing. It is dialectical if it takes either part alike, and apodictic if it takes one definite part because that one is true. A proposition is either part of a contradiction. A contradiction is an antithesis that has no intermediate as such; and a part of a contradiction is either an affirmation affirming something of something or a negation denying something of something. I call an immediate beginning of syllogism a 'thesis' if both it cannot be proved and a man can learn something without possessing it. But, if a man must possess it in order to learn anything at all, I call it an 'axiom'. (There *are* some such sentences, and it is to them that we mostly apply this word.) A thesis that takes either of the parts of a proposition (I mean such as says that something is so or is not so) is an hypothesis. Otherwise it is a definition. A definition is a thesis, for the arithmetician 'posits' that the unit is that which is indivisible in quantity; but it is not an hypothesis, for what a unit is and that there is a unit are not the same thing. (*Post. Anal.* I 2, 72ª8–24.)

What Aristotle means here is that, whereas an hypothesis is an assertion, a definition is not an assertion at all, but merely a convention or promise. The definer says 'I am going to use the word W to mean so and so'; and such an utterance is not a statement about the subject in hand, but a way of preparing to make a statement. An hypothesis, on the other hand, is the sort of thesis which does not define a term but makes an assertion, the sort of thesis which may be not merely wise or foolish but also true or false. The phrase τὸ εἶναί τι ἢ τὸ μὴ εἶναί τι is not his way of referring to existence-propositions, or of including such statements as 'There is a God' while excluding such as 'God is good'. It is his way of including all statements or assertions or propositions whatever and excluding sentences which are not statements but prayers or commands or promises or the like.

This interpretation is confirmed by a passage five pages later: 'Definitions require only to be understood; and that is not hypothesis, unless you call listening an hypothesis' (76ᵇ37). Aristotle does not mean that once you understand a definition you cannot help seeing it to be true; his name for a proposition that must be intuited without proof is 'axiom' (72ᵃ17). He means that truth and falsehood do not apply to definitions (although in the rest of the *Posterior Analytics* and elsewhere he habitually takes the contrary view).

Mr. Lee has pointed out (*CQ* XXIX 115) that in this passage Aristotle's 'axiom' corresponds to Euclid's 'common notion'; his 'definition' corresponds to Euclid's 'definition'; and his 'hypothesis' corresponds to Euclid's 'postulate'. We have only to recall the famous fifth postulate, about parallels, to see that a postulate need not be an existence-proposition.

This interpretation is still further strengthened by the strange phrase: ἀποφάνσεως τὸ ἕτερον μόριον. Aristotle says that 'a premiss is either part of a proposition' (72ᵃ8) and later that 'the thesis which takes either of the parts of a proposition . . . is an hypothesis' (72ᵃ19). If we keep to Waitz's text, we must apparently take μόριον or 'part' as meaning εἶδος or 'species', and understand Aristotle as referring to the two primary species of proposition which he distinguished in the *De Interpretatione* (17ᵃ8), namely affirmation and negation. It then appears that an hypothesis is always either an affirmation or a negation; and this must be a way of saying that an hypothesis is a proposition or ἀποφαντικὸς λόγος as opposed to another sort of utterance.

Possibly, however, we should abandon Waitz's text and read ἀντιφάσεως instead of ἀποφάνσεως in both passages. (This reading is given by one good manuscript for 72ᵃ19, and adopted by Ross into the text; but it would be an emendation for 72ᵃ8.) The meaning would then be that (in the first passage) a premiss and (in the second passage) an hypothesis is 'one part of a contradiction'. Now a contradiction naturally falls into two propositions: A is B, and A is not B. Aristotle would therefore be pointing out that every hypothesis, being a proposition, has a contradictory, whereas a definition, not being a proposition, has no contradictory.

It seems, then, that, whether we adopt the emendation or not, Aristotle is implying by this phrase that an hypothesis is a proposition as such, not a species of proposition. We may conclude, therefore, that this passage is no evidence that Aristotle held that an hypothesis is always of the form 'X exists' or 'There is X'.

Let us turn now to the fascinating question what sort of hypotheses Plato was referring to when he said that mathematicians, 'hypothesizing the odd and the even and the figures and three kinds of angle and other related things in each procedure, making them hypotheses as if they knew them, expect to give no explanation about them either to themselves or to others, as being plain to everyone' (*Rp.* 510C). And there is the further question whether Plato thought that these hypotheses were as a matter of fact false. Cornford and Mr. Hardie, following the view that Plato's hypotheses were normally existential in form, hold that the hypotheses here are the existence of odd and even and the rest. Professor Solmsen says that the hypotheses are the actual concepts themselves, not any axioms or axiom-like propositions; and he infers from the passage that definitions were unknown in mathematics at the time of writing. Sidgwick held that Plato hardly made the distinction between existence and definition, and meant that the geometers suppose both the existence of the odd and even and so on, and the truth of their definitions. Taylor, taking a very different view, has suggested that the hypotheses are (1) that all numbers are integers, (2) some assumption about the possibility of constructing regular figures or regular solids, such as that you can construct more than five regular solids, (3) that every plane angle is made by the meeting either of two straight lines or of two curved lines or of one straight and one curved line; and that Plato saw or strongly suspected that these statements are false (*Mind* XLIII (1934) 81–84). The first guess of an ordinary reader of today might be that the hypotheses are (1) that every number is either odd or even, (2) that three or more straight lines will enclose a plane figure, (3) that every plane angle is either right or obtuse or acute.

It is improbable that Plato was here indicating hypotheses that he believed to be actually false. There is (if we omit this disputed passage) no place where Plato suggests that there were actual errors in contemporary pure mathematics. His criticisms of the pursuit seem to be of two kinds only. Sometimes he blames men for studying sensible objects instead of intelligibles, that is to say, for not getting their mathematics pure. And sometimes he complains that the mathematicians attain merely consistency and not also knowledge; since they do not really know their hypotheses, they also do not know any of the propositions they consistently deduce therefrom. The latter criticism seems to be his whole point in our present passage. This interpretation is confirmed by a later passage which seems intended as a summary or restatement of the present one: 'We see that geometry and the allied sciences dream about reality, but cannot see it with waking eyes so long as they use hypotheses which they do not criticize, being unable to give an explanation of them; for if the beginning is not known, and the end and the middle parts are constructed out of what is not known, how can you ever contrive knowledge out of such consistency?' (533C). Plato's point is not that the hypotheses are false, but that the mathematician does not know that they are true. He might, of course, have offered, as an argument for the conclusion that the mathematician does not know that they are true, the premiss that they are in fact false. But he does not take this line. On the contrary, he seems to imply later that these hypotheses could be known, and therefore are true; for he says that the objects of mathematics 'are intelligible with a beginning' (καίτοι νοητῶν ὄντων μετὰ ἀρχῆς 511D). The premiss he uses to prove that the mathematicians do not know their hypotheses to be true is the quite different statement that they give no explanation or logos thereof.

This conclusion obliges us to reject Taylor's interpretation, according to which Plato was pointing to real errors. That interpretation seems to have other difficulties as well. (1) Plato's choice of examples suggests that he is trying to give representative instances from the whole field of mathematics as known at the time; but if so he would on this theory be implying that there were fundamental errors throughout the whole field of mathematics. (2) This theory makes Plato throw out tremendous and far-reaching criticisms of mathematics in an incredibly brief and obscure phrase. Is Glaucon supposed to understand what Socrates means, and if not what does he take him as referring to? (3) Either Taylor's principle that the dialogues are historical must be abandoned for this passage, or Socrates displayed a perfectly enormous and amazing mathematical foresight; for the theory of the five regular solids was not finished until half a century after the dramatic date of the *Republic*, and the error lurking in the so-called 'mixed' angle was, according to Taylor, not definitely exposed until much later again.

We have answered the question whether Plato was here indicating hypotheses that he believed to be actually false; but to the other question, what precisely these hypotheses are, we must say that there is not sufficient evidence to tell. Our previous conclusion, that an hypothesis for Plato was not normally existential or of any other special form, prevents us from giving an answer on general grounds, and weakens the view of Cornford and Mr. Hardie.

§ 2. THE USE OF HYPOTHESIS

Returning now from our digression on the question whether there is any restriction in Plato as to the kind of proposition that may be hypothesized, let us examine his conception of the use of hypothesis as distinct from his conception of hypothesis itself. It is never discussed with full explicitness. His four main passages on hypothesis differ in important respects; and each will have to be studied separately. Nevertheless, there is a certain procedure that may with fair accuracy be called his hypothetical method.

Plato's hypothetical method is, in the first place, an *hypothesizing*. In other words, he implies that we should adopt our opinions deliberately rather than slide into them unconsciously, and also that we should adopt opinions rather than suspend judgement. There is nothing in the dialogues that comes anywhere near being an explicit statement of either of these points; but they seem to be implied by what he does say about the use of hypotheses; and the second, that we should adopt opinions rather than suspend judgement, seems inherent in the dialectical procedure of question-and-answer, according to which the respondent makes an answer to every question however ignorant he may be of the subject.

Secondly, it is a method of *deduction*—deduction as opposed not to induction but rather to intuition. It is a procedure in which we explore implications, drawing the consequences of hypotheses and carefully distinguishing premises from conclusions. Socrates says 'I put together the things that are said, in order that I may learn' (συμβιβάζω τὰ λεγόμενα, ἵνα μάθω, *Hp. Mi.* 369D). This deductiveness comes out most clearly in the Divided Line; for there Plato seems to make the hypothetical method, at least as found in mathematics, consist in nothing else but deduction.

Thirdly, the hypothetical method consists in paying the utmost attention to *the avoidance of contradiction*, in valuing at zero any set of opinions that contradicts itself. 'Either therefore refute her and show that doing injustice and not being punished is not the ultimate evil; or, if you leave this unrefuted, then, by the dog that is the Egyptians' god, Callicles will not agree with you, Callicles, but be discordant throughout your life. Yet surely, my dear man, it is better for me that my lyre should be discordant and out of tune, and the opera that I am producing, and that most men should disagree with me and contradict me, than that I myself, though only one, should be out of tune with myself and contradict myself' (*Grg.* 482BC). The same metaphor of concord and discord occurs in the *Phaedo*'s statement of the method of hypothesis: 'Hypothesizing on each occasion the proposition I judge the strongest, I lay down as true whatever seems to me to accord therewith, both about cause and about everything else; and as not true what does not seem to do so' (100A). Plato's portrait of Hippias clinging to common sense in spite of the inconsistencies Socrates reveals therein shows the sort of thing to which the ideal of consistency is opposed; and the paradoxes which he puts into Socrates' mouth in the *Gorgias* and elsewhere show the price he was willing to pay for this ideal.

We must avoid both the direct contradiction of saying that this proposition is both true and false, and also the indirect contradiction of asserting a set of propositions such that some of them, by a shorter or longer train of implication, imply the falsity of another. Avoiding direct contradiction does not mean never changing one's mind, but never positing at the same time the truth and the falsity of the same proposition. 'Whatever you say, abide by it. Or if you change your opinion ($\mu\epsilon\tau\alpha\tau\iota\theta\tilde{\eta}$), change it openly and do not deceive us' (*Rp.* 345B). Changes of opinion must be explicit and open; in other words, they must be 'positings' in the sense we have given to that term. If we try to make all our opinions explicit hypotheses rather than unconscious assumptions, we shall be less liable to direct contradictions.

Avoiding indirect contradictions does not mean having very few opinions and those quite unrelated to each other, but systematizing our opinions into a body of 'concordant' beliefs. This is achieved by the exploration of their implications. The Socratic elenchus is the exploration of the implications of a set of hypotheses, bringing to light an indirect contradiction. When this happens the ideal of consistency compels us to choose among our hypotheses and abandon one of them. Socrates frequently puts such a choice before his companions in the dialogues; e.g. Simmias has to choose whether to abandon his belief that learning is recollection or his belief that the soul is a tuning (*Phd.* 92C).

In the fourth place, the hypothetical method consists in holding one's opinions *provisionally* and not dogmatically. While we ought to form hypotheses rather than suspend judgement, we also ought to bear in mind that these hypotheses may be false, and be ready to abandon them if consistency demands. 'We must be persuaded by the argument, until someone persuades us with another and better' (*Rp.* 388E). This is brought out very clearly in *Republic* 436–7, which is in general an excellent example of the method of hypothesis. 'But nevertheless, said I, in order that we may not be forced to delay long enough to go into all such objections and make sure that they are untrue, let us hypothesize that this is so and go on to the next thing, agreeing that, if these things ever appear to be otherwise, all our inferences therefrom shall be cancelled' (437A). This provisionality implies a willingness to reconsider all hypotheses and all deductions, or even an intention to do so. We do not in fact often find Socrates reconsidering in the dialogues; but that is only because such a thing is difficult to depict without making tiresome reading. We often find him laying down that there should be reconsideration. 'The first hypotheses, even if you are confident of them, should nevertheless be examined more clearly' (*Phd.* 107B). 'My dear Cratylus, I have been astonished myself at my wisdom for a long time, and I am suspicious of it. It seems to me that I ought to reconsider what I am saying. For being misled by your own self is the worst thing of all. It must be so, since the misleader does not let you alone even for a little, but is always present! One ought, surely, to turn back frequently to what has been said before, and try, as the great poet puts it, to look "hind and fore at once"!' (*Cra.* 428D).

The *Crito* professes to be such a reconsideration of hypotheses and deductions previously adopted.

Dear Crito, your insistence would be very valuable if it had some justice; but if it has not, then the greater it is the worse it is. We must consider whether we should do these things or not; for I am and always have been a man to obey none of my familiars except the reason that seems best to me when I reason. The arguments I used to put forward I cannot reject now that this fortune has come upon me. They seem to me pretty much as they did; and I honour and reverence the same arguments as before. If we cannot find better ones at the present, be assured that I shall not yield to you, even if the power of the many were to frighten us like children with bogies more than they are already doing, sending chains and deaths and confiscations of property. What then would be the most suitable way of considering them? If first we took up your argument about what men will think? Were we right or not, when we used to say that some men's opinions should be respected and others' not? Or were we right up to the time when I had to die, whereas now it has become evident that I was only talking childish nonsense for the sake of talking? I want to consider together with you, Crito, whether it will seem different to me now that I am in this situation, or the same, and whether we shall let it go or obey it. It used to be put, I believe, in this way by those who thought they were saying something, as I put it just now, namely that, &c. (*Cri.* 46).

By this provisionality, however, Plato does not understand a timidity or weakness in maintaining one's opinions. If the question had been put to him, he would have said that, so long as an hypothesis is *not* refuted, it should be maintained with vigour and acted upon with confidence. 'Either therefore let us refute these things and show that they are not well said, or, so long as they remain unrefuted, let us never say that', &c. (*Rp.* 610A). 'Let a man either persuade us by means of a refutation that we do not say well, or, so long as he cannot, he too must say as we say, that', &c. (*Sph.* 259A).

The method of hypothesis therefore seems to be a method of *approximation*, though there is no such description of it in the dialogues. We are perpetually making alterations in our whole set of opinions, according as contradictions are revealed among them by the process of deduction. In this manner we render them more and more adequate as time goes on. But it does not appear that we could ever render them final. The possibility that another contradiction will turn up is always present; and the method seems to provide no way of converting the provisional into the certain. Plato came to feel this a defect; and we shall see how he dealt with it.

The previous paragraph may perhaps be admitted to be interpretation rather than comment; but what is now to be said is certainly comment, and possible only from a later age. Plato's hypothetical method, if it is as above described, involves the habit of trusting our insight into the argument rather than our insight into the conclusion. It is opposed to the oracular Heraclitean mode of thought that presents itself as a direct intuition of reality and is unconscious of reasons for its pronouncements. The assumption that truth comes in independent, selfcertifying packets is abandoned in favour of the assumption that our intuition that these propositions entail this proposition is more likely to be right than our intuition of any other sort of truth. Hence the decision to follow the argument wherever it leads, and to accept paradoxical conclusions. Socrates asks 'What is your answer?' And Theaetetus replies: 'If, Socrates, I say what I think with regard to the present question, my answer is that it cannot; but if with regard to the previous question, in order to avoid contradicting myself, my answer is that it can' (*Tht.* 154CD).

This is not to say that intuition is entirely banished in the method. In the first place, the method entails the greatest possible cultivation of one sort of intuition, the intuition that this logically entails that. In the second place, the hypotheses from which we start have to be chosen somehow; and at first, before conclusions have been drawn and contradictions revealed, there is nothing to do but choose those that commend themselves to intuition. That is how hypotheses are actually obtained in the dialogues. Theaetetus simply intuits that knowledge is perception. Charmides simply intuits that temperance is a sort of quietness. What the method does is rather to *economize* intuition, by restricting it almost entirely to the intuition of a logical implication performed again and again, and to *criticize* and dispose of other intuitions by examining their mutual consistency. The unique beauty of Euclidean geometry down to the nineteenth century was that it seemed to combine in perfect harmony complete logical rigour and the complete satisfaction of all our intuitions about the subject-matter.

The general nature of Plato's hypothetical method may, therefore, be suggested by the words hypothesis, deduction, consistency, provisionality, approximation. If we compare this with the method recommended by Descartes, we see that it agrees in the element of deduction and disagrees in everything else. Descartes holds that, besides the intuition that this implies that, we can find other equally trustworthy intuitions. These therefore must form the starting-point of our reflections, not as provisional hypotheses but as certainties. The rest of science will consist in discovering what they imply. Their consequences must always be consistent, because they are true; and hence there is no point in looking out for contradiction, and no question of approximation arises. Descartes did, however, propose to himself, according to the second part of his *Discourse*, to proceed in practice as Plato proceeds in theory, that is, to act on his hypotheses with as much confidence as if he were certain of them, so long as they remained his adopted hypotheses.

Plato regarded his hypothetical method as a second best. He is ironical in the *Phaedo* when he calls it inferior to the procedure of the physicists; but even there he is at the same time implying that it is really inferior to some method that he had hoped to find in Anaxagoras. In the *Meno* Socrates makes clear, both at the beginning and at the end of the hypothetical part of the dialogue, that he is adopting a makeshift procedure in response to Meno's undesirable haste to reach a conclusion. Those remarks about the inadequacy of the present inquiry and the possibility of a better way, which are so common in the dialogues, refer in large measure to the hypothetical procedure. In the *Cratylus* and in the *Republic* Plato emphasizes the unsatisfactoriness of a deductive system whose starting-points are not known to be true; and in the latter work he tries to outline the superior method.

Is an hypothesis a proposition to be proved or a proposition adopted in order to prove something else; is it a premiss or a demonstrand? Today we should probably say that the purpose of an hypothesis is never to *prove* something else, that it is usually suggested in order to *explain* something else, but that it then requires to be itself proved. Is this also Plato's view?

At any rate Plato's conception of hypothetical procedure differs from ours to this extent, that with him there is no question of testing the hypothesis by an appeal to sensation. That an hypothesis should be disproved by being shown to entail a contrary of what actually occurs in sensible experience is no part of what he contemplates; and would conflict with his belief that true science does not use the senses. It can be disproved only by being shown to contradict either other hypotheses or itself. Nor does he have our distinction between verifiable and unverifiable hypotheses. 'Discussing a matter which they cannot determine' (περὶ πράγματος διαλεγόμενοι ὃ ἀδυνατοῦσι ἐξελέγξαι, *Prt.* 347E) is a contemptuous suggestion that all interpretations of a poet's meaning are unverifiable; but Plato never suspects that any of the hypotheses he himself deals with might be flatly unverifiable for any reason.

There is a strong reason for believing that Plato regarded an hypothesis as something to be proved (or disproved), namely that in the elenctic dialogues both the noun and the verb and the uncompounded verb τίθεμαι are often applied to the answerer's thesis, that is, to the proposition which is professedly to be either established or refuted, and which in the event is always refuted. (Examples of ὑπόθεσις or ὑποτίθεμαι referring to the refutand: *Chrm.* 163A, 171D, 172C; *Euthyph.* 11C; *Phd.* 94B; *Tht.* 165D.) Burnet appears to take this view in his note on *Euthyph.* 9D8:

> The verb ὑποτίθεμαι in the sense of setting before oneself or another a task to be done or a thing to be proved is properly Ionic, and it is from the Ionic dialect that Greek scientific terminology is mainly derived. In the sense of proposing something to be done or said it is as old as Homer (cf. e.g. *Od.* iv. 163 ὄφρα οἱ ἤ τι ἔπος ὑποθήσεαι ἠέ τι ἔργον), and easily passes into the sense of 'counsel', 'advise' (e.g. *Il.* xxi. 293 αὐτάρ τοι πυκινῶς ὑποθησόμεθ', αἴ κε πίθηαι), whence the title ὑποθῆκαι given to didactic poems. When geometry arose the term was naturally used of the proposition to be proved or the construction to be performed, and the method adopted was to deduce the consequences (τὰ συμβαίνοντα) from each ὑπόθεσις in order to see whether they led to anything impossible or absurd. In that case the ὑπόθεσις is 'destroyed' (ἀναιρεῖται, *tollitur*).

Yet, in spite of the above evidence and the view of Burnet, it must be maintained that Plato did not usually or primarily think of an hypothesis as a statement put forward for proof or disproof. Against the above-mentioned passages in which he calls the refutand an hypothesis we can put other passages of the early dialogues in which he gives this name to one of the premisses of the refutation, in other words to propositions posited solely in order to prove something *else*, and never themselves either proved or disproved (unless in a subsequent argument). Such are *Charmides* 160D; *Meno* 87D; *Phaedo* 92D; *Protagoras* 339D. The Socratic elenchus uses 'hypothesizing' both of the refutand and of the premisses from which the refutation proceeds. The hypothesizing of the Law of Contradiction in *Republic* 437A, though preceded by a page of recommendation, is quite obviously performed for the sake of testing not the hypothesis itself, but something else, namely the proposition that the soul of man has three parts. Burnet's note apparently implies that in the beginning all geometrical proofs were reductions to absurdity of the contradictory of the demonstrand. But this is improbable on general grounds; and Plato's account of mathematics in the Divided Line seems to imply that geometrical proofs were usually direct, and also to distinguish the hypotheses quite sharply from the demonstrand (τοῦτο οὗ ἂν ἐπὶ σκέψιν ὁρμήσωσι 510D). These considerations make for holding that Plato regarded an hypothesis as a proposition posited in order to prove something else and not a proposition posited in order to be itself tested. But the main reason for so holding is just the above development of the view that ὑπόθεσις takes its meaning from the meaning of ὑποτίθεμαι, which is to posit as a start, as a preparation for future activity, for something else. The notion of 'positing in order to test the very proposition you are positing' is sophisticated and subsequent; first comes the simpler and more natural notion of 'positing in order to act thereon in the future'. That is what the simple verb τίθημι overwhelmingly means; and that is what the compound ὑποτίθεμαι merely intensifies without significantly altering. There is indeed another compound that comes much nearer to meaning 'posit a proposition in order to test that very proposition', namely προτίθεμαι. But Burnet is mistaken if he implies that προτίθεμαι and ὑποτίθεμαι mean the same in Plato (on Euthyph. 11B7). An hypothesis is always a proposition posited *at the beginning* of a train of thought. Therefore it is naturally and normally a proposition posited for the proof of some *other* proposition, a premiss and not a demonstrand.

How then are we to explain those passages where the refutand is referred to as an hypothesis? There are two ways in which 'hypothesis' came to have the more sophisticated, apparently self-contradictory meaning of 'positing X in order to discover whether you ought to posit X'; and both of them pass through the Socratic elenchus. In the elenchus the answerer's thesis is the first event. It is the cause of all the subsequent activity, beginning with Socrates' acquiring the premisses he needs, going on to the syllogizing of those premisses, and ending with the conclusion that contradicts the thesis. Thus it is very decidedly the *beginning* of a train of thought; it fulfils that condition of being an hypothesis. Furthermore, it is *posited* by the answerer, as an hypothesis must be. Here, then, is a way in which the answerer's thesis can be thought of as an hypothesis in the original sense. And once this connexion has been made, then, since the answerer's thesis is tested in the event, the word 'hypothesis' can begin to assume the new sense of a proposition to be tested. But there is a second and surer way. If the elenchus is indirect, then the refutand is itself one of the premises in its own refutation; for the indirect refutation of p consists in showing that p, together with q which is admitted, entails r which cannot be so. Thus, whenever the elenchus is indirect, the answerer's thesis is posited as a beginning not merely of the whole train of thought but also of the actual syllogism that refutes that thesis. The very great influence that this had in causing the word 'hypothesize' to assume the sense of 'posit in order to test' is due to the fact that, as we have seen (above, p. 27), Plato regarded all elenchus as indirect.

The conclusion is that the modern notion of hypothesizing as 'positing p in order to ascertain the truth of p' is to be found in Plato, but only subordinately to the original notion of 'positing p in order to infer q', from which it arose owing to Plato's conception of the Socratic elenchus.

VIII

HYPOTHESIS IN THE *MENO*

LET us now turn to the special passages in which Plato reflects on the use of hypotheses. They occur in the *Meno*, the *Phaedo*, and the *Republic*, and there is also something about the matter in the *Parmenides*. Of these the earliest in time is the *Meno*. There Socrates professes to borrow a way of using hypotheses from the geometers. He explains this use by a geometrical example which is very difficult to interpret from the geometrical point of view. Fortunately, however, the geometrical details are irrelevant to the methodological point; and they will be omitted from the following translation.

Shall we then, since we agree that one ought to inquire into what one does not know, try to inquire together what virtue is?

Certainly. Although, Socrates, what I should most like to inquire into and hear about is the question I put at the beginning; whether we should approach virtue as being teachable, or as coming to men by nature, or in what way?

If I were the governor not merely of myself but also of you, Meno, we should not inquire whether virtue is teachable or not teachable until we had previously examined what it is; but since you make no attempt to govern yourself, in order that you may be a free man, but attempt and succeed in governing me, I will yield to you. What else can I do? It seems then that we must inquire of what sort a thing is when we do not yet know *what* it is. Or perhaps you would relax your government just slightly and allow me to inquire on an hypothesis whether it is teachable or how. By 'on an hypothesis' I mean thus, as the geometers often inquire, when someone asks them, for example about a rectangle, whether it is possible for this rectangle to be inscribed in this circle as a triangle, they might reply: 'I do not yet know if it is so; but I think some such thing as this would be useful in the matter as a sort of hypothesis: if this rectangle is [such and such], one thing seems to me to follow, and another thing if it is not such. So I should like to make an hypothesis and tell you the consequences regarding the possibility of inscribing it in the circle.' In the same way about virtue let us, since we know neither what it is nor what sort of thing it is, hypothesize it and so inquire whether it is teachable or not teachable, saying as follows: 'If virtue were what sort of thing concerning the soul would it be teachable or not teachable? In the first place, if it is other than knowledge, is it teachable or not—or recollectable, as we said just now—do not let it matter which word we use—but is it teachable? Surely thus much is plain to everyone, that the only thing a man can be taught is knowledge?

It seems so to me.

If virtue is some kind of knowledge, it would clearly be teachable?

Of course.

That did not take long then. If it is of this nature it is teachable; and if it is of this, it is not.

Certainly.

The next thing, apparently, is to ask whether virtue is knowledge or other than knowledge.

That seems to me the next thing to ask.

Well, now. We say, do we not, that it is good, virtue; and this hypothesis stands, that it is good?

Certainly.

If, therefore, there is something good apart from knowledge, perhaps virtue may not be a sort of knowledge; but if there is no good that is not included in knowledge, then we should suspect rightly if we suspected it to be a sort of knowledge?

That is so. (*Men.* 86C–87D.)

They proceed to prove that only knowledge is good, from which they conclude that virtue is a kind of knowledge. Then comes the following:

So we say that virtue is intelligence, either the whole or a part of it?

It seems to me, Socrates, that what has been said is well said.

Then if this is so, the good are not good by nature?

I think not.

And there would be this too, I suppose. If good men came by nature, we should have men who knew which children had good natures, and following their advice we should take these children and guard them in the citadel, sealing them up much more than gold, in order that no one should corrupt them, but when they came of age they should be useful to the cities.

I suppose so, Socrates.

Since then the good do not become good by nature, is it by learning?

I think that is now proved; and it is clear, Socrates, according to the hypothesis, if virtue is knowledge, that it is teachable.

Perhaps indeed. But I fear we were wrong to admit this.

It seemed all right a moment ago.

But it must seem all right not merely a moment ago, but also now and in the future, if there is to be any health in it.

What now? What makes you dislike it and doubt whether virtue is knowledge?

I will tell you, Meno. That we did well to say that, if it is knowledge, it is teachable, I do not take back (ἀνατίθεμαι); but see whether you think I am right in doubting whether it is knowledge. (*Men.* 89A–89D.)

There follows a long argument that virtue is not knowledge (the contradictory of what they had argued previously); and they conclude that virtue is not teachable. Let us therefore distinguish:

1. The geometrical example, 86E–87B.
2. The first deduction, as part of which virtue is proved to be knowledge, 87B–89C.
3. The second deduction, as part or the whole of which virtue is proved not to be knowledge, 89C–end.

The hypothetical method intended here seems to be as follows. It is a method for deciding whether a given proposition, say *q*, is true or false; and it consists in abandoning the attempt to prove or disprove *q* directly, and finding some other proposition, say *p*, which is equivalent to *q*, so that *q* must be true if *p* is true, and must be false if *p* is false. We then prove or disprove *p* directly, and from this we know whether the original object of our inquiry, *q*, is true or false, because *q* is equivalent to *p*. In this procedure *p* is called the 'hypothesis'. In the geometrical example the original subject of inquiry is the proposition that 'it is possible for this rectangle to be inscribed in this circle as a triangle', and the hypothesis is the complicated statement (87A) which I have passed over in my translation. In the subsequent application the original subject of inquiry, or *q*, is the proposition that virtue is teachable, and the hypothesis *p* is that virtue is knowledge. Socrates first ascertains that this hypothesis, *p*, is equivalent to the original proposition *q*; that takes only a few lines (87B5–C10). It is not argued because it is considered 'plain to everyone'. Secondly, Socrates gives a proof of the hypothesis that virtue is knowledge. This takes him two pages (from 87D to 89D). Meno then infers that virtue is teachable, his words being: 'It is clear, Socrates, according to the hypothesis, if virtue is knowledge, that it is teachable' (89C).

This is probably the end of the hypothetical procedure, for

after page 89 neither the word 'hypothesis' nor any methodological remark occurs in the dialogue. But it is important to notice that Socrates now reverses himself and disproves the proposition that virtue is teachable in a long argument occupying the rest of the dialogue, and that he concludes (99A) that since virtue is not teachable it is not knowledge. In doing this he is, though he does not say so, directly disproving the proposition that was originally in question, and inferring therefrom the falsehood of the hypothesis which was declared equivalent to the original proposition.

Assuming that the hypothetical procedure ends at page 89, we may say that it is probable that hypothetical method according to the *Meno* consists in recommending a proposition q, not exactly by proving q, but by proving another proposition p, where p has been hypothesized because it is equivalent to q.

I owe this interpretation of the *Meno* on hypothesis to the reviews of my first edition by Professors Friedländer and Cherniss. It is the most satisfying I have found; but there seems to be no perfectly convincing interpretation of this passage, and here follow the chief objections to the interpretation I have now adopted.

1. Whereas on this interpretation the hypothesis in question is that virtue is knowledge, there are two other propositions which Socrates calls 'hypotheses' much more distinctly than he ever calls this proposition an 'hypothesis'. In 89D he says that he does not 'take back' the proposition that if virtue is knowledge it is teachable. The Greek is ἀνατίθεμαι, suggesting 'withdraw the hypothesis that'. In 87D he speaks of the 'hypothesis' that virtue is good. Against these very explicit expressions we can set only the two following expressions suggesting that the proposition that virtue is knowledge is an hypothesis in the dialogue. (1) It is suggested by Meno's obscure remark: 'It is clear, Socrates, according to the hypothesis, if virtue is knowledge, that it is teachable' (89C). (2) Socrates' first sentence after his geometrical illustration proposes to hypothesize 'it', where 'it' certainly means virtue. If we look in the context to find what proposition Socrates had in mind when he spoke of hypothesizing virtue, there is no obvious and convincing answer, but the most probable one seems to be that 'virtue is knowledge', in view of 'if it is other than knowledge' (87B7) and 'if virtue is some kind of knowledge' (87C5).

The force of this objection may be lessened as follows. The two indications that the hypothesis is that virtue is knowledge, though not as unmistakable as we distant readers need, are strong enough, in view of the way this account fits into a general account of the hypothetical method here. The two contrary indications may be met as follows.

The notions of hypothesis and hypothetical method are running in Socrates' mind, and so he has a tendency to use them on any suitable or even speciously suitable occasion. The introduction of an unargued proposition from which other propositions are inferred is such an occasion. Both the propositions in question appear as unargued foundations of argument. The proposition that if virtue is knowledge it is teachable is the unargued and indispensable link between the propositions that virtue is knowledge and that virtue is teachable. The proposition that virtue is good is the start of the proof that virtue is knowledge.

In calling the proposition that virtue is good an 'hypothesis' Socrates is exemplifying a part of hypothetical method as described in the *Phaedo*. He presents the proposition that virtue is knowledge first as an hypothesis or premiss from which to infer a conclusion, and then as itself a conclusion inferred from the prior hypothesis that virtue is good. This seems to be covered by the *Phaedo*'s sentence: 'And when you had to discuss the hypothesis itself, you would do so in the same way, hypothesizing another hypothesis which seemed best of those above' (*Phd.* 101D). This was pointed out by Professor Cherniss in his review of the first edition of this book (*AJP* LXVIII (1947) 140).

2. A second objection to the above interpretation is as follows.

The interpretation makes hypothetical method no more hypothetical than any other Socratic argument, but on the contrary just as 'iron and adamantine' as they all claim to be; for the hypothesis that virtue is knowledge is proved in just the same way as any ordinary Socratic conclusion, and this hypothesis is found to be equivalent to the proposition that virtue is teachable, and therefore the proposition that virtue is teachable is proved in the ordinary Socratic way.

This objection may be met as follows. On general grounds we could not be sure that what seems to us an unimportant difference in procedure also seemed unimportant to Plato. And we have special evidence that this particular difference did seem important to Aristotle, namely his doctrine of the 'syllogism from hypothesis'. Aristotle's conception of this was that, to prove that C is D, you first get your answerer to agree, as to an hypothesis, that if A is B then C is D. You then obtain the necessary premisses and prove syllogistically that A is B. (See *Anal.* 50ᵃ16–28.) Aristotle considers this procedure inferior. It is not real demonstration, according to him, because it does not syllogize that C is D, in the sense of obtaining premisses from which C's being D follows by one of the three figures of syllogism. It syllogizes something else, namely that A is B; and the step from that to the required conclusion is merely hypothesized. It is a second best, to be employed only when you cannot directly syllogize that C is D. Thus Aristotle's hypothetical syllogism resembles our hypothetical syllogism with the addition of a categorical proof of the minor premiss.

Ours	*Aristotle's*
1. If A is B then C is D.	1. If A is B then C is D.
2. ..	2. Now A is X.
3. ..	3. And X is B.
4. But A is B.	4. Therefore A is B.
5. Therefore C is D.	5. Therefore C is D.

Aristotle concentrates attention on propositions 2–4; and regards 1 and 5 as unfortunate additions which prevent the argument from being a real demonstration. We, however, think it as strict a demonstration as any other; and we concentrate on propositions 1 and 4 and 5 to classify their valid and invalid forms. Thus the procedure which, on the above interpretation, constituted arguing 'from an hypothesis' in the *Meno* is the same as the procedure which Aristotle in his *Analytics* called 'the syllogism from hypothesis' and held to be importantly different from ordinary syllogism. It is probable that Aristotle had the *Meno* in mind while writing the *Analytics*, as Shorey said in his explanation of Aristotle's syllogism from hypothesis (*AJP* X (1889) 460).

Although the form of reasoning which Aristotle has in mind is the same as that which Plato has in mind in the *Meno*, the part of it which Aristotle calls the 'hypothesis' is different from the part which Plato calls the 'hypothesis', on the present interpretation of the *Meno*. To Aristotle the hypothesis is the proposition that 'if A is B, then C is D'; but to Plato it is the proposition that 'A is B'. This difference of nomenclature, however, does not affect the point that Aristotle and Plato are talking about the same form of reasoning, and that Aristotle considers this form importantly different from ordinary syllogism, and that therefore Plato may well have considered it importantly different from ordinary deduction.

3. A third difficulty is as follows.

Our interpretation involves that the reasoning, or most of it, takes place *to* the hypothesis and not *from* it. Socrates requires two pages of syllogizing to deduce the hypothesis that virtue is knowledge, but only a line to go from this hypothesis to the demonstrand that virtue is teachable, a step which he considers 'obvious to everyone' (87C2). Now this is difficult in two ways. First, it seems an odd use of the word 'hypothesis' to apply it to the last stage but one of a train of reasoning. Second, two phrases in Socrates' explanation of his method seem to imply that the hypothesis really was to have a long train of consequences deduced from it, and not be, as our interpretation implies, itself the last consequence but one. One of these phrases is 'let us hypothesize it and so inquire' (87B4), where 'inquire' suggests a substantial chain of reasoning proceeding *from* the hypothesis. The other is 'So I should like to make an hypothesis and tell you the consequences' (87B1), which suggests the same.

That it seems odd nowadays to give the title of 'hypothesis' to a proposition which, in a rigorous formal statement of your reasoning, would appear last but one and would be strictly deduced from what preceded, is true; but it is not a strong argument against the present interpretation, for we must expect thoughts created 2,000 years ago to seem odd to us sometimes. That the two lines, 87B1 and 87B4, fairly obviously suggest substantial trains of reasoning *from* the hypothesis, whereas on our interpretation Plato did not intend this, is more difficult to explain. We shall have to say that the consequences which he speaks of here are not the logical consequences of the hypothesized proposition, but the practical consequences of our hypothesizing it, namely, that we proceed to construct a chain of reasoning leading *to* the hypothesized proposition. The practical 'consequences' of the hypothesized proposition are its logical antecedents, here regarded as being uttered consequently upon our hypothesizing the proposition. This explanation appears to reconcile the lines with our general interpretation, at the cost of implying that Plato was here writing in a rather confusing way.

I conclude, then, that in spite of these serious objections the interpretation is to be adopted.

Farquharson has suggested that the method Plato here recommends is that which Greek geometers afterwards came to call analysis (*CQ* XVII 21). This method of analysis is described in the histories of Greek mathematics and also in my note in *Mind* (XLV 464). It consisted in hypothesizing the proposition to be proved and deducing consequences from that proposition until you reached a consequence which you knew independently to be true or to be false. You could then, if the consequence was a true one, use it as the premiss of a proof of your demonstrand; and if it was a false one, you could use its contradictory as a disproof of the proposition you had hoped to establish. Thus by making an hypothesis you were led beyond hypothesis to the discovery of a conclusive proof based on indubitable premises.

The method of analysis and the method in the *Meno* both include the act of hypothesizing. But they have no further resemblance; they do not use the act in the same way. In the geometrical example in the *Meno*, analysis would begin by hypothesizing the proposition to be proved or disproved, namely, that 'it is possible for this rectangle to be inscribed in this circle as a triangle', and then draw consequences from this hypothesis; but Plato represents the geometer as hypothesizing something else. In the discussion proper, since the question is whether virtue is teachable, the method of analysis would begin by assuming that virtue is teachable and draw conclusions therefrom. Other things being equal, it might be possible to hold that this is how Socrates does begin in the *Meno*, and that the first consequence he draws is that virtue is knowledge; but it is not possible to hold that he goes on to infer something from virtue's being knowledge. He goes on quite explicitly to prove that virtue is knowledge by a direct deduction.

On the theory of this chapter, hypothetical method as Plato conceived it in his *Meno* is not very like Platonic hypothetical method in general as I described it in the previous chapter. It contains, indeed, something which the speakers call 'hypothesizing', and it contains deduction; but the deduction is almost wholly to the hypothesis instead of from it, and the elements of provisionality and approximation seem to be absent, or present only in that the same question is answered first in the affirmative and then in the negative. The fact is that hypothetical method in the *Meno* is considerably different from what it is in the *Phaedo* and in the *Republic* and in the *Parmenides*, and my general account in the previous chapter is based mainly on the latter works. Hypothetical method according to the *Meno* also seems considerably less interesting and valuable than it later became; for it appears to differ from the ordinary Socratic deduction only in a point that now seems unimportant, namely, in not being Aristotelian syllogism but some other form of strict deduction. But, however that may be, the *Meno*'s discussion of hypothetical method seems to have value as the symbol of a valuable change in Plato's writings. With the introduction of this method he is passing from destructive to constructive thinking, from elenchus and the refutation of other men's views to the elaboration of positive views of his own. The dialogue begins with refutations of Meno's definitions of virtue, and ends with attempts to say something positive about virtue, even if tentative and non-essential, by means of the hypothetical method. It is thus a microcosm of the whole series of Plato's dialogues; for on the whole those previous to the *Meno* are merely destructive and those after it are definitely constructive.

IX

HYPOTHESIS IN THE *PHAEDO*

§ I. TRANSLATION OF THE PASSAGE

THE *Phaedo*'s account of the method of hypothesis is the main account of it in Plato. It is much more serious and full and precise than those in the *Meno* and in the *Republic* and in the *Parmenides*.

The aim of the speakers in the *Phaedo* is to establish that 'soul is immortal'. Some good arguments are brought forward; but a searching objection from Cebes seems to make everything doubtful again. Socrates then says that a general discussion of the cause of generation and destruction is required (95E); and proceeds to tell of his own experiences in that inquiry. In his youth he was greatly exercised by natural science. But the more he studied it the more ignorant and incompetent he came to think himself. None of the alleged causes seemed to be really a cause. Hope sprang in him anew when he heard that Anaxagoras taught that the cause and disposer of everything is mind; for he supposed that Anaxagoras would explain each case of generation or destruction or existence by showing that it was for the best; and he felt that if this were shown no further cause of any sort would be required. But when he read the book he was completely disappointed; for Anaxagoras said no more about the best than the other scientists. They all seemed to Socrates to take for the cause what was merely something without which the cause would not be the cause. They supposed the cause of Socrates' sitting to be certain arrangements of his muscles and bones; whereas these arrangements were merely the means of his sitting, and the cause was his decision that it was best to do so.

And so one makes the earth stay beneath the heaven by putting a whirl around it, and one presses down the air to make a foundation as if with a broad kneading-trough; but the power that makes them stand now as well as it was possible for them to be placed, they neither look for nor believe it to have any wonderful strength. They expect to find some Atlas who is stronger and more immortal than that power, and does more to hold all things together. That the good and the fitting do truly fit and hold things together they have no conception. Now I should have been very glad to learn from anybody the truth about this sort of cause; but since I was deprived of it, and could neither discover it for myself nor learn it from anyone else, would you like me, Cebes, he said, to give you an exhibition of how I have conducted my second best way of looking for the cause?

I should like it exceedingly, he said.

Well, he said, after this it seemed to me that, since I was exhausted by my study of things, I ought to take care that there did not happen to me what happens to those who observe and study the sun in eclipse. For some of them ruin their eyes, unless they study the sun's image in water or something of that kind. Something of the kind occurred to me; and I was afraid I might become totally blind in soul through looking at facts with my eyes and trying to grasp them with each of the senses. It seemed to me that I ought to resort to discussions (logoi) and study the truth of things in them. Perhaps my likeness is in a way unlike; for I do not altogether admit that he who studies things by discussions (logoi) is more a user of images than he who studies them in the concrete. Anyway that is how I proceeded; and hypothesizing on each occasion the proposition (logos) that I judge the strongest, I posit as true whatever seems to me to accord therewith, and as not true whatever seems not to, both about cause and about everything else. Let me tell you more clearly what I mean; for I think that as yet you do not understand.

No, by Zeus, said Cebes, not much.

Well, he said, I mean this. It is nothing new, but what I have always continually said both in the previous discussion and at other times. I am trying to exhibit to you the kind of cause I deal with; and I come back to those well-worn matters and begin from them, hypothesizing that there is a fine itself by itself and a good and a tall and all the others. If you grant me them and admit that they exist, I hope to exhibit the cause to you from them and discover that soul is immortal.

Well, I grant it, said Cebes; so you cannot be too quick with your conclusion.

Observe, he said, what comes next; and see if you think as I do. For it seems to me that if anything else is fine besides the fine itself, it is fine simply and solely because it shares in that fine; and so with all the others. Do you agree to such a cause?

I agree, he said.

I no longer understand, said he, and I cannot recognize these other ingenious causes. But if anyone tells me why something is fine, either because it has a blooming colour or shape or some such thing, I let everything else go (for everything else muddles me) and simply and solely and perhaps stupidly keep to this, that nothing makes it fine but the fine itself by its presence or communion or whatever sort of relation it is. What that relation is I do not assert, but that it is by the fine that all fine things are fine. That seems to me the safest answer to give both to myself and to others, and I think that if I cling to this I shall never fall. It is safe both for me and for anyone else to answer that it is by the fine that the fine are fine. Or don't you think so?

I do.

And by tallness the tall are tall and the taller taller, and by shortness the shorter shorter?

Yes.

Then you too would not allow anyone to say that one man was taller than another by a head, and that the shorter was shorter by this same. You would insist that for your part you only say that everything that is taller than something else is taller by nothing but tallness, and taller because of tallness, and the shorter is shorter by nothing but shortness, and shorter because of shortness. For you would be afraid of encountering a contradiction, I think, if you say someone is taller or shorter by a head, because you would be saying first that the taller is taller and the shorter is shorter by the same thing, and second that the taller is taller by the head when a head is short, and it is portentous to say that anything is tall by virtue of anything short. Would you not be afraid of this?

I should, said Cebes laughing.

And you would be afraid to say that ten is more than eight by two, and exceeds it through this cause, instead of saying that it is more by multitude and through multitude? Or that two feet are longer than one by a half and not by length? For that is the same danger.

Certainly, said he.

And when one is divided or added to another one, would you not refuse to say that the division or addition was the cause of its becoming two? And you would cry out that you know no other way in which a thing can become or enjoy the peculiar nature it does enjoy, and in these matters you see no other cause of its becoming two but the enjoyment of duality, and that any things that are going to be two must enjoy this, or unity if it is going to be one? And these divisions and additions and other such refinements you would dismiss, leaving them to cleverer persons to produce as answers. But you, fearing your own shadow, as they say, and your inexperience, would answer by hanging on to that safe hypothesis. And if anyone hung on to the hypothesis itself, you would dismiss him and refuse to answer until you had considered its results to see if they accord or disaccord with each other. And when you had to discuss the hypothesis itself, you would do so in the same way, hypothesizing another hypothesis which seemed best of those above, until you came to something adequate. But you would not confuse the two as the contradiction-mongers do, discussing the beginning and its results at the same time, if you wanted to discover some truths. They perhaps never even think or care about this. Their cleverness enables them to mix everything together and yet be satisfied with themselves. But I think that you, since you are one of the philosophers, would do as I have said. (*Phd.* 99B–101E.)

§ 2. THE METAPHOR OF ACCORD IN 100A

What is the meaning of the metaphor of 'accord and disaccord' in this passage? It occurs twice, and each occurrence requires separate study. The first is as follows: 'hypothesizing on each occasion the proposition that I judge the strongest, I posit as true whatever seems to me to accord therewith, and as not true whatever seems not to' (100A). The following are the two most natural conjectures as to Plato's meaning:

(1) consistent with—inconsistent with.
(2) deducible from, entailed by—not deducible from, not entailed by.

It is very hard to think of anything else that he could possibly have meant by the metaphor. At first sight we prefer the interpretation 'consistency–inconsistency', because it seems a much more natural and obvious metaphor. But a serious difficulty arises. If 'accord' means 'be consistent with', then Socrates is saying (100A) that he takes every proposition for true if only it is consistent with his hypothesis. 'I posit as true whatever seems to accord therewith.' This seems a rash and unwarrantable thing to do. We are not justified in adopting every proposition that is not contradicted by our hypothesis.

In view of this check we must explore the possibility of the other interpretation, 'is deducible from'. In favour of 'deducibility' there is not only the difficulty we have found in 'consistency', but also our general account of the hypothetical method. According to that account, after you have hypothesized a proposition, you do not inquire what is consistent with it but what is deducible from it. This is not an entirely circular argument; for that general account was not based merely on the *Phaedo*. And in the *Phaedo*, too, after Socrates has actually made his hypothesis, he and his answerer seem to imply that the next thing is to draw deductions from it. '. . . hypothesizing that there is a fine itself by itself and a good and a tall and all the others. If you grant me them and admit that they exist, I hope to exhibit the cause to you from them and discover that soul is immortal.—Well, I grant it, said Cebes; so you cannot be too quick with your conclusion.— Observe, he said, what comes next.' Here 'what comes next' seems to mean 'what logically follows'; and the 'conclusion' seems to be the logical conclusion.

Yet this interpretation also involves a difficulty at least as serious as that of 'consistency'. It makes Socrates say (in 100A) that whenever he finds a proposition not deducible from his hypothesis he sets it down as false. 'I posit . . . as not true whatever seems not to (accord with the hypothesis).' Now this seems very queer logic indeed. No one today would hold that, if p is true and q is not deducible from p, then q must be false. It seems impossible to believe either that Plato ever held this or that he here slipped into it by error.

Thus both our interpretations of the metaphor of accord and discord have run into grave paradox, and there seems to be no third interpretation. What is the way out of this difficulty?

There is no third interpretation. We have to choose between consistency and deducibility as the meaning of 'accord'. The better is consistency, for more than one reason. The paradox to which it leads is much less than that to which deducibility leads. To set down propositions as true because they are consistent with the hypothesis is far more defensible than to set them down as false because they are not deducible therefrom. And our feeling that 'consistency' is the more natural metaphor is confirmed by Plato's use of the words 'accord' and 'discord' elsewhere. There is no passage in which they certainly indicate deducibility or the absence thereof; but there are several in which they certainly indicate consistency or inconsistency. 'We must examine what the argument says as well as what Hippocrates says, and see if they accord' (*Phdr.* 270C). 'The assertion of these two propositions together is not very musical; they are not consonant or agreeable to each other' (*Prt.* 333A); here, though the words are different, the metaphor is the same. 'But what you are now saying seems to me neither consequent nor even accordant to what you said at first' (*Grg.* 457E, cf. 461A).

How then are we to mitigate the paradox that Socrates sets

down propositions as true because they are consistent with his hypothesis? One line of defence is this: 'There is no real queerness in positing as true what merely consists with your hypothesis. It is reasonable to posit everything that occurs to you as true, until the emergence of an inconsistency compels you to reject something. Socrates is going on the principle that every proposition is true until it is found to be inconsistent with the hypothesis or one of its real consequences, just as every prisoner is innocent until he is proved guilty; and, though the scientists frown on unsupported theories, this is an excellent principle in some theoretical inquiries as it is in law.'

This defence is inadequate because such an activity would not amount to a method. The hypothetical method is intended to reach some particular conclusion. Socrates here wishes to conclude that soul is immortal. But the mere activity of positing every proposition that was consistent with the hypothesis would not lead in any given direction. It would merely amass a heap of assertions. Or, if you deliberately make it lead to your desired conclusion, there is nothing to prevent your positing that conclusion immediately after positing the hypothesis itself. Your activity would then be finished almost as soon as it began; but you could not feel that you had rendered your conclusion any more probable. While on the one hand 'accord' means consistency and not deducibility, yet on the other hand Plato's hypothetical method, in the *Phaedo* as elsewhere, was surely a deduction of consequences from the hypothesis and not merely a further hypothesizing of propositions consistent with the first hypothesis.

It is necessary to conclude that Plato here does not say quite all that he means. He only says that the second step of the method is to find propositions consistent with the hypothesis; but he means that it finds propositions not merely consistent with them but also deducible from the hypothesis. Although the word 'accord' never meant definitely deducibility in his writing, and cannot mean it here, yet the metaphorical locution makes it possible on an uninterrupted reading to feel that the whole hypothetical procedure has been expressed.

'But why should Plato be so careless and vague?' The whole idea in his mind is that that which follows from the hypothesis is to be set down as true, and that whose contradictory follows from the hypothesis is to be set down as false. This idea has two parts;

and, since they are not contradictories (for the contradictory of 'that which follows from X' is not 'that whose contradictory follows from X' but 'that which does not follow from X'), the accurate expression of the whole idea is somewhat cumbersome. Plato chooses to be inaccurate, or at least inadequate, in order to preserve conversational simplicity. The two things he really has in mind, namely deducibility and inconsistency, cannot be neatly expressed by a single verb and its negative, because they are not contradictories but contraries. So he drops something of his meaning, trusting to its being 'divined', and takes consistency and inconsistency, which are contradictories and can be thus compactly expressed.

§ 3. THE METAPHOR OF ACCORD IN 101D

The metaphor of 'accord and disaccord' occurs once more in our passage, and in a still more puzzling way. 'If anyone hung on to the hypothesis itself, you would dismiss him and refuse to answer until you had considered its results to see if they accord or disaccord with each other' (101D). In using the word ὁρμη-θέντα (and ὡρμημένων 101E), which I have translated 'results', Plato seems to be thinking of the hypothesis as an impulse that gives rise to a string of events or produces a quantity of material. He had used the same notion earlier: 'anyway that is how I proceeded' (ὥρμησα 100A). And there are other dialogues in which a discussion is regarded as the gradual exhaustion of an original impulse (*Rp.* 510D, 511B; *Smp.* 185E; *Tht.* 184A). None of these other passages is at all definite on the question whether these 'results' are logical consequences or results of another kind. There appears to be no place in Plato where ὁρμηθέντα means logical consequences as technically and unmistakably as συμβαίνοντα can, with the possible exception of the present one. For here probably every reader feels that the results Plato has in mind are only the propositions the hypothesis entails.

It appears then that Plato is saying: 'until you had considered the logical consequences of the hypothesis, to see if they accord or disaccord with each other'. This puts us in a slightly better position to answer the question whether 'accord and disaccord' here means 'entail and do not entail' or 'be consistent and inconsistent with'. Now there is a very strong argument indeed for supposing that 'accord' here means entailment. This is that, if it meant consistency, Plato would be assuming a logical impossibility; for he would be assuming that the consequences of an hypothesis can contradict each other, whereas they cannot. The various propositions that follow from a given proposition are necessarily consistent both with the given proposition and with each other. This absurdity is avoided if we take him to be saying: 'you would refuse to answer until you had considered the (supposed) consequences of the hypothesis to see if they follow from each other or fail to follow'. If they fail to follow they are not really consequences. Thus the whole procedure would consist in (1) making an hypothesis, (2) drawing its consequences, (3) checking these consequences to see that they are really such (this is the step described in our present passage), and (4) positing these consequences as true (as described earlier, 100A).

Yet this will not do. Somehow or other it is necessary to get over the apparent logical absurdity and take 'accord' as meaning consistency here also, for the following reasons. (1) On the above interpretation, Plato in our present passage puts a disproportionate emphasis on the minor activity of checking one's logical calculations. In logic as in arithmetic it is always desirable to check any long operation; but there is little point in referring to that here, and no point at all in mentioning it to the exclusion of the other steps and as if it were the most important of them all, especially in what purports to be a first introduction of the procedure to a man as yet unacquainted therewith. (2) There are the general arguments, previously rehearsed, for believing that in Plato's logic the metaphor of 'accord' never meant entailment and often meant consistency. In the present passage 'disaccord' or διαφωνεῖ seems a particularly unnatural metaphor for 'does not follow from'. (3) It seems very unlikely that in two passages so closely connected in time and significance Plato would mean different things by the metaphor; and we have concluded that in the earlier he means consistency. It still seems unlikely, even when we recall that in this very passage there is an outrageous case of such ambiguity. 'You would answer by hanging on to that safe hypothesis. And if anyone hung on to the hypothesis itself', &c. The first 'hang on' means something like 'insist on believing'; but the second means 'object to'. When what a writer wishes to say could be expressed by a word he has just used in another sense, this word frequently presents itself to him in the new sense without

his realizing that he has just used it in another; and that is probably the manner of Plato's 'hangings on' here; but such an accident is hardly likely to happen to a word so central to the context
as is 'accord' here. (4) Even those readers of the *Phaedo* who have
expressed most dismay at our passage have never, so far as I know,
ventured to escape by reinterpreting 'accord' as entailment. (Mr.
Murphy interprets it thus [*CQ* XXX 41]; but he does not do so
as the conclusion of an exposition of the difficulty of the other
view.) They have supposed instead either that Plato here made
an error or that his text has been interpolated. For these reasons
we must hold that 'accord' here too means consistency; and we
must wrestle with the logical absurdity that appears in consequence.

The supposed logical absurdity is that Plato here implies that
the consequences of an hypothesis can be inconsistent one with
another. Now in discussing the distinction between direct and
indirect elenchus, we found reasons for believing that Plato regarded all elenchus as indirect, that is, as working by showing
that the refutand entails a falsehood; and further that he thought
that this falsehood was always the selfcontradiction of the refutand; and further that he regarded the elenchus as making the
refutand lead to this selfcontradiction without the aid of any
additional premisses. (Above, pp. 29–32.) If these things are so,
Plato believed that any hypothesis (for a refutand is an hypothesis and is often called so in the dialogues) can have as one of
its consequences the contradictory of itself; and if he believed
that, he surely may have believed also that it can have as one of
its consequences the contradictory of another of them. That an
hypothesis may by itself entail the contradictory of itself is in fact
the general assumption of the elenctic procedure; and every particular elenchus is supposed to be precisely the eliciting from a
given proposition of its own contradictory. It is a very short step
from this to holding that a proposition may have a pair of conflicting consequences; and we can make it even shorter by reflecting that, as Mr. Murphy has suggested to me, Plato's phrase
'the results of the hypothesis' (τὰ ἀπ' ἐκείνης ὁρμηθέντα) may very
well include the hypothesis itself. It means 'all the propositions
you have when you have exhausted the impulse that began with
the hypothesis'; and the hypothesis itself is one of these. Mr.
Hardie (*A Study in Plato* 67, referring to *Cra.* 436D) says that

Plato in the *Cratylus* recognizes that it is paradoxical to imply that the consequences of a single hypothesis can be inconsistent with each other; but he has mistaken the meaning of the passage, which merely says that even if all the consequences are consistent with each other and with the hypothesis they may still be false, because the hypothesis itself may be false.

There is a good enough sense in which an hypothesis really can give rise to a consequence that contradicts another of its consequences or the hypothesis itself. The hypothesis may be a whole of parts, and one of them may be latently inconsistent with another. Plato offers no criterion to distinguish a complex from an atomic proposition; and it is not clear that a perfectly watertight distinction could ever be made. That is one reason for holding that what Plato says here is not a logical absurdity; and it is perfectly sufficient in itself. Nevertheless, in view of the stumbling this passage has caused, we may add a second.

Whitehead and Russell, by their *Principia Mathematica*, have made familiar to most mathematicians and philosophers the idea of complete axiomatization. This is the idea of enumerating exhaustively and explicitly all the premisses required to deduce a given body of propositions. A system is completely axiomatized if nothing whatever is required in order to deduce its theorems except what is explicitly stated in its axioms. The notion of logical 'rigour' includes the notion that all the required premisses have been mentioned.

For our present purpose we need to notice two facts about this great idea. The first is that perhaps it is only an ideal and can never be realized. For it assumes a sort of isolability which perhaps cannot be had. It assumes that we can construct a system in which the theorems will follow from the axioms *no matter what happens outside the system*. It also assumes that our symbols can enter new combinations without relevant alteration of their meaning; and, as Whitehead has himself suggested (*Philosophical Review*, March 1937), perhaps this cannot be guaranteed. There might be a fluidity or an interdependence in the nature of things that defeated the ideal of axiomatization. The *Principia* may come to seem as little axiomatized as Euclid does now, and this process may continue indefinitely.

The second fact for us to notice about the ideal of axiomatization is that it has not always existed in men's minds, and still exists only in those of mathematicians and philosophers. It is not the common way of looking at deduction. In ordinary thought a conclusion is regarded as following from only one or two of the many premisses it requires according to this ideal. Not merely do the formal principles of the deduction remain wholly implicit. Many of the material premisses required remain so too. The inference that John is in because his hat is on the peg demands many other premisses that we never think of formulating. It even happens that we do formulate some of these other premisses and still regard the conclusion as flowing not from them but only from some special premiss; and that is the fundamental point for understanding Plato here. We habitually divide the logically necessary premisses (or rather as many of them as we are aware of) into two groups, the one or two or three that we regard as the 'efficient causes' of the conclusion, and the mass of others that we regard as merely the 'conditions' without which the true premiss would not have had the effect it does. What leads us to place a premiss in the group of 'conditions' is usually its relative permanence in our beliefs or in nature. The proposition we have only just thought of, and the proposition that states a fleeting event, are regarded as the premisses of the inference; those we believe year in and year out are merely its conditions.

This is the sense, the natural and ordinary sense, in which Plato speaks of an hypothesis' having conflicting consequences. It may have conflicting consequences on our standing assumptions, that is, when combined with some of our permanent beliefs. There is no logical absurdity in the passage.

What is the relation between the procedure described in this passage and that of the previous one? Previously he said: 'hypothesizing on each occasion the logos that I judge the strongest, I posit as true whatever seems to me to accord therewith, and as not true whatever seems not to' (100A). Now he says: 'hanging on to that safe hypothesis ... you would ... refuse to answer until you had considered its results to see if they accord or disaccord with each other' (101D). The connexion is as follows. The main outline of the hypothetical method is given in the earlier passage, as we have interpreted it: (1) make an hypothesis, (2) posit as true what follows therefrom and as false that whose contradictory follows therefrom. But in exploring the consequences of an hypothesis you may find two that contradict each other, or one that contradicts the hypothesis itself. This is the possibility contemplated in the second passage and unmentioned in the first. When this happens, Plato means, the hypothesis must be abandoned; for it has been refuted in the very way in which the elenchus always works. Only when it does not happen, or so long as it does not happen, can we apply the procedure of the first passage, which is the proper aim of the hypothetical method, namely, draw the consequences of the hypothesis and posit them as true. In drawing the consequences of an hypothesis we are in fact advancing the main aim of the method, which is to deduce something from the hypothesis, and at the same time to some extent testing the hypothesis; for if it should lead to a contradiction it would be refuted, and the longer it fails to do so the more it grows in our confidence. The two passages have seemed contradictory to some readers only because they took each as a full account of the method. But each is partial, and the second much more so than the first. In the first Plato regards the method as constructive, which is what it aims at being. In the second he brings out the critical element in it, in response to an imaginary critic. The whole method as so far described comes to this: in order to reach a desired conclusion, (1) hypothesize whichever hypothesis seems strongest to you of those that seem likely to lead to the conclusion; (2) draw the consequences of this hypothesis; (3) see whether they give rise to any contradiction; if they do, begin from the beginning again with another hypothesis; but, so long as they do not, (4) posit as true that which the hypothesis entails, and as false that of which the hypothesis entails the contradictory. In this description the third element is a test of the hypothesis; and to that extent the procedure here outlined is a test of the hypothesis and not a proof of something else by means of the hypothesis. But the *Phaedo* as a whole entirely supports the general statement (above, pp. 111-12) that to Plato an hypothesis was primarily a premiss and not a demonstrand, a proposition posited in order to prove something else and not in order to be itself established or refuted. The original statement of the method makes the hypothesis unequivocally a premiss (100A). The employment of the method in the dialogue is equally unequivocal. The hypothesis chosen is the theory of Ideas. There is no question of testing or recommending this theory in any way; but it is used as a premiss for inferring another proposition, namely that soul is immortal. Socrates introduces the notion of testing only when he comes to imagine somebody objecting to the hypothesis (101D). Even then he never thinks of an empirical test; the whole inquiry is 'by discussion' merely, σκέψις ἐν λόγοις. And the testing never becomes an end in itself; he seeks to confirm the hypothesis only because he thereby confirms the conclusion that follows from the hypothesis.

But here a difficulty occurs. What has just been declared to be a testing of the hypothesis seems to be regarded by Plato as not so. He seems expressly to distinguish it therefrom. He urges that we ought to keep the activity of 'seeing whether the results accord or disaccord with each other' quite separate from that of 'discussing the hypothesis itself . . . by hypothesizing another hypothesis which seemed best of those above, until you came to something adequate'; and his language implies that whereas the second of these is a testing of the hypothesis the first is not.

One way out of this difficulty would be to abandon the view that 'seeing if the results accord' really is a sort of test of the hypothesis; and this would enable us to maintain a simplified and more universal form of the general doctrine that an hypothesis to Plato was not primarily a proposition to be tested. But 'seeing if the results accord' is so strongly reminiscent of the elenchus that we must retain the view that it is a sort of test, and explain Plato's apparent implication to the contrary thus. (1) Because he is urging that we ought to keep the two activities separate, he emphasizes their difference; and because the second is simply and solely a means of recommending the hypothesis, he tends to represent the first as not such a means. (2) Whereas the second is merely a means of establishing the hypothesis, the first is not merely so but also an integral part of the hypothetical method. For the activity of seeing whether the results accord, though it has the effect of testing the hypothesis and is here expressed in a way that brings out that aspect, is identical with the activity of inferring consequences from the hypothesis, and that is one of the main elements of the method. It is not primarily concerned with the truth of the hypothesis, which the other is. It is thus intrinsic to the method. However little you reck of testing your hypothesis, you cannot help testing it to this extent. But the other procedure is wholly extrinsic. It is nothing but a test of the hypothesis, and tests are not the purpose of the method. (3) 'Seeing whether the results accord', considered as a test, is merely negative. It can sometimes show that the hypothesis must be abandoned, but never that it must be retained. 'Hypothesizing a higher hypothesis', on the other hand, positively confirms it. These considerations show, first, that 'seeing whether the results accord' is not primarily a test, in spite of the manner of its expression here; and, second, that there is good reason why Plato should represent it as not a test at all when he was anxious to distinguish it from something that was merely such.

Phaedo 100A refers only to the development of a hypothetical system. *Phaedo* 101D1–5 notes that this development may reveal a defect which requires you to abandon the hypothesis, and refers mainly to this but partly to development. *Phaedo* 101D6–E1 points to the further task of confirming an hypothesis whose system develops no internal defect.

§ 4. HYPOTHESIZING A HIGHER HYPOTHESIS

We have been carried imperceptibly into a discussion of the next phrase, 'hypothesizing a higher hypothesis', and have already made several assumptions about Plato's meaning here. These must now be brought into the open. The passage is as follows: 'And when you had to discuss the hypothesis itself, you would do so in the same way, hypothesizing another hypothesis which seemed best of those above, until you came to something adequate.' The sort of 'discussion' in question is recommendation or defence. Socrates is thinking of the objector who says: 'Yes, your conclusion follows from your hypothesis; but how do you know the hypothesis is true?' The defence he indicates is to apply the hypothetical method to the hypothesis itself. The purpose of this method is to establish a given conclusion, and it does so by positing an hypothesis and deducing the conclusion therefrom. Very well then. Let the suspected hypothesis be your given conclusion, and prove it by deducing it from some other hypothesis. In other words, institute a new train of thought, having as its conclusion the proposition that was the hypothesis in the earlier train.

The new hypothesis is to be the one that seems best of those 'above'. What does the metaphor of 'above' mean here? Since the essential characteristic of the second hypothesis is that it entails the first, this metaphor must include the notion of entailment in its meaning. Hypothesize the best of those hypotheses that entail the first hypothesis—or better, perhaps, that seem likely to entail the first hypothesis, since at first you may not be clear whether the deduction will succeed. But does 'above' mean any more than this? Some readers feel that it means also 'more comprehensive, more universal, farther removed from the particulars'; and Archer-Hind quotes Aristotle: 'By "up" I mean towards the universal' (*Post. Anal.* 82ª23). The second hypothesis entails the first because it includes it. In the extreme form this interpretation is certainly wrong. Plato is not thinking of definitions, as Archer-Hind supposed; and he does not mean by 'a higher hypothesis' the definition of a concept wider than that defined in the 'lower' hypothesis. We have seen that there is no necessary connexion between hypothesis and definition (above, p. 100). He may, however, be thinking that the higher includes the lower as Newton's laws included Kepler's. He may also be thinking that the higher, as nearer to the source of entailment, is grander and more important. But both these are only overtones to his fundamental meaning of entailment.

'Until you came to something adequate.' This phrase indicates, in the compactest possible form, that the opponent might object to your second hypothesis too, in which case you would have to deduce it from a third. And if he objected to the third, you would have to deduce it from a fourth. And so on. But this process might be terminated by your reaching 'something adequate'. This surely means 'some adequate hypothesis'; and two questions arise. (1) Adequate to what? (2) What sort of hypothesis would Plato consider adequate to whatever it is? The answer to the first is determined by the context. The whole passage (101DE) is about the possibility of objection's being taken to your hypothesis; and so an 'adequate' hypothesis cannot be anything but an hypothesis to which your hearer will not object, one that he will be as willing to take for true as you are. 'Adequate' is 'adequate to satisfy your objector, and thus prove, as far as you and he are concerned, the conclusion you set out to prove'. It is not 'adequate to satisfy yourself'; for you were already satisfied with the first hypothesis. Nor is it 'adequate to satisfy anyone'; for dialectic takes no account of anyone except those present. This enables us to answer the second question also, namely, What sort of hypothesis would Plato consider adequate to satisfy the objector? There is no sort of hypothesis which as such satisfies objectors. The characteristic of satisfying objectors is not uniquely correlated with any other characteristic of hypotheses. The question was raised in the expectation that some epistemological answer would be relevant, such as 'The adequate hypothesis is the selfevident one'. But, since Plato is merely aiming at an hypothesis that the objector will agree to, epistemology does not enter into the matter at all. This has the important consequence that there is no connexion between the 'something adequate' of the *Phaedo* and the 'unhypothesized beginning' of the *Republic* (511). The latter *is* an epistemological concept; and it belongs to a somewhat different conception of the hypothetical method.

'Yet surely there is more in choosing an hypothesis than merely finding one that your interlocutor will accept. Plato's dialectic is not mere persuasion. It is an effort towards real knowledge, or at least rational opinion; and the dialectician must choose his hypothesis so as to convince himself along with others. Of all the thousands of hypotheses from which a man could deduce a desired conclusion, what makes one better than another? What makes one the "strongest", as Socrates puts it (100A)? Surely an hypothesis ought to be "adequate" in this sense too.'

These reflections are perfectly true, but they do not apply to this particular passage: 'until you came to something adequate.' There Plato is thinking merely of persuading the objector. At first it may seem odd to admit that Plato held that some hypotheses are better than others, and yet maintain that in the present passage he is thinking only of hypotheses that the objector will accept, and not of any other kind of betterness. But it will seem more reasonable if we inquire just what it is that makes one hypothesis better than another according to Plato. He speaks of 'an hypothesis worthy of acceptance' earlier in this dialogue, in a passage which at first seems to offer what we want:

How can this proposition of yours be brought into tune with that one? —Nohow, said Simmias.—And yet, said he, if any proposition ought to be in tune it is one about harmony.—It ought, said Simmias.— And this of yours, said he, is not in tune. But consider which of the propositions you choose, that learning is recollection or that soul is harmony?—Undoubtedly the former, Socrates, said he. For the latter came to me without demonstration through a certain specious probability, which is what recommends it to most people; and I know that arguments which make their 'demonstrations' through probabilities are charlatans; and if you do not watch them they deceive you nicely, both in geometry and in everything else. Whereas the proposition about recollection and learning was stated by means of *an hypothesis worthy of acceptance*. For we said that our soul existed even before it came into a body, in the same way as that essence to which is given the name of 'which exists'; and this I am persuaded that I am fully justified in accepting. (*Phd.* 92C–E.)

In this passage something logically better is contrasted with something logically worse, and mention is made of 'an hypothesis worthy of acceptance'. Yet, apparently, it is not better and worse hypotheses that are being contrasted, but the hypothetical method as such that is being contrasted with another way of reaching conclusions. Simmias says the proposition that learning is recollection was obtained by demonstration from the respectable hypothesis about the essence 'which exists'; in other words, it was obtained by the hypothetical method from the hypothesis of the Ideas, the ruling hypothesis in the *Phaedo*. But the proposition that soul is harmony was reached by a 'demonstration' that was merely probable. He seems to use the word 'demonstrations' derisively in this second occurrence; and his implication is that probable argument is not the hypothetical method at all. It contains no explicit, responsible hypothesizing, and no rigorous deduction of any sort. Thus after all this passage tells us nothing about what constitutes a good hypothesis except that the theory of Ideas is one. (A minor objection to the above interpretation of 92C–E is that it makes Simmias understand the hypothetical method before Socrates explains it to Cebes in 100A. But the failure in dramatic verisimilitude is small and of a likely kind.)

There is, however, another passage in the *Phaedo* that throws more light on the difference between a good and a bad hypothesis, although it does not use the word 'hypothesis':

With regard to such things it seems to me, as perhaps it does to you, Socrates, that to know them clearly in the present life is either impossible or extremely difficult, but not to attack (ἐλέγχειν) what is said about them by all means and refuse to give up until you have exhausted every way of looking at them is the part of a very soft man. For we ought to achieve one or other of these things about them: either learn or discover what the truth of them is; or, if that is impossible, at least to get hold of the best and least refutable (δυσεξελεγκτότατον) of human propositions and voyage through life mounted upon it like an adventurer on a raft, unless one could cross with less danger and risk on a steadier vessel, some divine proposition. (*Phd.* 85CD.)

For some purposes what is said here of 'propositions' or logoi may be taken as true of hypotheses. Plato is connecting the attainment of the best proposition or hypothesis with the notion of elenchus. If in reply to an objection or elenchus you can restate your hypothesis so that the objection fails, it is thenceforth inoculated against that particular objection, and so stronger. The best or 'least refutable' hypothesis is that which by a series of modifications has been rendered immune to all the refutations so far conceived.

But this procedure is just that internal and negative test that Plato expresses as 'seeing whether the results accord or disaccord with each other'. For the form which elenchus takes is precisely the attempt to prove that the results do disaccord with each other or with the hypothesis itself. This internal procedure then is the real test, the test about which the dialectician himself cares. The external process of deducing the hypothesis from a higher one is purely to satisfy the objector; and, if it is to satisfy the dialectician too, the higher hypothesis must pass the same internal test. There is nothing better within the confines of the hypothetical method. Only two things could be better; actual knowledge or 'some divine proposition'. Thus we have the curious fact that, of the two procedures mentioned in 101CD, the one that Plato there treats as a test of the hypothesis is the one that he did not regard as the real test. The real testing of the hypothesis is identical with the hypothetical procedure itself, namely, drawing consequences from the hypothesis. Deducing the hypothesis from a higher one is a test only from the point of view of an outsider who does not see the value of the hypothetical method; but it is represented as the only test here because Plato is here considering the outsider's point of view.

'But you would not confuse the two as the contradiction-mongers do, discussing the beginning and its results at the same time.' Here the 'beginning' is surely the hypothesis. This is perhaps the first appearance of the word ἀρχή or 'beginning' in its logical sense of 'principle', though the metaphysical sense is said to have been used by Anaximander (Simplicius *in Arist. Phys.* 150. 23). 'Discussing the beginning' must be a way of referring to deducing an hypothesis from a higher one; and 'discussing its results' must be a way of referring to 'seeing whether the results accord or disaccord with each other'. Plato's insistence on keeping these separate seems at first unnecessary because it is hard to see how they could be combined. But he says that certain 'contra-diction-mongers' do combine them; and in fact what he is inculcating is the most fundamental element of the hypothetical method, which consists in distinguishing at every instant between what you are assuming and what you are deducing. For thought to advance, a system of entailments must become visible; and the bigger the system the greater the possible advance. But no such system can ever become visible unless you are willing to assume a given proposition long enough to work out some of its conse-quences. If, each time you begin to deduce the results of *p*, you are distracted from your task by your own doubts about *p*, or by other men's attacks on it, the system cannot appear, and your opinions can only be a heap of intuitions. Hence the need for hypothesizing, which need is the origin of the hypothetical method.

Besides explicitly saying that you must keep the two activities separate, Plato seems to imply fairly definitely that you must take them in a certain order. You must first deduce the consequences of your hypothesis, and secondly deduce your hypothesis from a higher one; not the other way about. 'You would not answer (attacks on the hypothesis) until you had examined its conse-quences.' This accords with the views we have elucidated. Dedu-cing the consequences is both the real business of the hypothetical method (in order to prove the desired conclusion) and the only real test of the hypothesis. If the hypothesis fails to imply the conclusion, or if it develops an internal contradiction, it will have to be abandoned anyhow; and there would be no point in trying to defend it against outside objections by deducing it from a higher hypothesis. If it could be so deduced the higher hypo-thesis would itself involve the contradiction involved by the lower.

These reflections make it unnecessary to say that Plato is here thinking of attacks made by Protagoras and others on mathe-matics, as Burnet said; and false to say that Plato is enunciating the Aristotelian position that you must not ask for a proof of first principles, as Heinrich Maier seems to do (*Die Syllogistik des Aristoteles* II, 2, 46–56). The passage is like Descartes's *Discourse* in insisting on an order, as Taylor points out; but the items to be ordered have no resemblance in the two thinkers.

§ 5. MISCELLANEOUS QUESTIONS

How far is the method as Socrates describes it practised in the
dialogue? This question can be soon answered if we arrange
Socrates' account in three parts:

1. Hypothesizing a proposition and positing as true what agrees
therewith.

2. Seeing whether any contradiction arises out of the hypothesis.

3. Deducing the hypothesis from a higher one.

The first of these is performed at large throughout the dialogue.
The main proposition hypothesized is the theory of Ideas, and
the main conclusion deduced therefrom, by three different routes,
is that soul is immortal. A minor hypothesis is that soul is harmony
(called an hypothesis at 93C10 and 94B1), from which it is sought
to conclude that soul is mortal. The second part, seeing whether
any contradiction arises out of the hypothesis, is not a distinct
operation from the first, but rather a possibility for which we
look out while engaged in the first. This possibility is not realized
in the *Phaedo* in the deductions from the main hypothesis; the
theory of Ideas is not found to lead to contradiction here as in the
Parmenides. But it is realized in the deductions from the minor
hypothesis that soul is harmony. That proposition leads to the
'contradictions' that all souls are equally good (94A), and that
soul never rules over body; and has to be abandoned. The third
part, deducing the hypothesis from a higher one, is never undertaken in the *Phaedo*, which is another evidence that Plato considered it external and inessential.

A much more puzzling question is: What is the relation of this
account of method to its context? Why does it come in the *Phaedo*
where it does? It comes, in Socrates' account of his intellectual
life, at the moment when he gave up trying to show that the cause
of things is the Good. That he does describe himself as abandoning
the attempt to show that the cause of things is the Good seems
clear in these words:

> That the good and the fitting do truly fit and hold things together
> they have no conception. Now I should have been very glad to learn
> from anybody the truth about this sort of cause; but since I was
> deprived of it, and could neither discover it for myself nor learn it from
> anybody else, would you like me, Cebes, he said, to give you an
> exhibition of how I have conducted my second best way of looking for
> the cause? (99C.)

This passage, in combination with the fact that he goes on to introduce the Ideas as causes, and says no more about the Good as a cause, seems clearly to mean that he gave up the attempt to show that the Good is the cause of things.

Immediately after this passage, and before introducing his new cause, he describes his hypothetical method. The question is, therefore: What has the hypothetical method to do with the new kind of cause?

It seems a mere excrescence. Socrates might have said merely this: 'First I sought for causes as the scientists do. Then I saw that the real cause is the Good. But I could not find the Good. At last I invented for myself a third kind of cause, not so good as the Good but better than that of the physicists, namely, participation in the Idea.' Why does he talk about hypothesis before introducing the third kind of cause? The connexion seems perfectly accidental. Surely you could have the third kind of cause without the method, and have either of the two previous kinds of cause *with* the method? What is the relation between these two things: (1) abandoning the search for the Good, (2) adopting the hypothetical method?

It will not do to say that the hypothetical method and the belief in formal causes go together because the method eschews the senses and the formal causes are not accessible to sense. It is true that the method eschews the senses, and true that the Ideas cannot be sensed; but this does nothing to explain why Socrates adopted the method only when he had abandoned the Good. Surely he did not think at this time that the Good could only be found through the senses. The problem may be put in this way. When at last Socrates had abandoned the use of the senses and adopted the hypothetical method, why did he not try once again to ascertain the Good, now that he had much better instruments of research? Surely the abandonment of the senses and the adoption of this method offered the hope that now at last he *would* be able to explain things by means of the Good. But, according to the account, he never put his new weapons to the test upon his heart's desire. Instead he used them on a second-best sort of explanation.

There appears to be no satisfactory answer to this problem, and only two suggestions that have any plausibility at all. The first is that Plato wants to introduce his new method impressively in this dialogue, and this seems an impressive place to do so. In other words, there is no real connexion between the introduction of the method and the switch from final to formal causes. Plato is merely emphasizing the importance of the method by representing it as entering Socrates' life at a time of momentous change. The unsatisfactoriness of this suggestion is obvious. The only other solution that seems worth even a moment's consideration is that Plato believed at this time that the hypothetical method could not be applied to the Good. If he held that you could not hypothesize the Good, so to speak, and that the hypothetical method could never lead to valuable doctrines on this supreme matter, then when he made Socrates adopt the hypothetical method he would naturally make him also abandon the search for the Good. 'But', we at once exclaim, 'is there any reason why the method should be debarred from this particular subject, and is there any evidence that Plato thought it was?' If we interpreted the Divided Line in the *Republic* as contemptuous of the hypothetical method, and as implying that this method cannot be used to seek the Good, then the *Republic* would be evidence in support of this interpretation of the *Phaedo*; but, according to the view of the Line which will be recommended below, Plato in the *Republic* holds on the contrary that the method can lead us to the Good. Therefore he had changed his mind between the two dialogues if, when writing the *Phaedo*, he thought the method could not be applied to the Good. We remain without adequate reason for adopting any particular answer to the question why Plato in the *Phaedo* made the abandonment of the search for the Good simultaneous with the adoption of the hypothetical method.

If we now review our attempt to elucidate the *Phaedo* on hypothesis, we see that this dialogue contains fairly explicitly all the elements that we declared characteristic of the method in general. Socrates explicitly says that he makes an hypothesis. We have decided after some difficulty that he also means to say (though he does not quite say it) that he deduces consequences therefrom. The primary purpose of these two activities is to reach a desired conclusion and thereby prove it; Socrates does not say this in abstract language, but it is sufficiently obvious in his procedure in the last argument for immortality. But the consequences of the hypothesis might, according to Plato's logic, be contradictory either of each other or of the hypothesis itself. In that case the hypothesis would be untenable and no conclusion could properly be established by its means. It therefore becomes a secondary purpose of the deduction to see whether any such contradiction does arise, and this is explicitly stated (101D). If it does, the hypothesis must be reformulated to avoid it; and then we must begin our deductions again from the new hypothesis, again trying first to reach the desired conclusion and secondly to detect any contradiction. This procedure implies both a determination to avoid contradiction, which is often expressed in the dialogues, and a belief in the value of gradual approximation, which does not find expression. Since the primary purpose of the deduction is to establish the desired conclusion, the hypothesis is primarily a premiss; but secondarily it is a conclusion to be itself recommended or destroyed by the absence or presence of contradiction among its consequences. Plato adds, in the *Phaedo* alone, that it may be further recommended by being deduced from a higher hypothesis. The whole method functions solely in the dialectical plane; that is to say, it is an affair of question and answer and thinking, without any appeal to observation or experiment. It is a second best (99C), a raft, as it were (85D), with which to meet the waves as well as we can in default of 'clear knowledge' or divine inspiration; but Plato evidently thinks it a fairly stout raft, and he evidently does not think that using the senses would be superior.

X

HYPOTHESIS IN THE *REPUBLIC*

§ I. A CONFLICT BETWEEN PLATO'S EPISTEMOLOGY AND HIS METHODOLOGY

PLATO believed in the possibility of absolute, incorrigible knowledge. Intelligence, he said in the *Timaeus* 51DE, is not the same as true opinion, for these two came into being separately and are unlike in nature. 'The one comes to be in us through teaching, but the other owing to persuasion; and the one can always give a true account, but the other none; and the one is immovable by persuasion, but the other can be persuaded away; and it must be said that the one can be enjoyed by every man, but intelligence by gods, and by some small race of men.' In the *Theaetetus* he argued elaborately and energetically that knowledge would not be true opinion even if that opinion could give an account of itself. In the *Republic* he was, though brief, most definite of all; he bluntly said that knowledge could not be the same as opinion because the latter is fallible but the former infallible (477E). He rated opinion at a very low value compared with knowledge.

But his hypothetical method, if our analysis of the *Phaedo* has been correct, can never attain to absolute knowledge. It is merely approximative; and, however much work has been done, the possibility that the ruling hypothesis is false must always remain. It thus appears that Plato's methodology in the *Phaedo* is at variance with his epistemology as stated in the *Republic* and later works. The Aristotelian or the Cartesian methodology would have been, it seems, more suitable to this theory of knowledge; for both Aristotle and Descartes believed in absolute incorrigible starting-points, guaranteed by an infallible intuition, from which certain conclusions could be deduced.

We have seen that Plato regarded his hypothetical method as only a second best; but, when we recall that he believed in the possibility of absolute knowledge, we may think that he ought to have regarded it as a tenth best, and we must certainly wonder why he devoted so much space to its elaboration and so little, apparently, to the elaboration of a method for winning the real and not impossible prize, infallible certainty.

There is a passage in the *Cratylus* (436D) that seems to record the kind of dissatisfaction with mere hypothetical consistency that we should expect from a man with Plato's view of knowledge.

If the giver [of names] made a mistake in the first place and then distorted the rest to meet it and compelled them to accord with him, it would not be at all surprising, just as in diagrams sometimes, when a slight and inconspicuous mistake is made in the first place, all the huge mass of consequences agree with each other. It is about the beginning of every matter that every man must make his big discussion and his big inquiry, to see whether it is rightly laid down or not (ὑπόκειται); and only when that has been adequately examined should he see whether the rest appear to follow from it.

A much stronger statement of dissatisfaction, which the context proves to refer expressly to hypothetical procedure, is to be found in the dialogue we are about to examine (533C): 'For if a man's beginning is something he does not know, and the end and what comes between are constructed out of what he does not know, what contrivance can ever turn such consistency into knowledge?'

§ 2. TRANSLATION OF PASSAGES ON METHOD IN THE 'REPUBLIC'

The 'first-best' method, which seems to be demanded by these complaints and by Plato's epistemology, is indicated in the diagram of the Divided Line in the *Republic*; and to that we must therefore turn.

The main passages concerning hypothesis in the *Republic* appear in the part devoted to the higher education of the rulers, the part whose problem is 'how and through what studies and exercises the saviours of the republic will come to exist in it, and at what age each of them will take up each activity' (502C–541B). Socrates holds that these saviours must pursue 'the greatest study, the idea of the good' (505A). He does not himself know what the good is, except that it seems to be neither pleasure nor knowledge; but he suggests that it is to intelligence and the ideas as the sun is to sight and the visibles. It gives us all the knowledge and truth we have, but is itself superior thereto. And to the things we know it gives all the existence and reality they have, but is itself beyond reality in dignity and power.

Consider then, said I, that, as we say, they are two [namely, the good and the sun], and the one reigns over the intelligible sort and sphere, the other over the visible. . . . You have these two kinds, visible and intelligible?

I have.

Then take them as if they were a line cut into two unequal sections, and cut each section again in the same proportion, both that of the sort that is seen and that of the sort that is thought; and then, in degree of clearness relative to each other, you will have, in the visible, as the one section, images—I mean by images first shadows, next appearances in water and in things of a close and smooth and plain constitution, and everything of the sort, if you understand me.

I understand you.

Let the other section be what this one resembles, the animals about us and the whole class of everything that grows or is made.

Let it be, said he.

Would you be willing to say, said I, that we have divided it so that in degree of truth the likeness is to what it is like as the opined is to the known?

I certainly should, said he.

Now consider how we are to make the section of the intelligible part. How?

In that the soul, using as images what was previously imitated, is compelled to pursue one section of it from hypotheses, not proceeding to a beginning but to an end; but for the other, which leads to an unhypothesized beginning, the soul goes from hypothesis and without the images of the other, making the inquiry by ideas themselves through themselves.

I do not understand that very well, said he.

Once again, then, said I. You will understand it easier if I say this first. I think you know that those who study geometry and calculation and such matters hypothesize the odd and even and the figures and three kinds of angles and related matters in each inquiry. Assuming that they know these things, and making them hypotheses, they do not expect to give any account (logos) of them either to themselves or to others, as being plain to all; but beginning from them they go through the rest consistently and end with what they set out to examine.

Certainly, he said; I know that much.

And they use the forms that we see and make their arguments about them, although they are thinking not about them but about what they resemble, making their arguments for the sake of the square itself and the diagonal itself, not of that which they draw. And so with the rest. What they model and draw are things of which there are shadows and images in water; but they use these things themselves as images again, their aim being to see those very things that can be seen only by thought.

That is right, he said.

Well, then, I meant that this kind is intelligible, but yet the soul is obliged to use hypotheses in pursuing it, and does not go to a beginning because it cannot get above the hypotheses, and uses as images the very things that are themselves imitated by those below them and honoured and valued as clear in comparison therewith.

I see, he said. You mean the object of geometry and the related sciences.

Then understand that by the other section of the intelligible I mean that which is grasped by pure discussion through the power of dialectic, making the hypotheses not beginnings but really hypotheses, like steps and sallies, in order that, going as far as the unhypothesized to the beginning of everything and grasping it, it may descend again thus to an end, clinging to the things that cling to that, using absolutely nothing sensible but only ideas themselves through themselves on themselves, and ending with ideas.

I see, he said, not indeed sufficiently, for I think you mean a big job. But I see this much, that you want to distinguish the part of intelligible reality which is the object of dialectic as being clearer than that which is the object of what are called the sciences, for which hypotheses are beginnings; and, while those who study them are obliged to do so by thought and not by senses, yet, because they inquire from hypotheses and do not ascend to a beginning, you think they do not have intelligence about them, although they are intelligible with a beginning. And to the state of the geometers and such persons I think you give the name 'thought', as being something between opinion and intelligence.

You have understood me perfectly, said I. And now take it that to the four sections there correspond these four effects in the soul: intelligence to the highest; thought to the second; to the third give conviction, to the last conjecture, and arrange them proportionately, giving to each as much clearness as its correspondent has truth.

I see, he said, and I agree and arrange them as you say. (509D–511E.)

Socrates next illustrates 'our nature regarding education and the lack of it' by the image of the Cave (514A ff.). He supposes men chained from childhood in a cave so that they see only the shadows of themselves and of certain statues and other objects that are being carried along behind them, and hear only their own voices and the echoes of the voices of the men carrying the objects. Such men, he says, would take these shadows and echoes for the truth; and, if they were afterwards unchained and made to look at the reality, they would be dazzled and take it for illusion. Becoming accustomed to the truth would be a long and painful process; and it would have to be repeated at many stages of increasing brightness before they were at last able to look directly at the sun itself. But once it was achieved they would pity the state of their fellow prisoners. If they returned to the cave they would be unable to see in the dimness; and those who had never been released would be confirmed in their belief that it was a bad thing to go upwards. In this image, Socrates says, the upward progress symbolizes the ascent of the soul to the intelligible place. The idea of the good is seen last and hardest among known things; but when we see it we infer that it is the cause of all that is right and fine everywhere. Education is not putting sight into blind eyes, but turning round eyes that are looking in the wrong direction. The question thus arises which studies drag the soul away from that which becomes to that which is. Arithmetic does so, because its object, the one, &c., never appears to sense except along with its opposite. What looks one also looks a multiplicity; and this confusion in the report of the senses compels the reason to intervene. As successive stages in the education of the rulers Socrates appoints plane geometry, solid geometry, astronomy (which he converts into kinematics), and harmonics. The final study, the grasping at the good itself, will be dialectic.

This at any rate, I said, no one will allege against us, that any other inquiry [than dialectic] attempts methodically and universally to ascertain with regard to each thing what that very thing itself is. All the other sciences are either concerned with men's opinions and desires or with productions and manufactures, or they are aimed at the care of what grows and is manufactured. As to the rest, geometry and those connected therewith, which we said grasped something of reality, we see that they dream about reality, but cannot see it with waking eyes so long as they use hypotheses and do not canvass them, being unable to give an account of them. For if a man's beginning is something he does not know, and the end and what comes between are constructed out of what he does not know, what contrivance can ever turn such consistency into knowledge?

None, said he.

Then, said I, the dialectical method alone proceeds in this way, destroying the hypotheses, to the very beginning, in order to obtain confirmation. It gently pulls and draws upwards the eye of the soul that is literally buried in a sort of Philistine filth, using the sciences we have detailed as its assistants in the conversion. 'Knowledge' we often called them owing to custom; but they need another name, clearer than 'opinion' and not so clear as 'knowledge'. I think we previously defined it as 'thought'. But men do not dispute about a word when they have such great matters to examine as we have proposed.

No indeed, said he. [I follow Adam's excision of the next sentence, and keep the MS. ἀρέσκει thereafter.]

We are content, then, said I, as before, to call the first part knowledge, the second thought, the third conviction, and the fourth conjecture; and the last two together opinion, and the first two together intelligence; and to say that opinion is about becoming but intelligence about being; and that intelligence is to opinion what being is to becoming; and knowledge is to conviction, and thought is to conjecture, what intelligence is to opinion. But let us not go into the proportion and division of their objects, the opinable and the intelligible, Glaucon, in order not to involve ourselves in many more discussions than we have had already.

Anyhow I agree with you about the rest, he said, as far as I can follow it.

And do you call dialectical the man who takes the account of the essence of each thing? And if he cannot give an account to himself and others, then, so far as he cannot, you will not call him intelligent on the matter?

How could I? said he.

And the same with the good? If a man cannot by his account separate and distinguish the idea of the good from all else, and persevere through everything in the battle of refutation, eager to refute in reality and not in appearance, and go through all these things without letting his argument be overthrown, you will not say he knows the good itself or any other good; but, if he is somehow grasping some copy of it, he is grasping it by opinion and not by knowledge, his present life is a dreaming and a dozing, and before he wakes up here he will have gone to Hades and be completely asleep?

Yes, by heaven, said he, I say all that emphatically.

Well, then, your children, whom you are training and educating in the discussion—if you ever trained them in reality, I presume you would not let them govern the city and decide the most important things until they had ceased to be as irrational (ἀλόγους) as lines.

No, indeed, said he.

You will legislate for them to lay hold especially of the discipline that will make them capable of asking and answering questions most scientifically?

I shall, said he, along with you.

Then does it seem to you, said I, that dialectic lies on top of the sciences like a coping-stone, so that no other science could properly be placed above it, and the matter of the sciences is concluded?

Yes, he said.

Then the allotment is all you have left, I said; to whom we shall give these sciences and how. (533B–535A.)

Socrates then proceeds to answer this last question.

§ 3. MATHEMATICS

Let us begin our attempt to understand what Plato says about hypothesis in these passages by considering what he says about hypothesis in mathematics. And first let us notice a remarkable feature that seems to contradict our previous account of hypothesis. This is that Plato here treats as hypotheses certain propositions which the mathematicians think they know, which they consider 'plain to all'. Thus every element of provisionality and approximation is removed. The mathematicians' procedure is represented as a single forward march once for all. And so, though the word 'hypothesis' is here, no element of what we thought it meant remains. There is no question of hypothesizing in the sense of deliberately assuming, for the time being, a proposition which you know that you do not know.

The explanation of this anomaly is that Plato is regarding the mathematicians as not treating certain propositions as hypotheses when they ought to, as not using the hypothetical method when they ought to. He thinks they are wrong to take the propositions from which they begin, 'the odd and even and the figures and three kinds of angles and related matters', as evident and known to be true. They should take them as tentative hypotheses. His complaint is that mathematicians do not use the hypothetical method although they should. The word 'hypothesis' is Plato's interpretation of their procedure, and not the word they themselves would use. Contemporary mathematicians did not describe themselves as starting always from hypotheses. This passage is not evidence for that; and the *Meno*, which explicitly borrows from mathematical procedure, surely implies that what they called the 'by hypothesis' method was not their regular procedure but a special method, frequent indeed (πολλάκις *Men.* 86E) but not preponderating.

Plato means, then, that the mathematicians, who usually proceed dogmatically and only occasionally hypothetically, ought to proceed always hypothetically, because in reality they never know their ultimate premisses to be true. In the *Meno* he borrowed a special mathematical method for philosophy. This method afterwards came to seem to him very important indeed, as we see in the *Phaedo*. And now that he is writing the *Republic* he has come to think that this procedure should be not a special but the general method of mathematicians. He wants to extend the use of their method far beyond what they themselves would do, because he has come to think that, besides the hypotheses which they themselves recognize as such, all their other starting-points are hypotheses too.

What makes Plato think that the mathematicians do not really know their starting-points? One answer to this has already been rejected in the general discussion of the hypothetical method (above, p. 104); it was not that he thought he saw that some of them were in fact false. The context seems to suggest that it was his opinion at this time that nothing is really known unless it is deduced from the idea of the Good; and that was perhaps his opinion when he wrote the *Phaedo* too. It might also be that by using his hypothetical method he was led to believe in the merely provisional nature of all ordinary starting-points, including those of mathematics, whereas formerly he had without realizing it assumed that there are plenty of certain starting-points. There is very little in his text by way of a direct answer. When he says that 'they do not expect to give any account (logos) of [these hypotheses] either to themselves or to others' (510C), he seems to think of this as the consequence of their supposing that they know them rather than the cause of their really not knowing them; but his similar language in a later passage ('they use hypotheses and do not canvass them, being unable to give an account (logos) of them' 533BC) implies rather that the cause and the proof of their not really knowing their starting-points is precisely their inability to give a logos of them. The only other direct statement on the point seems to be this: 'because they inquire from hypotheses and do not ascend to a beginning, you think they do not have intelligence about them, although they are intelligible with a beginning' (511CD). This would apparently come to the same as the former passage if giving a logos of a proposition were sufficient to turn it from an 'hypothesis' into a 'beginning'. It is noteworthy that the *Phaedo* also speaks of giving a logos of an hypothesis. What this giving a logos would consist in will appear if we can elucidate what Plato understands by dialectic in the Line; for he holds that dialectic does give a logos of everything. First, however, let us consider one more side of his discussion of mathematics.

What the Divided Line says about mathematics falls into two distinct parts. Separately from the mathematicians' attitude to hypothesis, Plato brings out the fact that they use sensible images in order to deal with the supersensible realities they are talking about. (To the Greeks this was as true of arithmetic as of geometry.) The question thus arises whether he thought there was a necessary connexion between these two marks of mathematics. Did he think that geometry must use hypotheses as it does because of its employment of images, or that it must use images because of the way it treats hypotheses, or both? Or was he merely noting a chance conjunction in contemporary mathematics, an accident of history?

That he thought it merely a chance conjunction is strongly suggested by the consideration that in the *Phaedo* he declares that the hypothetical method makes no use of the senses. At the very least this means that that method *need not* use the senses; and, if so, surely there cannot be a necessary connexion between the two marks. Furthermore, according to the Divided Line mathematics is not alone in using hypotheses. Dialectic uses them too. One of the curious things about the Line is the way in which Plato says that mathematics starts from hypotheses, as if he were going to say that dialectic did not, and then says that dialectic does so too. 'The soul, using as images what was previously imitated, is compelled to pursue *one* section of it *from hypotheses*, not proceeding to a beginning but to an end; but for the *other*, which leads to an unhypothesized beginning, the soul goes *from hypothesis*', &c. (510B). But Plato is quite definite in the Line that dialectic does not use the senses; it follows that the use of hypotheses does not entail the use of the senses. This impression is strengthened by the fact that the *Republic* contains no statement that such a connexion exists, and still less a statement as to what sort of thing it would be if it did. The only text that carries even the shadow of an implication that it exists is this: 'The soul, using as images what was previously imitated, is compelled to pursue one section of it from hypothesis' (510B). Here the fact that the use of images is attached as a participle to the use of hypotheses in the main verb perhaps gives a faint indication that they are necessarily and not merely historically connected. And that is all. Burnet could only say that the special sciences 'depend on hypotheses of which they can give no account, and are therefore obliged to use sensible diagrams' (*Greek Philosophy* 229); he offered no justification for his 'therefore'.

Yet we should prefer to believe that Plato found some necessary connexion between the two marks, not merely because a philosopher systematizes whenever he can, but further because Plato regards mathematical procedure as the work of a distinct type of mental activity which he calls thought or διάνοια as opposed to intelligence or νόησις. If these two marks were connected only historically, 'thought' would not be a real species of mental activity, but a conjunction of two real species. And he does seem, in a vague and general way, to make Socrates regard what he describes as an organic whole.

Jackson suggested that the hypotheses of the mathematician are still dependent on the particulars or 'many' from which they were originally derived, because they have not been shown to be correct and complete accounts of Ideas. We may perhaps interpret this as saying that an hypothesis, being arbitrary, is not a sure grasp of an Idea, and therefore can be accepted as true only so far as it agrees with the particulars in which the Idea is exemplified. If, however, we came to know the Idea itself and see it face to face, all appeal to the sensibles would be irrelevant, and at the same time our attitude to the Idea would not be an hypothesis but something better.

There is, however, no evidence for Jackson's acute suggestion in the text, and it seems to be gravely damaged by the fact that, according to the *Phaedo*, hypothetical method is independent of the senses. If we are to show any necessary connexion between the two characteristics ascribed to mathematics in the Line, we must do it without violating this fundamental fact that the hypothetical method has nothing to do with the senses.

A much more probable suggestion is that Plato is connecting geometry's use of the senses not with its use of hypothetical method but with its *failure to use the hypothetical method*. His view is that geometry treats its starting-points as certainties when it ought to treat them as hypotheses, because that is what they really are, though the geometer does not recognize the fact. Its material only justifies it in being hypothetical; yet it proceeds dogmatically. Plato felt, though without full explicitness, that no one would be as confidently dogmatic as the mathematicians were unless he had sensible experiences to go upon, that what made the mathematicians so convinced of their 'hypotheses' was that they seemed to be directly given in sensible intuition. They were 'plain to all' or παντὶ φανερά in the physical sense of being there to see in the geometer's sand. In geometry the appeal to spatial intuition and the claim that one's postulates are certainties go together. Plato's contemporaries accepted both. Plato and the twentieth century reject both.

§ 4. THE UNHYPOTHESIZED BEGINNING

In contrast to the procedure of mathematics the Divided Line indicates a method that makes a proper use of hypotheses and a proper disuse of the senses; and to this let us now turn. Dialectic, in contrast to mathematics, does not take for certain propositions that ought to be merely hypothesized. It makes hypotheses 'really hypotheses'. By that Plato means that dialectic not merely uncovers and confesses its premisses (mathematics does that much), but also admits that it does not know those premisses (which mathematics ought to do but does not). It openly declares, and it always bears in mind, that its premisses are merely 'hypothesized', that is, assumed to be true until we learn better.

Plato further explains that dialectic takes its hypotheses οἷον ἐπιβάσεις τε καὶ ὁρμάς. The odd thing about this phrase is that it seems to couple an instrument with an action; for ἐπιβάσεις is apparently passive but ὁρμάς surely active in sense. Most translators seem to have felt that, coupled as they are, these words must really be either both active or both passive, and have chosen to make them both passive. They have thus given to ὁρμάς a passive sense which, if we may argue from Liddell and Scott's silence, it never bears. If we must accept this dilemma, it would surely be easier to take ἐπιβάσεις as active for once. But it is better to go between the horns and say that Plato coupled active and passive here, or at least did not make up his mind whether he meant ἐπιβάσεις actively or passively; and so I translate ἐπιβάσεις by an ambiguous and ὁρμάς by an active word: 'steps and sallies'. In any case the phrase is merely a metaphor for what Plato has already told us in saying that dialectic treats its premises as hypotheses. They are not laid down as definitive parts of science; they are merely posited temporarily in the hope that they will lead us towards science.

So far this sounds like the hypothetical method of the *Phaedo*. But Plato introduces a most striking addition. He now proposes, by means of this tentative and hypothetical attack, to reach in the end an absolute certainty. It is not a matter of perpetual improvement and approximation, as in the *Phaedo*, but of attaining incorrigible truth. For he is not merely blaming the mathematicians for thinking they have absolute certainty when they only have hypotheses, as we have remarked. He is furthermore, as we must now observe, declaring that a proper method, while recognizing hypotheses for what they are, can so manipulate them as to reach incorrigible truth. Thus he is making a double criticism of mathematics. On the one hand, it assumes a certainty to which it is not entitled; on the other, it ought to obtain a certainty which it does not possess. The peculiarity of the Line is that, while Plato is trying to get away from the dogmatism of mathematics, he himself hopes to arrive at a dogma, namely the anhypotheton.

Plato expresses dialectic's claim to certainty mainly by denying the term 'knowledge' or ἐπιστήμη to mathematics. '"Knowledge" we often called them [i.e. the mathematical sciences], owing to custom; but they need another name, clearer than "opinion" and not so clear as "knowledge". I think we previously defined it as "thought"' (533D). And it is to mathematics that the following applies: 'For if a man's beginning is something he does not know, and the end and what comes between are constructed out of what he does not know, what contrivance can ever turn such consistency into knowledge?' (533C). Plato is not nearly so ready to assert the complement, that dialectic or right manipulation of hypotheses *is* knowledge, although that is here the obvious and inevitable tendency of his thought. He does once name the highest of his four faculties 'knowledge' (533E); and, since his whole description of this faculty is in terms of its use of hypotheses (511BC, cf. 533CD), that must really mean that this use of hypotheses can yield certainty. But mostly he prefers to wrap up the conception of certainty in that of the 'unhypothesized', or in the still vaguer conception of a 'beginning' as something opposed to an hypothesis. We must examine these two latter conceptions.

The word 'anhypotheton' or 'unhypothesized' was apparently coined by Plato in the Divided Line. He used it twice in this passage and never again. In view of the context and especially of the passages just quoted about mathematics' not being knowledge, what he understood by 'not hypothesized' must have been something to which the provisionality and arbitrariness of an hypothesis did not attach, something in other words that was known and certain once for all. Shorey wrote that 'Plato, except in mystical passages, has no absolute ἀρχαί'; and that 'methodologically and in its most important sense for the Platonic dialectic [the anhypotheton] denotes the habit of the flexible disciplined intelligence which is able and willing to revise, correlate, and unify its opinions through a virtually infinite receding series of hypotheses' (*The Idea of Good*, &c., 232, 234). This amounts to making 'anhypotheton' signify the hypothetical method as we have found it in the *Phaedo*, a perpetual approximation based on the exploration of implications. Now the Line certainly does suggest that dialectic is tentative and approximative as mathematics is not. But that is only the one half of what it suggests; and the other is that through this provisionality dialectic finally reaches a certainty that is real and not, like that of mathematics, illusory. It says in effect that mathematics is dogmatic from the start, and unjustifiably; whereas dialectic is dogmatic only at the end, and is then fully justified in being so. We greatly misrepresent Plato's account of dialectic here if we leave out either the preliminary tentativeness or the final certainty.

'Anhypotheton' and 'beginning' seem to be equivalent in Plato's terminology here. One way in which he expresses his criticism of mathematics is by saying that it mistakes hypotheses for beginnings. He speaks of those sciences 'for which hypotheses are beginnings' (511C7); and he tells us that dialectic 'makes the hypotheses not beginnings but really hypotheses' (511B5). This seems to mean that mathematics treats propositions as incorrigible which it ought not to. A beginning, then, is a proposition that we are fully justified in taking for incorrigible, as an hypothesis is one that we must maintain only tentatively. And thus a beginning is the same as an anhypotheton. The root notion of perfect certainty is described as a 'beginning' when it is regarded as the best or the only real basis for deduction, but as an 'anhypotheton' when it is regarded as differing from an hypothesis, which is also in a sense a beginning of deduction, by not being provisional.

Nowhere in the dialogues is any proposition put forward as an anhypotheton or a beginning. Nearest comes the proposition put forward in the *Crito* as 'the beginning of the inquiry' (48E), of which Socrates says that those who believe it and those who do not have no common ground, and must despise each other when they see each other's decisions (49D). But there is a great difference between the notion implied here and the notion expressed in the *Republic* by 'beginning'. The idea of certainty or incorrigibility is absent from the *Crito*. And there must be some common ground between the supporters and the opponents of a proposition if that proposition can be reached by a method. The general impression left by the dialogues is that no proposition there enunciated is to be taken as more than a corrigible hypothesis. Although a certain manipulation of hypotheses can according to the Line result in an unhypothesized beginning, this kind of manipulation is apparently either not practised or at most never brought to a successful conclusion in the dialogues.

Could there be more than one genuine 'beginning'? Most students of Plato believe that he thought there was really only one, namely, the Idea of the Good. This might be divided into several propositions; but they would form a single, closely knit organic whole. The evidence for this view is indirect; for Plato does not explicitly say that the anhypotheton is the Good. We infer it from the following facts. First, the simile of the Sun has told us that the Good has a unique place in all our knowledge, and now the Line gives a unique place in our knowledge to the 'unhypothesized beginning'. Secondly, while the Line tells us that we reach the 'unhypothesized beginning' at the end of an upward path of reflection, the Cave says that the released prisoner sees the sun last of all, and here the sun probably means the Good as it did in the simile of the Sun. Lastly, there is a passage in Book VII which, while it does not mention the 'beginning', describes dialectic in language reminiscent of the Line as pressing on until at last it reaches—the Good: 'When a man attempts by dialectic without any of the senses through the logos to press on to what each thing itself is, and does not desist until he grasps what Good itself is by means of intelligence itself, he arrives at the end of the intelligible' (532AB).

This, apparently, is the evidence for our belief that the 'un-hypothesized beginning' mentioned in the Line is the Idea of the Good. The value of the last point is diminished by the fact that this passage recalls the Cave far more than it recalls the Line; so that it is perhaps only a form of the second argument. It must also be said on the other side that a later passage suggests that the Good is only one of the crowd of dialectic's objects ('And the same with the good' 534B). But on the whole the evidence seems sufficient.

Plato does not mention the 'beginning' or the 'anhypotheton' again after the *Republic*. But that he always retained the conception of the logical 'beginning' is suggested by its reappearance in Aristotle.

§ 5. THE UPWARD PATH

What was the nature of that 'upward' path by which, according to Plato, we pass from hypotheses to an unhypothesized beginning? The material for an answer is scanty. Socrates four or five times says that dialectic goes *from* hypotheses *to* beginnings; but, if we ask him *how it can*, or even what makes him think that perhaps it might, he hardly seems to answer. There are only two passages that are anything like descriptions. The first is as follows: 'Making the hypotheses not beginnings but really hypotheses, like steps and sallies, in order that, going as far as the unhypothesized to the beginning of everything and grasping it, it may descend again thus to an end' (511B). This really contains no description of the manner at all. It says that we start by real hypothesizing and that we end by grasping the beginning. But as to how the trick is done, no word is said. One might almost suppose that Plato thought it obvious *how* you did it, or that he thought his readers would no more expect an explanation than a cook expects the recipe-book to tell her how to boil water.

The other passage is this. 'The dialectical method alone proceeds in this way, destroying the hypotheses, to the very beginning, in order to obtain confirmation' (533C). Here there does seem to be a mite of description; but it is very hard to interpret. What receives confirmation? And what is 'destroying' hypotheses?

The latter question is so difficult that many readers take the text for unsound, and emend. Certainly the phrase cannot have its most obvious meaning of 'refuting'. Plato cannot be thinking of proving an hypothesis to be false (although that is what Aristotle meant by the phrase, *E.E.* 1222^{b}28); for he implies that dialectic 'destroys' *all*, or at least all relevant, hypotheses, and he surely would not think that every hypothesis mooted would by some strange accident turn out to be false, that we should never hit upon a true one. He cannot have thought it the function of dialectic to disprove all hypotheses whatsoever; some of them must be true.

It seems equally unlikely that all the hypotheses would turn out to be true. Hence 'destroying' hypotheses apparently does not consist necessarily in deducing them from a higher hypothesis, which in turn will be deduced from a still higher hypothesis, and so on up to the 'unhypothesized beginning'.

Thus 'destroying' hypotheses appears to be neither refuting nor establishing them. Plato seems to be telling us of something that the dialectician will do to *all* the hypotheses he deals with, regardless of whether they are in fact true or false propositions. What then could dialectic possibly destroy with regard to *all* hypotheses? Why, precisely their hypothetical character, of course. Plato is not referring to the destruction of the proposition itself, i.e. to its refutation. It may be refuted but it may be established. He is referring to the destruction of our attitude towards it, which consisted in hypothesizing it. To 'destroy hypotheses' is not 'to prove the falsity of certain propositions which we formerly hypothesized' (nor to prove their truth), but 'to cease hypothesizing certain propositions which we formerly hypothesized, and take another attitude towards them'.

Hypothesizing a proposition includes both holding it as the beginning of a train of thought, and holding it tentatively. Which of these attitudes are brought to an end in the dialectician's destruction of hypotheses? The tentativeness will apparently be brought to an end in every case; for, after the dialectician has done his work, every proposition considered is either a certain truth or a certain falsehood. This seems to be implied by Plato's account of the downward path. The other element, the being a beginning of a train of thought, will apparently be brought to an end in nearly every case but not quite all. Nearly every proposition considered will be either rejected as certainly false or deduced from a higher proposition; but one proposition will still be underived, namely the 'unhypothesized beginning'.

If this is the correct interpretation of 'destroying the hypotheses', we have the unfortunate consequence that this passage, which at first raised our hopes, really tells us no more than the other about the *method* by which the dialectician gets from tentativeness to certainty, from hypotheses to the anhypotheton. This 'destroying the hypotheses' turns out to be merely another name for the fact that he *does* start with hypotheses and uncertainty and *does* end with perfect certainty and without hypotheses; but *how* he does so is said no more here than there. But these are the only two passages in which Plato is quite explicitly referring to the upward path in unmetaphorical language. It follows that all interpretations of this path are doubtful; and that they have to be based on the adduction of passages whose relevance is never certain. We will now review the principal kinds of interpretation that have been suggested.

§ 6. THE SYNTHESIS-THEORY OF THE UPWARD PATH

First there is what may be called the synthesis-theory of the upward path. According to one passage in the Line, the work of dialectic consists of two distinct operations, first the upward path towards the 'beginning', and then a downward path away from the 'beginning' (511B). Now Plato's later dialogues also tell us that dialectic consists in two opposed operations. This is very clear in the *Phaedrus* (265–6), hardly less clear in the *Statesman* (285) and the *Philebus* (16–18), and perhaps to be discerned also in the *Sophist* (253). In these passages the two parts of dialectic are (1) synthesis or generalization and (2) division or classification. Now —so interpreters have thought—it is very unlikely that Plato would twice in his life distinguish dialectic into two separate operations and mean different things by the distinction each time. We must suppose that he means by it in the *Republic* what he tells us that he means by it in the later dialogues. It is not as if these processes were totally unknown to the middle dialogues. The lover's ascent towards absolute beauty in the *Banquet* is very similar in tone to the upward movement of dialectic in the *Republic*, and it is a process of generalization. The *Republic* itself mentions generalization at least twice (531, 537) and division at least once (454), and in two of these passages the activity is said to belong to dialectic. These are the considerations that have led to the view that by the upward and downward paths of dialectic in the *Republic* (511B) Plato meant the synthesis and division described in the *Phaedrus* (265–6). They are weighty enough to have convinced Zeller and Heinrich Maier and Rodier. The upward path would thus be, apparently, a gradual assembling of related species under their appropriate genus, and then the treatment of that genus as itself a species to be placed along with its fellow species under an appropriate genus, and so on repeatedly, always ascending towards a higher genus, always unifying a larger manifold. Thus the metaphor of 'upward' would here mean towards the more universal, though it does not in the *Phaedo*.

What should be our judgement on the synthesis-theory of the upward path? It seems rather doubtful whether Plato would think of the Idea of the Good as being the *summum genus*, which he would have to do on this interpretation; and very doubtful that he could ever think that the process of finding the genus in a group of species was in any sense 'destroying hypotheses' or 'treating hypotheses as steps and sallies towards the unhypothesized'. In what sense would the Good be 'unhypothesized' if it were the result of this procedure? These considerations presuppose a certain community between Plato's logic and ours; but the following are independent of that. Although the notions of synthesis and division occur in the *Republic* in some sense, the actual nouns that are technical for these notions in the later dialogues (συναγωγή and διαίρεσις) do not occur in the *Republic*; nearest to them are συνοπτικός, κοινωνία, διαιρεῖσθαι. Moreover, neither the words nor the notions occur in the Divided Line itself, but only in other parts of the dialogue.

If the upward path were generalization, it would surely have to be empirical. Generalization picks the universal out of the particulars given to sense. *Phaedrus* 249BC, which seems to describe generalization, mentions 'many sensations'. Rodier saw this necessity, and accordingly maintained that Plato believed the upward path to be empirical; only when the 'anhypotheton' had been reached and the downward path begun did the dialectical procedure dispense entirely with the senses. Now, while what Plato says is not explicit enough to make this interpretation impossible, it does make it very improbable. The most obvious way to take the passage that distinguishes the two paths is as meaning that both of them proceed entirely without the senses. 'By the other section of the intelligible I mean that which is grasped by pure discussion through the power of dialectic, making the hypotheses not beginnings but really hypotheses, like steps and sallies, in order that, going as far as the unhypothesized to the beginning of everything and grasping it, it may descend again thus to an end, clinging to the things that cling to that, using absolutely nothing sensible but only ideas themselves through themselves on themselves, and ending with ideas.' The phrase 'using absolutely nothing sensible' is contiguous to the description of the downward path, and so might conceivably refer to that alone. But the 'absolutely' or παντάπασιν seems to embrace the whole of dialectic. Certainly the whole is referred to by the initial phrase, αὐτὸς ὁ λόγος ἅπτεται τῇ τοῦ διαλέγεσθαι δυνάμει; and my translation of this is based on the belief that it refers to the process of dialectical question and answer which Plato held to be independent of the senses: 'that which is grasped by pure discussion through the power of dialectic.' Moreover, the passages where dialectic is described without distinction of paths as dispensing with the senses (510B6–9, 532A6), and the whole contrast between dialectic and mathematics, seem to tell us definitely that dialectic is beyond experience throughout its course.

Another difficulty for the synthesis-theory is as follows. If the synthesis of the *Phaedrus* is the upward path of the Line, where does the division of the *Phaedrus* come in? We naturally think that it constituted the downward path; but there are reasons for believing that, if synthesis and division were applied to the Line by Plato at all, they both went in the upward path. Proclus seems to have understood division as belonging to the upward path (*in Euclid.* 211 Friedlein). In *Republic* 534BC division seems to be a process of arriving at the Idea of the Good; and therefore would come in the first part of dialectic. If *Sophist* 253D explains the upward path, as Maier thought, then again division would belong to the upward path. Above all, the following reflection seems to make it impossible for division to come in the downward path: Plato surely conceives of the downward path as a proof, a deduction, a demonstration, in which conclusions are drawn from the anhypotheton as from an axiom; but how could division ever prove anything? If for these reasons we come to think that both synthesis and division must go in the upward path of the Line, we have sawed off the branch we were sitting on; for what originally led us to use these conceptions in the interpretation of the Line was precisely that the later dialogues present them as a dichotomy of dialectic and the Line also makes a dichotomy of dialectic. But it now appears that the dichotomy in the later dialogues is a subdivision of one side of the dichotomy in the *Republic*.

The synthesis-interpretation of the Line consists in reading into the Line what is said in some passages of the later dialogues, because both the Line and those other passages are dichotomies of dialectic. It is thus an argument from analogy: 'since the Line has certain features of these later passages, therefore it has the others too.' But it is not a strong analogy, because the points of difference are weighty and the points of resemblance are not. Here are nine points of difference. Unlike the Line, the later passages do not mention (1) the senses, or (2) hypothesis, or (3) the 'beginning', or (4) the metaphor of up and down, or (5) a fixed temporal order for the two processes. Unlike the later passages, the Line does not mention (6) synthesis, or (7) division, or (8) definition. Above all, (9) the *Republic* belongs to Plato's middle period, whereas the other passages, with the possible exception of the *Phaedrus*, are very much later. The resemblances are merely the following four: both sets of passages (1) refer to Ideas, (2) are about dialectic, (3) divide dialectic into two processes, and (4) use πάλιν or αὖ or πάλιν αὖ to pass from one process to the other. I mention the fourth resemblance because Rodier did so; but it is worth nothing at all, for Plato constantly uses those adverbs to mark any sort of transition whatever.

I conclude that it would be very wide of the mark to say that the upward and downward paths mentioned in the Line were thought of by the author as consisting either essentially or mainly in synthesis and division respectively. On the other hand, it is clear from certain passages in the *Republic* that Plato was already thinking of something at least faintly like the synthesis and division of the *Phaedrus* as being activities proper to the dialectician; and it is fairly likely that he would have agreed, if asked, that these activities might sometimes aid the activities of the upward and downward paths.

§ 7. MATHEMATICAL THEORIES OF THE UPWARD PATH

Let us turn to the theories that give dialectic a mathematical tinge. One of the most frequent of these is that the upward path is what the Greek geometers called analysis; and it has sometimes been said, following a tradition that Plato invented analysis, that the Line is the first statement of this method. Cornford is, so far as I know, the latest person to interpret the Line by means of geometrical analysis; but he assumes a heterodox view of analysis which I have argued to be false (*Mind* XLV 464). According to the ordinary view, which is really as certain as anything in the history of thought, analysis consists in finding a proof of p by hypothesizing p, observing that p entails q, inferring q, observing that q entails r, inferring r, and so continuing until you reach a proposition, say s, which you independently know to be true. Your proof of p is then as follows: 'we know s to be true, and s entails r entails q entails p; therefore p is true.' This statement of the proof was called the synthesis, in contrast to the analysis which was the discovery of the proof. The method requires that the implications observed shall be reciprocal; not merely must p entail q but q must entail p, and so on; and this condition frequently holds in mathematics.

Once we have realized what geometrical analysis was, there is little incentive to read it into the Divided Line. It would have to mean that dialectic hypothesizes some proposition and goes on deducing its consequences until it arrives at the Idea of the Good, which it independently knows to be true. It then (and this synthesis would be the downward path) asserts the Idea of the Good, and deduces consequences therefrom in the reverse order until it arrives at the original hypothesis, which is thus established. But the Idea of the Good is not antecedently known to be true; it is just the task of the upward path to lead us to our first knowledge of the Good. It would be slightly less absurd to say that the original hypotheses or 'steps and sallies' of the upward path are propositions about the Good itself, proposed definitions of the Good; that the analysis consists in inferring consequences from these until we come to something we know (if we can), and the synthesis in proving our definition of the Good from the known fact. But the Line is equally fatal to this; for the Good does not come at the end of the downward path. It comes at the beginning thereof, and is the presupposition of all categorical proof.

Another of the mathematicizing interpreters of the Line is Milhaud. He holds that if we think of mathematics when we read what Plato has to say about science, everything becomes astonishingly clear. Plato's theory of science was an analysis of rational geometry as he knew it and practised it. The domain of intelligence is distinguished from that of opinion by two things. The first is logical rigour; for in both its parts intelligence forms chains of propositions closely bound to each other, whereas opinion never gives us any necessity. The second is the creative initiative of the soul, making her own hypotheses (*Les Philosophes-Géomètres de la Grèce*, 245).

These and other reflections of Milhaud's can be guaranteed to stimulate a person interested in Plato's epistemology; but the conclusion must nevertheless be that Milhaud is mistaken. Like many other readers, he has attributed to Plato something that he himself admires, but Plato did not think of. His interpretation seems to leave no place for the unhypothesized beginning, which is the keystone of the doctrine. It illuminates particularly clearly the great fault of most mathematicizing explanations, which is that they ask us to believe that Plato is here borrowing something from mathematics, although he quite explicitly says that he is producing something which mathematics lacks. There really can be no doubt that the Line examines mathematical method and finds it wanting, that Plato here presents dialectic as a procedure distinct from that pursued by the geometers, and better. If in the face of this we insist on saying that nevertheless the dialectical method *is* something Plato learnt from mathematics, we shall inevitably imply one of two unpleasant things: either that he was mistaken in supposing he had a non-mathematical method, or that he was dishonourably denying the mathematicians a credit he knew to be their due.

The proposition, that Plato did not receive from contemporary mathematics the notion of the method which he attributes to dialectic in the Line, does not settle the question whether he thought his new method would or could be adopted by mathematicians in the future. This problem, whether mathematics could become dialectical, seems identical or vitally connected with these others. Could mathematics become knowledge (for only dialectic really knows, according to the Line)? Could it dispense with sense? Could it cease to take hypotheses for beginnings?

Could it obtain a real beginning? Are its objects possible objects of dialectic? What are its objects? These questions are so doubtful and have been so much argued that we must postpone their discussion until we have completed our present inquiry into the method of passing from hypotheses to the anhypotheton.

A more attractive kind of mathematicizing interpretation of the Line was put forward by Julius Stenzel. He said that the Line 'is unambiguously the proposal to axiomatize'. By this he seems to have meant that mathematics starts with a welter of propositions and proofs, and the upward path consists in gradually reducing them to the order of a system entirely deducible from a few precise propositions. The unhypothesized beginning is the unity of the whole that we thus obtain; and from this unity the logos itself, reversing its direction, can, without making use of sense, render all the earlier stages evident and intelligible. Thus the important thing is not in the least whether the propositions refer to anything sensible, but only that they shall be logically connected together and made to depend on principles. (*Verhandlungen des internationalen Mathematiker-Kongresses Zürich* 1932, Bd. I 331.)

This interpretation, which we may call the axiomatization-theory of the Line, is a valuable insight. The word 'axiomatization', as now used in mathematics and logic, evokes a conception of which a seed is to be found in the Line. Plato expresses here the notion of minimizing the number of one's unmediated assertions by deducing as many of them as possible from the rest; this idea bore fruit in Aristotle's theory of science and Euclid's axiomatization of geometry.

It is important, however, to realize the distance and difference between the idea of axiomatization in the Line and that in a mathematician like Hilbert. For one thing, Plato's conception of logical rigour, if he can be said to have one at all, is much less exacting than that of twentieth-century logic (see above, pp. 132–3). Its looseness appears, for example, in his habitual assumption that a single axiom might suffice to generate a whole system. Phrases like 'the first hypotheses' (*Phd.* 107B) are unusual in his works. Ordinarily he thinks of a single hypothesis as fertile by itself, ignoring in his methodology the other premises to which he is allying it; and in the Line above all the 'beginning' is invariably referred to in the singular. *Principia Mathematica*, because of the plurality of its primitive propositions, would have been a disappointment to him. Thinkers have been working recently to reduce the number of postulates required for logic; but Plato is not confining himself to logic. He seems to hope for nothing short of deducing the whole of knowledge from his single 'beginning', a goal which now appears infinitely far removed.

So much for the far less rigorous nature of Plato's conception, but there is another important difference between his Divided Line and the present idea of axiomatization. Today axiomatization is an autonomous ideal, at least in mathematics. Perhaps we have ulterior motives for trying to axiomatize chemistry; but we axiomatize mathematics for the sake of the axiomatization itself. We enjoy the elegance of a deductive system as such; the fewer the postulates, and the faster they generate the theorems, the better we like it. Hence we sometimes feel no interest in the question whether the postulates are *true*, or even go so far as to say that the question has no meaning, since 'true', which means 'deducible from a given set of postulates', is a term that can apply only to theorems. Now this attitude is foreign to the Divided Line. To Plato, the question whether the 'unhypothesized beginning' is true is perfectly legitimate and supremely important. To Plato, on the other side, axiomatization has no value as such; and is desirable only because, if we can certify the 'beginning', axiomatization thereby certifies all the rest. Axiomatization, like many other human activities, arose as a means to something else and later became an end in itself. In modern logic it is pursued for its own sake; but Plato valued it only as a means to sure knowledge. It was an instrument in his passionate 'quest for certainty'. He could not feel as certain as he wished about any proposition in mathematics or physical science. He had hopes that he could find a lake of certainty in the mountain of the Good, and could then, by channels of axiomatization, conduct its water down to the shifting deserts of mathematics and physics. The axiomatization-theory, therefore, is an incomplete account of the Line because it ignores Plato's quest for certainty, and does not tell us how he hoped to find certainty. It seems to be an account of the downward rather than of the upward path.

§ 8. THE 'PHAEDO'-THEORY OF THE UPWARD PATH

Let us now consider the suggestion that the upward path of the Line is the hypothetical method described in the *Phaedo*.

The method described in the *Phaedo* was to defend a proposition by deducing it from an hypothesis, and to defend this hypothesis first by drawing all its consequences to see if they were self-consistent, and secondly by deducing the hypothesis from a higher hypothesis, and so on until you came to something adequate. The original defence of a proposition by deducing it from an hypothesis would no doubt be regarded by Plato in the *Republic* as belonging to mathematics and not to dialectic; but were the *Phaedo*'s subsequent operations on the hypothesis itself what Plato had in mind in the Line under his metaphor of the upward path of dialectic?

The first of these subsequent operations (Socrates in the *Phaedo* insisted that it should come first) was to draw the consequences of the hypothesis to see whether they were selfconsistent. This, I have argued, was to subject the hypothesis to the Socratic elenchus, for Plato thought of the elenchus as making a thesis lead to selfcontradiction. If, then, the upward path of the Line was, or included, the hypothetical method of the *Phaedo*, it was, or included, the Socratic elenchus.

Plato probably did, in the *Republic*, think of his upward path as including the elenchus of hypotheses. To treat the hypotheses as 'really hypotheses', which the mathematician fails to do, included making a methodical attempt to show that they led to a selfcontradiction. When he wrote that 'by the other section of the intelligible I mean that which is grasped *by pure discussion through the power of dialectic*', τοῦτο οὗ αὐτὸς ὁ λόγος ἅπτεται τῇ τοῦ διαλέγεσθαι δυνάμει, he was referring to the dialogue between two or more persons in which by question and answer and elenchus, without any appeal to the senses, Socratics earnestly and laboriously pursued consistency and enlightenment.

If we turn to the description of dialectic in Book VII, which is universally recognized to be an expression of the same ideas, we find a passage in which the elenchus is prominent:

And do you call dialectical the man who takes the account (logos) of the essence of each thing? And if he cannot give an account (logos) to himself and others, then, so far as he cannot, you will not call him intelligent on the matter?

How could I?, said he.

And the same with the good? If a man cannot by his account (logos) separate and distinguish the idea of the good from all else, and persevere through everything in the battle of refutation (ἐλέγχων), eager to refute (ἐλέγχειν) in reality and not in appearance, and go through all these things without letting his argument be overthrown, you will not say he knows the good itself or any other good? (534BC.)

A further confirmation of this view, that the upward path in the *Republic* would contain elenchus as the hypothetical method of the *Phaedo* did, may be drawn from the *Republic*'s use of hypothetical method in establishing that the soul has three parts. Socrates there hypothesizes a proposition 'in order that we may not be obliged to waste time examining all such objections and making sure that they are not true' (*Rp.* 437A). This seems to imply that, if you want to use a proposition as a premiss, the alternative to hypothesizing it is examining and disarming all the objections to it. But the alternative to hypothesizing a premiss should be the upward path of dialectic. That path, therefore, seems to involve attempting to refute the hypotheses.

The other part of hypothetical method according to the *Phaedo* was the deduction of the hypothesis, after it had been tested for selfcontradiction, from a higher hypothesis posited for the purpose. Was Plato in the *Republic* envisaging this as also part of the upward path of dialectic? The answer appears to be yes, for the following reasons. First, there appears to be nothing in this part of the *Phaedo*'s method that conflicts with anything said in the Divided Line, and hence it seems more likely than not that on this point Plato's view in the *Republic* does not differ from his view in the *Phaedo*. Secondly, since the downward path sounds like a deduction of theorems from axioms, it is quite likely that the upward path would proceed from as yet unproved theorems to as yet uncertified axioms from which the theorems followed. Thirdly, if we do not count this second part of the *Phaedo*'s method as part of what Plato intended in the upward path of the *Republic*, we have not yet shown any reason for Plato's metaphor of 'upward'. The elenctic procedure, which is all of the content that we have yet given to the upward path, has nothing upward about it. In this procedure an hypothesis is tested by having its consequences drawn, which is a downward path. If no contradiction appears, that is the end of the elenchus. If a contradiction does appear, we proceed to take another hypothesis which, we hope, will not develop the same defect. But this new hypothesis will not necessarily be in any natural sense 'higher' than the discarded one; it

is much more likely to be 'on the same level', since it is intended
to fulfil the same function. These reasons seem to suggest that we
should take the upward path of the *Republic* as including the
second element of the *Phaedo*'s hypothetical method as well as
the first.

§ 9. THE INTUITION-THEORY OF THE UPWARD PATH

The upward path of the *Republic* includes, then, the hypothetical
method of the *Phaedo*. On the other hand, the hypothetical
method of the *Phaedo* does not seem to exhaust the upward path
as Plato conceived it in the *Republic*, because it cannot give, and
does not claim to give, the infallible certainty, the sure grasp of
an 'unhypothesized beginning', which is emphasized in the
Republic. The characteristic and new element in the *Republic* is
the claim to have a method that gives absolute certainty. It will
not do to say that the upward path is merely selfcriticism that
never reaches any absolute at all, merely the readiness to reconsider and go behind any postulate, or 'the habit of the flexible
disciplined intelligence which is able and willing to revise, correlate, and verify its opinions through a virtually infinite receding
series of hypotheses' (Shorey, *The Idea of Good, &c.*, 234). It is true
that Plato in the Line is pointing to a contrast of intellectual
temperaments, and that 'the scientific habit of reasoning from
unquestioned assumptions does differ from the philosophical
readiness and ability to extend indefinitely the analysis of the
presuppositions either of science or of common sense' (Shorey,
What Plato Said 233). But it is false that that is all he is doing. In
the few words of the Line he manages to convey not merely this,
but also that the philosopher, just because he leaves no assumption unquestion*ed*, will finally reach one that is unquestion*able*.

The question therefore seems to arise: What method has Plato
in the *Republic* in addition to the hypothetical method of the
Phaedo, through which he thinks the dialectician can escape from
the tentativeness of the *Phaedo*'s procedure and reach indubitable
certainty? I believe, however, that the true answer to this question is to deny part of what it implies. I believe that Plato in the
Republic claims the possibility of certainty for the dialectician
without having any more method at his command than the
Phaedo gave him. He merely claims that the man who competently
and conscientiously practises this hypothetical and elenctic pro-

cedure will, or may, one day find himself in the possession of an unhypothetical certainty. He conceives that the dialectician takes an hypothesis and deduces its consequences, trying his hardest to discover some contradiction in those consequences. If he does discover one, the hypothesis is thereby refuted. He then takes another hypothesis, usually a modification of the first one designed to avoid the contradiction which refuted that. He then deduces the consequences of this second hypothesis, again trying his hardest to make it lead to a contradiction. He continues this process for a long time, making a great effort to be patient and thorough. Some day, after months or years of labour, he reflects that he has now been attempting to refute the same hypothesis for many weeks, and that this last hypothesis has endured every test and stood consistent in all its consequences, which he has deduced on every side as far as it seems possible to go. With this reflection (if he ever gets so far) it dawns on him that this hypothesis is certainly true, that it is no longer an hypothesis but an anhypotheton.

In this process the last event, the 'dawn', is something like what was afterwards meant by the doctrine of intuition, for 'intuition' means certain knowledge not reached by method.

On this 'intuition-theory' of the upward path, that path is not a process of *proof* at all. It does not *demonstrate* the 'beginning' at which it arrives. Socrates never says that it does; he uses only vague language such as 'proceeding' to a beginning. If we get the opposite impression, it is because he compares the path of dialectic to that of mathematics and the latter is a chain of inference; but, because they are both paths, it does not follow that they are both demonstrations. The 'beginning' at which dialectic arrives is the Good; and Plato's view seems to be that the Good, far from being proved, is the presupposition of all proof that is not hypothetical.

But if the path does not prove the beginning, what is its use? What confidence can we have that our beginning is less arbitrary than that of mathematics? Or, if we can be confident of this, why do we need the path at all? Why not begin at the beginning instead of a long way before it! The answer to this is the positive side of the intuition-theory. The prisoner released from the Cave goes through a series of objects graduated in brightness before he can look at the sun, which is the brightest of all. But the series of preliminary objects does not demonstrate the existence of the sun; it only enables him to see it. The prisoner by this process gradually strengthens his eyes. By practising on effects he gains the power to see the cause of those effects. So the dialectician on the upward path is gradually strengthening his mental vision until he can apprehend not merely the effects with which he had to start but also the cause of these effects; but he is not demonstrating the existence of that cause except in the sense in which the raising of the curtain demonstrates the existence of the stage. The upward path is an intellectual discipline that results in knowledge and yet does not prove anything. 'Plato constantly uses metaphorical expressions taken from the senses of sight and touch to denote the immediate character of his highest knowledge' (Lutoslawski, *Origin and Growth of Plato's Logic* 294; see the references there). What makes the beginning a real beginning and 'unhypothesized' is simply the fact that it is the first thing to be really known. Mathematics is not knowledge. The upward path is not knowledge. We have our first perfect knowledge when at last we apprehend the Idea of the Good; and that is why this Idea is our true 'beginning' although it comes late or never in our lives.

A similar view is implied by the account of the lover's progress in the *Banquet*. The beautiful itself is known through itself; but a long apprenticeship among the many beautifuls is necessary before this direct knowledge can occur. Because this knowledge requires many preliminaries, and yet is direct when it comes, it may suitably be represented by the language of vision and of the sights revealed to the religious after a laborious initiation. A similar view is implied again in the *Seventh Letter*, with the two differences (1) that here Plato does not imply anything about the nature of the object known by this process, and (2) that he describes the illumination when it comes as 'sudden'. 'It cannot anyway be expressed like other learning, but after community of life with much discussion of the matter itself it suddenly appears in the soul like light kindled from leaping fire, and thenceforward sustains itself' (341C). 'Hardly when each of these things is compared with the others, names and definitions, sights and perceptions, and men criticize them in question and answer with benevolent criticisms and without envy, does wisdom and intelligence about each thing flash out, straining human power to the utmost' (344B).

In the downward path we for the first time possess categorical demonstrative knowledge, knowledge obtained by sure inference from a sure premiss. Many of the steps we then take will, no doubt, have been already contemplated during the upward; but at that time they were only hypothetical, because we did not know whether their premisses were true. The downward path distinguishes the true from the false hypotheses of the upward; and it will probably add some entirely new propositions.

If the intuition-theory is right, the Line contains a doctrine similar to Aristotle's. For Aristotle too has an upward and downward movement of thought. In the downward, which he calls apodeixis or syllogism, we are rigorously demonstrating incorrigible conclusions from incorrigible premisses of a universal character; and in the upward we are obtaining those universal premisses by a process that is not demonstration and yet gives them to us without doubt. His word for this upward path, νοῦς, is closely related to Plato's word for the faculty of dialectic in the Line, νόησις. His word for the basic premisses that νοῦς, or intuition, obtains is Plato's word 'beginning'. If we accept the intuition-theory we ought, in view of these resemblances, to suppose that Aristotle's theory of science was a descendant of the theory recorded in the Line.

On the other hand, we ought not to lose sight of the fact that Aristotle greatly developed and altered the theory. According to him, there is a plurality of these 'beginnings' and each special science has some of its own. And, while the path towards them may be dialectic (*Topics* I 2), it may also be something else, such as habituation (*N.E.* I 4, 1095^{b}4–8). It may even be 'epagoge', which in this connexion appears to be a kind of abstraction and to start from the senses (*Anal.* IV 19). Plato has none of Aristotle's proof that there must be beginnings, none of his long and varied discussion of the nature of a beginning, none of his discussion of the downward path or his epoch-making division of it into the three figures of syllogism, nor even his surely fundamental point that our grasp of the beginning and our grasp of the demonstration are distinct mental faculties (for according to Plato the upward and the downward paths of dialectic belong to the one faculty of 'intelligence'). Nor would Plato have approved of the slovenly argument by elimination which is all that Aristotle offers to prove the existence of intuition (*Anal.* IV 19 and *N.E.* VI 6).

The doctrine of intuition is present in the Line only to this extent, that Plato there exhorts us to acquire the habit of uncovering the premisses of our arguments and asking how we know them; that he realizes that all certainty obtained by inference presupposes a certainty obtained without inference; and that he has faith that there might be such a thing as valid certainty obtained without inference.

The upward path on this theory is identical with something which in the *Phaedo* was not supposed to lead to final certainty. But that is just the difference between the *Phaedo* and the *Republic*; the former does not maintain that the elenchus could ever establish a proposition with certainty, and the latter does. What has caused our bewilderment about the Divided Line is partly the feeling that, since Plato is now claiming a dogmatic certainty which he did not before, he must have some new method which he did not have before. The disappointing conclusion to which we have come at last is that he has not. The new claim for certainty is made on the ground of the old hypothetical method.

Did Plato think of the 'beginning' as a proposition that would necessarily be seen to be true as soon as it was entertained, or as a proposition that could be entertained indefinitely without being seen to be the ultimate truth? Would the dialectician who finally discovered it have a new proposition before him, or an old one at last known to be true? Probably the question as such did not occur to Plato. But he says that in the ideal city the soldiers would hold as steadfast beliefs certain ethical propositions which the rulers knew to be true. If the definition of the Good were such as to convey any meaning to the common man, then surely the rulers would teach it to the soldiers along with the definitions of courage and the other virtues; and thus the few who finally came to know the Good would have been believing it for a long time. Plato actually envisages the case of a man to whom the lawgiver has taught 'what is the fine' (538D). Apart from these considerations, if the upward path includes a thoroughgoing elenchus before it culminates in intuition, it seems that a man could not actually perceive the truth of the true account of the Good until he had submitted it to a very long and very serious examination. Thus the intuition that is faintly suggested by the Line is not the sort of intuition in which conception and confirmation occur simultaneously. The confirmation, that is, the apprehension that the proposition is true, may be sudden, as it is implied to be in the *Banquet* and the *Seventh Letter*; but it occurs long after the first conceiving of the proposition.

§ 10. COMMENTS

A few remarks may be added in evaluation of Plato's statements about hypothetical method in the *Phaedo* and the *Republic*, so far as they can be evaluated without first pleading a whole system of methodology.

The question how far Plato was bringing something new into human consciousness with his hypothetical method is not one that we can answer with any precision, owing to the scantiness of our evidence for previous thought. The previous forms of methodological consciousness to which he owed most were no doubt those present in Socrates, the mathematicians, and the Eleatics. His dialogues make it probable that he thought he obtained his conception of the elenchus from Socrates; but any statement as to how far he really did so, and how far his own mind had unconsciously remoulded what he found in his teacher, would be worth asserting only at the end of a long study of the evidence for the historical Socrates. Probably, however, it was his own idea to make the elenchus serve positive and constructive ends. In Socrates it had been purely refutative, as its name implies; Plato was responsible for the view that it could serve to suggest more and more improvements in an hypothesis until it became practically unassailable. He was thus reproducing in philosophy the methodical constructiveness that had previously appeared only in mathematics, and paradoxically using for the purpose a method that was essentially destructive. The originality of this would have been much less if, as Burnet suggested, mathematics itself at that time made all its constructions by a destructive method, by reduction to absurdity; but we have rejected this view (above, p. 112).

Part of his originality lay, then, in demanding the generalization of certain aspects of mathematical thought, and their extension to all thinking. These aspects were its constructiveness, its deductiveness, its clear distinction between conclusions and premisses, and its open confession of its premisses. But he not merely borrowed these elements for philosophy. He also made an advance on them, which could be applied with benefit in all fields of thought, including mathematics itself. For he demanded that the premises should be not merely confessed but criticized. He is the first person to show any sign of at once believing and disliking the proposition that every proof has unproved premises; a linked insight and dissatisfaction which are of great importance in methodology. He is really the author of 'the quest for certainty', because he was the first to appreciate the obstacle to certainty. Out of this appreciation arose a seed that grew in Aristotle's mind as the doctrine of intuition, the faculty that gives certainty without proof. Out of it also grew, in Plato's own mind, the hypothetical method, with its emphasis on tentativeness and provisionality, which are now seen to be very necessary until intuition is achieved. The hypothetical method, suggested according to the *Meno* by a device often used by contemporary mathematicians, but perhaps in truth merely crystallized thereby, came to be in Plato's view not an occasional dodge but the sole and universal method of all responsible thinking.

It seems reasonable to ask what it is in the nature of things and the nature of men that makes the hypothetical method desirable. For if a method is suitable, that must surely be because the reality sought to be known is such and such, and the human mind that seeks to know it is such and such. That a method is good ought to be derivable from the situation to which it applies. But Plato's insight did not go so far as that. He does not give us a reasoned derivation. Like most expounders of method, whether in abstract thinking or in aesthetic composition or in physical skill, he writes out of an uncriticized conviction that these are the things that have caused the successes he is conscious of having achieved.

We must evidently accept Plato's provisional and tentative method of using hypotheses, and his call for tentative constructions, for deduction and the confession of premises and the criticism of them. As to the method by which these premises are to be tested, we should all of us today want to make some use of a way that he rejected altogether, the appeal to sense. We believe that in the interpretation of nature the main test of an hypothesis is whether its consequences contradict what is given to sense, or, on the contrary, truly predict sensations that were not expected. Most of us would allow to Plato that there is another test as well; but we should want to reformulate his description of its nature. He supposed that an hypothesis might generate a consequence that contradicted another of its consequences or the hypothesis itself. We should perhaps agree that this might occur; but we should say that the vast majority of the cases Plato thus classified demand another explanation. The contradiction is really generated by the conjunction of the hypothesis with one or more of our standing beliefs. The aim of the hypothetical method thus becomes the establishment of consistency among our standing beliefs; and on occasion the appearance of a contradiction may call for the abandonment not of the hypothesis under consideration but of some other proposition.

With these corrections we should most of us accept the hypothetical method as stated in the *Phaedo*. But few would nowadays agree with the *Republic*'s claim that this process might culminate in intuitive certainty. The above correction makes this claim even more dubious. That Plato vaguely supposed that somehow or other his dialectical procedure would illuminate the premisses, and so make everything as certain as the conclusions are, provided you assume the premisses, was largely because he remained under the impression that an hypothesis can by itself give rise to contradictory consequences. This made it appear that the dialectical examination of a premiss did not itself assume other premisses. Thus an infinite regress did not arise; and if an exhaustive examination of the consequences of the premiss revealed no contradiction, it was possible to feel that the premiss had been established. But what seemed to Plato the gradual forging of an hypothesis to which there were no objections turns out, on this correction, to be merely the gradual forging of a consistent set of beliefs; and it therefore does not escape the stricture passed in the *Cratylus*, that consistency is no guarantee of truth. If an epistemological intuition can ever supervene upon our reflections, it might seem more likely to do so when our reflections took the form of analysis than when they were devoted to the construction of a consistent system. Surely Descartes was nearer the probabilities when he advised us to seek the simplest elements in any field. There seems more chance of intuiting a relation between simple elements in an analysed complex, than of intuiting the truth of a set of propositions ascertained to be consistent.

XI

THE LINE AND THE CAVE

HAVING completed our examination of Plato's account of the best method in the *Republic*, let us consider the question we formerly postponed, namely whether mathematics could become dialectical. It was possible to give an adequate discussion of the main subject in the Line without seeking a general view of the three passages known as the Sun and the Line and the Cave. But it is not possible to do the same for this minor question. In order to determine whether in Plato's view mathematics could ever adopt that superior method which it now lacks, we must have an opinion about the whole 'simile of light', to borrow Professor Ferguson's description; and this will also be useful towards the main question, though only negatively, as removing objections that might be made to our interpretation of the central passages of the Line on the ground of certain views of their context.

§ 1. THE 'CAVE' IS NOT PARALLEL TO THE 'LINE'

The usual English interpretation of the Line, as found, for example, in Adam and Hardie, is mainly based on the premiss that Plato tells us (in 517BC) that his Line corresponds exactly to his Cave. If this is true, it follows that the four 'states' of the Line, 'intelligence', 'thought', 'conviction', and 'conjecture', are all discernible in the Cave. In particular, it follows that the lowest 'state' of the Line, 'conjecture', corresponds to the lowest estate in the Cave, the situation of the unreleased prisoners; and this conclusion is fundamental to all the rest of the usual interpretation, because it gives rise to the two following lines of reasoning.

1. The unreleased prisoners symbolize something more than mere vision; they symbolize the whole life and experience of the ordinary man. Therefore, it is argued, the corresponding notion of 'conjecture' in the Line must mean something different from or more important than just an attitude towards visible images of visible things. It must be something that could engross the whole of a man's life, as the shadows and echoes wholly engross the prisoners. This inference seems to be confirmed by certain pas-

sages where Plato calls the two lower states in the Line 'opinion';
and it is concluded that by 'conjecture' he meant some attitude
towards opinable images of opinable objects. That is the first line
of reasoning.

2. The other deduction, also proceeding from the assumed correspondence between 'conjecture' and the state of the unreleased
prisoners, is as follows. The unreleased prisoners regard the
shadows and echoes as originals. They take them, not as means
of knowing a reality beyond them, but as themselves the only
reality to be known. It follows that 'conjecture' is not trying to
apprehend originals through their images but taking the image
for the original. Adding this result to Plato's statement that
'thought' is to 'intelligence' as 'conjecture' is to 'conviction', we
obtain the probable conclusion that 'thought' or διάνοια is also a
form of taking the image for the original. Since the original is in
this case the Idea (for the object of 'intelligence' is said to be
Ideas), we infer that 'thought' takes images of the Ideas for the
realities themselves. But these images cannot be what Plato usually
points to as images of the Ideas, namely the world of becoming,
for that is clearly the object of 'conviction'. What can they be?
And how tantalizing of Plato not to say! Aristotle now comes
most opportunely to our rescue with the information that Plato
believed in 'mathematicals', intermediate between Ideas and
things because unchanging like Ideas and yet multiple like things.
This conclusion is strengthened by the discovery of passages in
the neighbourhood of the Line where Plato's language entails a
plurality of such objects of mathematics as the unit. Such is the
second line of deduction.

The whole of these two chains of deduction depends fundamentally on their original premiss that Plato in 517BC tells us
that the Line is in exact correspondence with the Cave. If this
premiss had to be abandoned, it would be unreasonable to retain
the hypothesis that the objects of 'thought' are the 'mathematicals'
and the lower objects are all opinables. These hypotheses could
not be supported by the scraps of incidental evidence that would
be left.

It will now be demonstrated that this premiss is false. (1) Whatever Plato may say about them, his Line and Cave are not as a
matter of fact in precise correspondence; (2) Plato in two places
quite distinctly asserts a relation between them which is other

than exact correspondence; (3) he is not referring to the Line at all in 517BC.

(1) First comes the evidence for the statement that, whatever Plato may say about them, his Line and Cave are not as a matter of fact in precise correspondence. (1.1) The Cave is mostly about motions or progressions from point to point; but the Line is not. The Line tells us that dialectic goes upwards and then downwards; it also tells us that mathematics goes downwards. It mentions no other forms of motion. It mentions no motion or progress from one to another of the four states, 'conjecture', 'conviction', 'thought', and 'intelligence'. This difference, however, would not prevent a close correlation between the two passages; for it might have been the case that the motions indicated in the Cave were between the points indicated in the Line. Four states would give three changes; and it might have been the case that the Cave presented just three changes or progressions, and each of these was between a pair of conditions recognizably the same as two adjacent states in the Line.

(1.2) But it is not the case. The prisoner's progress from captivity to the vision of the sun does not divide into three changes any more definitely than into two or ten; and the various stages at which he may be supposed to remain for a time are not more definitely four than three or any number. Evidently the first state is that of viewing the shadows, and the first change is the turning about from the shadows. Evidently the last state is looking directly at the sun, and the last change is turning to look at the sun from whatever was his previous occupation. But into how many states and changes should we divide the intervening matter? Plato mentions (1) looking towards the light (515C8) and the things going by (D4); (2) looking at the light itself (E1); (3) being dragged out of the cave into the light of the sun (E8); and then looking at (4) shadows (516A6), (5) reflections (A7), (6) things (A8), (7) the nocturnal heavens (A9), (8) the sun (B4). This is certainly not to define a set of changes that would fit precisely between the states enumerated in the Line. Plato's intention seems rather to describe a single continuous change, terminated in both directions, but infinitely divisible within those bounds. He does not seem to be inviting us to rediscover here the four states of the Line, and in addition to contemplate the three changes by which we proceed from the lowest to the highest.

(1.3) 'But perhaps the Cave *allows* us, even if it does not *invite* us, to divide this more or less continuous progression into three changes holding between four states. Plato may have thought the Cave parallel to the Line and yet not have wished to emphasize the correlation in his description. Surely, if external considerations invite us, it would not be *impossible* to find the Line's four states in the Cave.'

The answer to this suggestion is that Plato's description of his Cave not merely does not invite, but positively forbids, us to put it in exact correspondence with his Line. There is one point at which the correlation must break down completely, whatever interpretation we assume of the debated questions; and Professor Ferguson has shown very forcibly what it is (*CQ*, 1934, p. 203). If there were a precise correlation, the state of the unreleased prisoner would have to be 'conjecture', and the state immediately succeeding his release would have to be the adjacent state in the Line, namely πίστις. But πίστις, which means conviction or confidence, and refers at least primarily to our ordinary attitude to 'the animals about us and all that grows and everything that is made' (510A), bears no resemblance to the prisoner's condition immediately after his release; for the latter is expressly described as bewilderment and as the belief that his present objects are less real than his previous objects (515D). In view of this observation we must say that Plato's Cave is not parallel to his Line, even if he himself asserts that it is!

§ 2. PLATO'S ACCOUNT OF THE RELATION BETWEEN 'CAVE' AND 'LINE'

(2) But does Plato ever say that his Cave is parallel to his Line? We come now to the second point, which is that Plato in two places quite distinctly asserts a relation between them which is other than exact correspondence. The fuller and more explicit of these passages is 532A–C, where he unmistakably says that in the Cave the viewing of the sun and the stars and actual animals is dialectic (and dialectic is the method of 'intelligence', the highest state in the Line). He further unmistakably says that the viewing of shadows and reflections in the real world, and of the puppets in the cave, and everything down to the very moment of unchaining, is 'the work of the sciences we have gone through'

(which is certainly mathematics, and mathematics certainly falls entirely within 'thought', the second state in the Line). This accounts for every stage of the Cave except the original unreleased condition of the prisoners; and it follows quite inexorably that, according to this passage, either the prisoners' original state corresponds to *both* the lower states in the Line or one of the lower states in the Line has nothing corresponding to it at all in the Cave. That is something other than one–one correspondence of state to state.

To put the matter in the reverse order, this passage distinctly says that in the figure of the Cave everything from the first moment of the prisoners' release to the last moment of looking at shadows and reflections outside the cave is mathematics, and everything from the first look at real things outside the cave to seeing the sun is dialectic. It follows that the state of the unreleased prisoners is everything below mathematics; and if the distinction between conviction and conjecture is relevant here, the state of the unreleased prisoner is both. Here follows a translation of this fundamental passage.

Then, Glaucon, said I, this is already the very melody that dialectic performs? Which, though intelligible, would be copied by the power of sight, which we said tried to look at animals themselves and the stars themselves and ultimately the sun itself. Just so when a man by dialectic tries without any of the senses by means of the logos to press towards what each thing itself is, and does not desist until he grasps what the good itself is by intelligence itself, he comes to be at the very end of the intelligible, as that other man was then at the end of the visible.

Quite so, said he.

Well, don't you call this journey dialectic?

Of course.

And the release from chains, the turning from shadows to images and light, the ascent from the cave to the sun, and up there the inability at first to look at animals and plants and the light of the sun, the looking at wonderful images in water and shadows of real things, no longer at shadows of images shadowed forth by a light of the same sort, to judge it by the sun—all this work of the sciences we have gone through has this power of leading the best thing in the soul up to the sight of the best thing in reality, as then the clearest thing in the body was led up to the sight of the brightest thing in the bodily and visible place. (532A–C.)

This passage occurs after the exposition of the mathematical curriculum. If we look back to what Plato says just before this curriculum (521C), we find that there too he uses the imagery of the Cave.

Then would you like us to ask now how such men will come into existence, and how they will be brought up to light, as some are said to have gone up to the gods from Hades?
Of course I should, said he.
This is not the turn of a shell, it seems, but the conversion of a soul from a nightlike day to a true one, an ascent of reality, which we shall say is true philosophy.
Certainly.
So we must examine which of the sciences has such a power?
Of course.

This passage clearly implies that what Socrates is about to develop will include, in terms of the Cave, everything from the moment of conversion to some moment outside the cave in the real world, both conversion and the real world being actually named. But what Socrates is about to develop is the mathematical curriculum. Thus this passage also quite definitely understands the Cave as having only the single undivided stage of the original unreleased prisoners to correspond to both the lower divisions of the Line. We must infer that Plato considered the distinction between 'conviction' and 'conjecture' irrelevant to the purpose he had in mind in the Cave. The Cave distinguishes the domain of knowledge into the two parts dialectic and mathematics; but it regards the domain of opinion as an undivided unity, represented by the original state of the prisoners.

§ 3. INTERPRETATION OF 517

(3) There is only one passage which has been thought to show that Plato himself considered his Cave parallel to his Line; and that is this.

This image, dear Glaucon, said I, should be attached as a whole to what we said before, likening (a) the domain that appears through sight to the house of the prison, and (b) the light of the fire therein to the power of the sun. And, if (c) you make the upward progress and view of the upper things the ascent of the soul to the intelligible place, you will not miss my expectation, since you want to hear it. God knows if it is true. But at any rate the appearances appear thus to me, that (d) the idea of the good is seen last and hardest among known things; but when it is seen we must infer that it is the cause of all that is right and fair to everything, in the visible begetting light and the lord thereof, in the intellectual being itself the lord who provides truth and intelligence; and that a man must see it if he is to act prudently either in private or in public affairs. (517A–C.)

However difficult this passage may be to understand or to accept in certain respects, it is quite definitely not a statement that the Cave is parallel to the Line. (3.1) In the first place, neither the word 'Line' nor any unique description of the thing occurs in this passage; the phrase 'what we said before' would apply to any part of the first six books of the *Republic*, and Jowett is too specific in rendering 'the previous argument'. Therefore the view that it means the Line, or even includes the Line as part of the passage it refers to, must be based on some of the subsequent detail.

(3.2) The rest of the paragraph may be divided into four parts, namely three correlations and then a statement of doctrine without any metaphor. The statement of doctrine (d), to take that first, is ominous for the attempt to rediscover the Line in the Cave. 'The idea of the good is seen last and hardest among known things; but when it is seen we must infer that it is the cause of all that is right and fair to everything, in the visible begetting light and the lord thereof, in the intellectual being itself the lord who provides truth and intelligence; and that a man must see it if he is to act prudently either in private or in public affairs.' Here is not a mention of the Line's four objects nor of its four 'states', not a mention of mathematics or dialectic or hypothesis or method. Here on the contrary is mention of the Idea of the Good, which the Line never says to be seen last and hardest among known things, never says to be the cause of all that is right and fair to everything, never says to beget light and the lord thereof in the visible world, never says to be in the intellectual itself the lord of truth and intelligence, never says to be essential to all prudent action. The Line does not use these phrases about *anything*; and it could not use them about the Good because it does not mention the Good. (That is to say, the Good is neither named nor uniquely designated from 509D to 511E.) What these phrases do unmistakably recall to mind is primarily the simile of the Sun and secondarily the Cave itself. That the Idea of the

Good is seen last and hardest among known things is nowhere so forcibly suggested as in the Cave itself. The rest of the statements here made about the Good are faithful echoes of the Sun. They echo nothing whatever in the Line except the distinction visible-intelligible, which is common to the Line and the Sun.

(3.3) Let us turn to the three correlations. Still working backwards, we have (c): 'make the upward progress and view of the upper things the ascent of the soul to the intelligible place.' The upward progress and view of the upper things is a part of the image of the Cave; and we are here told quite satisfactorily what this part of the image means. Note that this meaning has nothing to do with the Line; for the Line does not mention any ascent except the dialectician's ascent from hypotheses to a 'beginning', which is not *to* the intelligible place but *within* it, and not within the lower part of it either. The fact is that this ascent from an inferior world to the intelligible is not clearly referred to anywhere prior to the Cave itself. The two worlds are distinguished; but there is no clear suggestion that men do actually pass from the lower to the higher. We must take it that by the time Plato reaches this third correlation he is no longer telling us to correlate something in the Cave with something that 'we said before', but is merely correlating a part of the Cave with its meaning. He has in fact begun a new sentence here; and the verb 'make' ($\tau\iota\theta\epsilon\iota\varsigma$) has replaced the previous 'likening' ($\dot{\alpha}\phi o\mu o\iota o\hat{\upsilon}\nu\tau\alpha$).

(3.4) Let us go back now to the second correlation (b): '⟨likening⟩ the light of the fire therein to the power of the sun.' The light of the fire in the image of the Cave is to be likened to some previously mentioned 'power of the sun'. Here again, Plato cannot mean the Line because the sun is never mentioned in the Line. (That is to say, the sun is neither named nor uniquely designated between 509D4 and 511E5.) He must mean the sun in the analogy of the Sun. He had previously given us an analogy between the sun and the Idea of the Good. He now tells us that the fire in his Cave-image is like the sun.

(3.5) Finally we come to the first correlation (a): 'likening the domain that appears through sight to the house of the prison.' Here the 'house of the prison', which is an element in the image of the Cave, is to be likened to 'the domain that appears through sight'. The visible world occurs in the Line; and therefore this correlation, alone of the four, could, taken by itself, be intended to connect the Cave with the Line. But the visible world also, and more evidently, occurs in the Sun; and this interpretation would accord much better with the other three points, of which we have seen that none can refer to the Line, and two strongly indicate the Sun.

It may be objected to the preceding argument that it assumes the Sun and the Line to be distinct and coordinate similes, whereas Plato intends the Line to be a further elaboration of the Sun. He introduces the Line as a continuation of 'the likeness about the sun' (509C), and it follows that whenever he refers to the likeness about the Sun he is necessarily also referring to the Line.

To this objection the reply is as follows. Although Plato introduces the Line as a continuation of the Sun, no reader can help feeling a considerable difference of subject and temper between them. The Line is definitely not merely more of the same thing as the Sun. Its methodology and epistemology are distinctly new, not in being more specific than the Sun, but in being generically different. No one could possibly guess from the Sun what Plato was going to say in the Line about the differences between mathematics and dialectic, or that he was going to discuss these differences at all. There is therefore a real and important sense in which the Line is not a continuation of the Sun but a new doctrine.

Now the passage in 517, to which scholars appeal to confirm their doctrine that Cave and Line are parallel, does not mention any element of the radically new material that appears in the Line. It mentions only material that is introduced before Plato begins to talk about a Line, that forms the substance of the simile of the Sun in the narrow sense, and is present in the Line only as an unstressed background. It is therefore correct to say that, while 517 does refer us to the Line in that it refers to the Sun and the Sun in a sense includes the Line, the only parts of the Sun that 517 mentions are those before the introduction of the Line. This fact, taken together with the fact that Plato twice indicates a relation between Line and Cave other than one–one correspondence, dictates the conclusion that, just as the Line and the Cave *are not* parallel, so Plato did not *think* they were.

The general nature of the passage in 517 will now appear if we briefly contemplate the meaning of the Cave. It means the following doctrines about education and the lack of it (514A). Most men are uneducated in the sense that they are occupied exclusively with the objects of opinion. These objects are half-real copies of the real, and as such they cannot be genuinely known; but most men can see no reality in the essences which concern the philosopher, and they violently resist any attempt to convert them thereto. Even if one is converted, he has a long and desperately hard struggle before he can really apprehend those essences, the culmination of which is the knowledge of the Idea of the Good, and the realization that this Idea is the cause of everything else, including all that has any reality in the objects of opinion themselves. Such a knowledge is the best basis for dealing even with the objects of opinion; but most men do not think so, and they are encouraged not to think so by the fact that it takes a little time before the philosopher can successfully apply his knowledge of the Ideas to practical matters. He fumbles at first, and men do not wait to condemn him.

The Cave is a passionate appeal to us either to become philosophers ourselves, if we can, or, if we cannot, to let the philosophers rule over us. It is a forcible statement of Plato's conviction that philosophy is both valuable and practical in spite of appearances to the contrary. Like the Ship (488), it presents us with a vivid picture and implores us to believe that political reality corresponds thereto. It is meant to be a picture of actual cities, as Professor Ferguson has said. Yet there would be a Cave in the ideal city, as Mr. Murphy has said, in the sense that philosophers would 'descend' from contemplating the Ideas to regulating practice in accord therewith, and that there as here the majority of the citizens would be preoccupied with the half-real objects of opinion.

The passage we are discussing (517BC) is essentially an explanation of the meaning of the Cave. It proceeds partly by stating that meaning in relatively unmetaphorical words ('the idea of the good is seen last', &c.), and partly by correlating elements in the Cave with elements having an analogous function in the simile of the Sun. The Sun deals mostly with the nature of reality; the Cave, relying on the Sun, deals mostly with our attitudes towards reality; but they are near enough to explain each other in part.

Having arrived at this interpretation of 517BC, we are able to say finally that neither is the Cave parallel to the Line nor does

Plato anywhere say that it is. We have also attained a view of the meaning of the Cave.

§ 4. CONJECTURE (εἰκασία) AND THE MATHEMATICALS

What then is the Line, and what is it doing between the Sun and the Cave? Before we take a general view of it, there is one point which we now have the premisses to determine, namely whether by 'conjecture' or εἰκασία Plato meant trying to apprehend realities through images or taking images as themselves the realities to be apprehended. We now know that no argument in this matter may be based on the premiss that the Line is parallel to the Cave, because the Line is not parallel to the Cave and Plato did not think that it was. The state of the prisoners in the Cave is therefore no evidence for what Plato meant by 'conjecture' in the Line. But there is something else to which he does make 'conjecture' parallel, and that is 'thought' or διάνοια, the habit of mind of the mathematician. He is quite explicit that 'conjecture' is to 'conviction' as 'thought' is to 'intelligence', as the procedure of mathematics is to that of dialectic. Now we have already arrived at an interpretation of his account of mathematics in the Line; and, as we did so without any use of what he says about 'conjecture', we can now use it to determine his conception of the latter. He brings out two characteristics of mathematics in the Line, first that its premisses are uncertified hypotheses, and, second, that it gets at its objects indirectly, through images, instead of taking them pure as dialectic does. It is reasonable to conclude that he saw an analogy between at least one of these marks and 'conjecture'. Suppose that he saw something in 'conjecture' analogous to the fact that the premisses of mathematics are uncertified hypotheses. What would this entail about 'conjecture'? The conclusion is not at all obvious; but it seems to be that in 'conjecture' there is an unjustifiable confidence. Now taking images as realities in their own right perhaps shows more of unjustifiable confidence than trying to know realities through images. On this supposition, then, the conclusion seems to be that Plato understood 'conjecture' as taking images as if they were realities in their own right; but it is far less certain than we could wish.

Now take the other supposition, that he saw something in 'conjecture' analogous to the fact that mathematics gets at its objects indirectly, through images, instead of taking them pure as dialectic does. The conclusion from this is much more evident and strong than from the other supposition, and it is that 'conjecture' was trying to apprehend realities through images. Unfortunately, it is opposite to that to which we were led by the first supposition! We must therefore say that mathematics and 'conjecture' are analogous in only one of the two marks assigned to mathematics, and we must determine which that is. The answer is that they are analogous in attempting to know realities through images; and 'conjecture' is not taking images as realities in their own right, but attempting to know the realities through their images. The reasons are as follows. (1) As we have seen, there is a much more evident and strong conclusion from the supposition that the relevant mark of mathematics is its use of images than from the supposition that it is its attitude to its premisses. (2) Plato would naturally connect 'conjecture' with mathematics' attitude to images and not its attitude to its premisses, for the whole nature of 'conjecture' is concerned with images. Its object is precisely images, and its name is formed from the name of images. (3) The word εἰκασία would surely suggest εἰκάζω to a Greek as strongly as φαντασία suggested φαντάζω; and εἰκάζω never conveyed any suggestion of taking copies as originals, but did most frequently suggest getting at originals by means of copies. Liddell and Scott give: represent by an image or likeness, portray, liken, compare, infer from comparison, form a conjecture. It will not do to say that the word means merely conjecture, and not specifically conjecture about the originals of images (Hardie 61). It does specifically and essentially refer to trying to know A through B, where B is *like* A. Εἰκασία is a σκέψις ἐν εἰκόσι (cf. *Phaedo* 100A: τὰ ὄντα ἐν εἰκόσι . . . σκοπεῖν). (4) We scarcely ever do, as a matter of fact, take for originals the things Plato mentions as objects of εἰκασία: 'shadows, . . . appearances in water and in things of a close and smooth and plain constitution, and everything of the sort.' In view of these examples, and of the associations of the word εἰκασία, Plato was almost bound to be misunderstood by his readers if he meant it to convey the idea of taking copies as originals.

We thus reach without circularity the further conclusion that by 'conjecture' Plato understood trying to know originals through their copies; and it was in this respect that he held 'conjecture' analogous to the 'thought' of the mathematicians.

What evidence is now left for the theory that Plato meant the objects of 'thought' to be the mathematicals? It is urged, first, that otherwise this object seems to be left empty; and, second, that Plato does speak of mathematical objects both as eternal and as plural. The second argument must be dismissed; for it is a clear case, particularly obvious in Adam, of that fallacious principle of interpretation which I have called misinterpretation by inference (above, p. 2). The fact that Plato speaks of the mathematician's objects in one place as eternal, and in another as plural, while in a third place he tells us that there is only one Idea of each kind, is no evidence that he had formulated the doctrine described by Aristotle. He does not even get so far as to call these objects 'many', though Adam misleadingly suggests that he does. He merely says things which logically imply that they are many, such as 'the one that is equal every one to every one'. There is no evidence that he himself saw this implication; and, even if there were, it would still remain a question whether he saw the further fact that this plurality conflicted with the singleness ascribed to Ideas in Book X. To suggest that he did not is not in the least to belittle his insight; for it is perfectly certain that all of us all the time are failing to perceive implications which will seem obvious when they are pointed out. Thus there remains in favour of the hypothesis of mathematicals only the fact that otherwise this object seems to be empty; and of this another explanation will be offered below.

What evidence is now left for the theory that Plato meant the lower Line to cover all opinion and opinables? This has lost all the force it gained from the premiss that 'conjecture' is equivalent to the state of the unreleased prisoners. There remains only the fact that towards the end of the Line (511D4), and again in the recapitulation (534A), the two lower states of the Line are summed as δόξα or opinion, while in the latter passage the two lower objects are also summed as δοξαστόν or the opinable. (That this also occurs in 510A seems a misinterpretation.) Of these also I shall offer another explanation.

§ 5. A GENERAL VIEW OF THE 'LINE'

Let us now take a general view of the Line. It has a framework of four objects; for the intelligible and the visible, which are objects by nomenclature, are each to be divided into two (509D).

The two parts of the visible are described; one is images and the other their archetypes (510A). The two parts of the intelligible are not described in any analogous manner; but that there is such a division is implied on three subsequent occasions (510B2, 511C3–6, 534A5–7). These four objects, however, seem to remain *only* a framework. The body of the Line, and its serious message, is the distinction between mathematics and dialectic which we have elucidated. The difference between the two sorts of intelligible object is never explained or described or even named, except by the indirect statement that one is grasped by mathematical method and the other by dialectic. One passage suggests that Plato did not know what to say about them.

We are content, then, said I, as before, to call the first part knowledge, the second thought, the third conviction, and the fourth conjecture; and the last two together opinion, and the first two together intelligence; and to say that opinion is about becoming but intelligence about being; and that intelligence is to opinion what being is to becoming; and knowledge is to conviction, and thought is to conjecture, what intelligence is to opinion. But let us not go into the proportion and division of their objects, the opinable and the intelligible, Glaucon, in order not to involve ourselves in many more discussions than we have had already. (534A.)

The last sentence here is strange. If the proportions of the objects are the same as those of the mental states, it would have been just as short a sentence to say so; there would be no question of 'many more discussions'. But if they are not the same, it seems very important that we should know how they differ. The passage gives an impression of perfunctoriness, of evading a description because there is none to give. And the truth is that nothing philosophically important is ever said about these four objects. They do not appear outside the Line and its recapitulation in Book VII; and in those places they are at best a framework on which to hang the comparison of mathematics and dialectic, at worst an empty play with the idea of mathematical proportion.

Against its four objects the Line sets four 'effects' ($\pi\alpha\theta\dot\eta\mu\alpha\tau\alpha$) or 'states' ($\xi\xi\epsilon\iota\varsigma$). (Plato never calls them 'faculties' or $\delta\upsilon\nu\dot\alpha\mu\epsilon\iota\varsigma$, as some commentators have implied.) He seems to be even less interested in these. They have a suggestion of afterthought, as Stocks pointed out; for they appear only at the very end of the

Line, and are never explained or discussed. The Cave, as we have seen, has only one state to correspond to the two lower states of the Line together; and this seems to suggest the unimportance of the subdivision of vision and the visibles. The four states reappear only once in Plato's writings, namely in the recapitulation of the Line in Book VII. This recapitulation begins by recalling the distinction between dialectic and mathematics, which was the meat of the Line. It then gives the four 'states' of the Line and some proportions among them (the passage just quoted). And with that it ends. The latter passage, naming the four states and giving their proportions, seems to come in by mere association, to have no real relevance to its context, and to convey no real message in itself. It is just a set of useless proportions among a set of algebraical symbols of unknown meaning. Like the famous Number in Book VIII, it is a mathematical fancy which pleased Plato.

There is thus a strange incoherence in the Line, namely that within a framework of four objects and four corresponding 'effects' what it actually gives us of philosophical matter is two methods. Plato describes a difference in method, but classifies it as a difference in mental state plus a corresponding difference in object. He offers us eight pigeon-holes, four objects and four 'states'; but it is scarcely an exaggeration to say that he leaves every one of them empty and instead gives us two methods.

The Line falls in a part of the *Republic* devoted to the higher education of the rulers. The fundamental fact upon which this education depends is that there exists a world of unchanging essences distinct from and more real than this world of change. The essences are grasped by knowledge; this world by opinion; and the two faculties are distinct. So much was laid down in Book V, and constitutes an enduring and undoubted part of Plato's doctrine. In the Line he introduces a further point, also very important for the education of the rulers; and this is that we must distinguish a lower and a higher way of getting at the intelligible world. That is the main point of the Line, the two 'ways' or methods of mathematics and dialectic. Now for Plato a division of method tended to imply a division of object. He was imbued with the Greek belief that like is known by like, as we see most clearly at the end of Book V, where he argues from the distinctness of two faculties to the distinctness of their objects. It was

therefore easy for him to talk of distinct objects corresponding to
the distinct methods. The objects are defined primarily in terms
of our attitude towards them. Thus the primary difference between the 'intelligible' and the 'visible' is, as their names imply,
that we grasp the one by intelligence and the other by vision. In
this case there are very decided further differences, ontological
differences. But of the subdivisions that is not true. Between the
objects of conviction and conjecture the primary difference, that
they are the objects of different attitudes, remains the only difference. Ontologically, they are identical; for conviction and conjecture are different ways of getting at the same thing. Nearly
the same is true of the objects of 'intelligence' and 'thought'. The
quantitative Ideas dealt with by mathematics are other than
the ethical Ideas dealt with by dialectic; but both are Ideas. The
mathematician seeks 'the square itself' 510D7.

In the preceding simile of the Sun Plato had used the visible to
explain the intelligible. Now that he is introducing a new point
about the intelligible, he again uses the visible to explain it. The
fact that dialectic gets its object pure, whereas mathematics seeks
that object with the aid of sensibles, is, he tells us, analogous to
the difference between grasping a visible object by direct vision
and grasping it through its shadow or reflection. Thus the original
purpose of the lower Line is to illustrate the upper. Not, of course,
that the lower Line is imaginary. There really are visible things;
they really have shadows and reflections; and we really seek information about them sometimes directly and sometimes through
their reflections. But these facts are cited here, not for their own
interest or importance, but as a convenient illustration of another
fact, namely the difference between dialectic and mathematics
in the matter of using images.

But the illustration invites Plato forward in two ways. On the
one hand, he now has four 'objects' of a kind, namely the objects
of dialectic, those of mathematics, visibles, and reflections of
visibles. The like-by-like theory suggests four corresponding
mental attitudes or 'habits' or ἕξεις. Plato adds them as an afterthought, attracted by the neat mathematical scheme they give.
'Geometrical equality has great power both among gods and
among men' (Grg. 508A).

On the other hand, the added importance thus given to the
lower Line suggests a new way of regarding it. Perhaps we can

take it not as a mere illustration of the upper, but as an intrinsically important subdivision of opinion and opinables, that is, of the whole of 'reality' other than what the upper Line refers to? That is the idea in Plato's mind as he begins to use 'opinion' to cover the lower Line.

But the suggestion remains only a suggestion. There is not, after all, any fundamental distinction among opinables to be represented by the distinction between visible objects and their reflections, or any fundamental differentiation of opinion corresponding to the difference between looking at a man in a mirror and looking at him direct. The scheme refuses to burgeon into anything more than the bare proportion with which it began; and so, after one repetition (534A), Plato drops it for ever. He had seriously meant his distinction between conviction and conjecture to illustrate his distinction between dialectic and mathematics; and he had played with the idea that it might have some importance in itself. But in fact he remains with only his original two objects, Ideas and things; with only his original two corresponding faculties, knowledge and opinion; and his sole significant and enduring addition is the distinction between the two *methods* which the faculty of knowledge may employ in its search for the Ideas.

The Line seems somewhat out of place. We do not see until later the relevance of its distinction between mathematics and dialectic. In dealing with the higher education of the rulers, Plato first indicates that which it is most needful for them to know, namely the form of the Good; and by the simile of the Sun he gives a sketch of the Good's relations to the rest of the universe, which shows why it is the most important thing for them to know. It seems as if it would have been a more natural introduction to go next to the Cave, which represents in a preliminary way the process of getting to know this form of the Good; and after that to the explicit description of this process in the curriculum of mathematics and dialectic; and last of all to the very abstract epistemological account of the difference between mathematics and dialectic which constitutes the Line. It is noteworthy that in his recapitulation Plato does put the Line (533B–534A) after and not before the Cave(532A–C).

§ 6. MATHEMATICS

It is an integral part of this view of the Line that the objects of mathematics are Ideas. In the simile of the Sun the 'intelligibles' were the Ideas; and we should naturally expect a subdivision of 'intelligibles' in the Line to be a subdivision in which both parts were Ideas. Our expectation is strongly confirmed by the statement that the mathematician's interest is in 'the square itself and the diagonal itself' 510D. 'Mathematicals' are nowhere explained or named in the *Republic*; and that such a striking doctrine, such an innovation on anything else that the middle dialogues say, would have been introduced here in this ambiguous fashion passes all probability. That interpretation of the Line is only probable on the assumption that 'conjecture' is taking images for originals; and this in turn is only probable on the assumption that 'conjecture' is the same as the state of the unreleased prisoner in the Cave; and this in turn is only probable, or indeed barely possible, on the false view that Plato in 517BC declares the Cave to be precisely parallel to the Line. Once we have freed ourselves from the shackles of this inference, the natural interpretation is that the objects of mathematics as well as those of dialectic are Ideas. Plato made mathematics a preparation for philosophy, not because he thought its objects belonged to a class intermediate between those of philosophy and the sensibles; but because it deals with the easiest Ideas, the Ideas most obvious and most obviously distinct from sensibles.

This general examination of the Line and Cave was undertaken in order to determine whether Plato held that mathematics could become dialectical in method, although at the time of his writing it was not so. The question whether mathematics could become dialectical is, in more precise language, the question whether the study of those objects which mathematics now studies could be successfully conducted in the dialectical manner. It is an element in the larger question whether there are according to Plato spheres that resist the application of dialectic.

An answer to this question would naturally follow from the mathematicals-theory, if that theory were true; since the objects of mathematics are not Ideas, it would run, they can never be grasped by dialectic, which is said to be concerned solely with Ideas. The contradictory answer would follow from another theory that we have rejected, namely the mathematicizing theory that sees in the Line precisely a proposal for the betterment of mathematics. But, since both these theories are false, a more laborious examination of the evidence is required.

The following considerations favour the conclusion that Plato thought that the objects of mathematics could never be successfully treated by dialectic. (1) He represents the objects of the two methods as distinct, although both are Ideas, and so grasped by distinct 'attitudes' of mind. This is an important point, when we recall that in Book V he said that distinctness of faculty entails distinctness of object. To this must be added two confirmations in detail. (2) In two places Plato says that in studying the objects of mathematics the soul is 'forced' to use hypotheses; and this seems like saying that the objects of mathematics cannot be grasped except by the mathematical method (510B5 and 511A4). (3) He says that the objects of mathematics 'could not be seen except by thought'; and 'thought' is his name for the 'attitude' of mind peculiar to the mathematician and distinct from the 'attitude' of dialectic (511A1).

What considerations are there on the other side? It will not do to bring forward his suggestion that mathematics ought to be pursued by means of 'problems' (530B, 531C). The method of 'problems' is not, in his opinion, one that would turn mathematics into dialectic. On the contrary, he regards it as the method already employed in geometry (530B); and his proposal is to extend it to astronomy and 'harmony', so as to make those studies truly mathematical instead of empirical as they now are.

There are, however, the following important considerations in favour of the view that Plato thought mathematics could become dialectical. (1) We have ascertained that its objects are Ideas; and Plato nowhere suggests that the activities of dialectic are necessarily confined to certain groups of Ideas. (2) We have ascertained the procedure of dialectic to consist in the application of the elenchus to hypotheses. Surely it must be possible to apply the elenchus to any proposition whatever, including the hypotheses of mathematics. (3) Plato once says that the objects of mathematics could, if they obtained a 'beginning', become 'intelligible'. Now a 'beginning' is what dialectic obtains by means of the elenchus, and 'intelligence' is the name for the 'attitude' of dialectic.

You want to distinguish the part of intelligible reality which is the object of dialectic as being clearer than that which is the object of what are called the sciences, for which hypotheses are beginnings; and, while those who study them are obliged to do so by thought and not by senses, yet because they inquire from hypotheses and do not ascend to a beginning, you think they do not have intelligence about them, *although they are intelligible with a beginning.* And to the state of the geometers and such persons I think you give the name 'thought', as being something between opinion and intelligence. (511CD.)

This passage must not be discounted owing to the fact that 'intelligible' is Plato's word not for the special object of dialectic but for the general object of dialectic and mathematics. For 'intelligible' here is evidently an echo of 'intelligence' just above; and 'intelligence' just above is evidently the peculiar state of the dialectician, since it is explicitly denied to mathematics. The passage unambiguously means that the special attitude of the dialectician is not being applied to the objects of mathematics but could be.

Such are the considerations, for and against, by means of which we have to reach a conclusion. There are three of them on each side. What is their weight?

One of the reasons for holding that Plato thought that mathematics could never become dialectical breaks down entirely on closer inspection, namely that from Plato's statement that the objects of mathematics 'could not be seen except by thought'. When we look at the context we see that he is explaining that, although mathematics uses visibles, it is not about them. He says that its objects 'could not be seen except by thought' by way of contrast with the possible view that they could be seen by the bodily eye. He is, so to speak, being accurate by reference to the distinction between thought and sense; but he is not here concerned to be accurate by reference to the distinction between 'thought' and 'intelligence'. That would have been irrelevant, and therefore a pedantry such as his conversational style forbids and he makes his characters condemn (e.g. 533DE). In any given context a word means as much of its total meaning as that context allows; and here the context allows 'thought' to mean any cognition that is not sense.

Consider now another argument on the same side, namely that, by the doctrine of like-by-like, a distinctness of object entails a distinctness of faculty; and hence the faculty by which we apprehend the objects of dialectic could not also be the faculty by which we apprehend the objects of mathematics. This too is weak; for, as we have concluded, Plato's subdivision of intelligibles in the Line is primarily only the objective reflection of his distinction between two methods. Its shadowy existence is itself maintained only by the doctrine of like-by-like working from the real difference between mathematics and dialectic, and has by no means the strength to generate a further difference of faculty. That Plato here speaks only of 'effects' and not of 'faculties' is probably due precisely to his feeling that the word 'faculties', by bringing the doctrine of like-by-like too powerfully into play, would have excluded the possibility of replacing mathematical by dialectical method in any given field.

Consider lastly the argument from Plato's saying that in mathematics the soul is 'forced' to use hypotheses (510B5, 511A4). This is the best of the three on its side, and cannot be wholly explained away. At first sight we might think to nullify its force by pointing out that dialectic too, according to Plato's account, always uses hypotheses (for it always starts from them); and mathematics could not be prevented from becoming dialectical by being forced to do something which dialectic itself does! But it would remain a very odd fact that Plato says mathematics uses hypotheses in a way which implies that he is going to say that dialectic does not, and then says that dialectic does so too. This apparently false contrast probably really means that mathematics is condemned never to get beyond hypotheses to a 'beginning'; both methods start with hypotheses, but only dialectic ever reaches an irrefutable starting-point.

The three arguments on the other side all seem to stand up to scrutiny. We have, therefore, three good arguments for, and one good argument against, the view that Plato held that mathematics could become dialectical.

This review of the evidence does not give as sure an answer as we could wish; but, basing ourselves upon it, the conclusion we must adopt appears to be the following. Plato probably held that the objects now studied by mathematical method could be successfully studied dialectically; for (1) he thought them Ideas and he thought dialectic competent about all Ideas, (2) the repeated application of the elenchus, which is what he understood by dialectic in the Line, surely could be practised on any proposition whatever, and (3) he said that 'they are intelligible with a beginning' (511D). Nevertheless, he did also use language (510B5, 511A4) which either contradicts 511D or is a false contrast.

In the Line Plato is evidently trying to do better than contemporary mathematics did. What he is there proposing is not primarily a change in mathematics itself, but a step right out of and beyond mathematics; so that we misrepresent him if we interpret the Line as primarily a proposal for the betterment of mathematics. However, the better world into which the Line would lead us is very large, and includes mathematics; and therefore enables us to improve our mathematics as well as other things. The objects of mathematics are 'intelligible' in the narrow sense if they receive that starting-point which dialectic can give them. Mathematics would become knowledge if it gave a logos of its hypotheses. Probably, however, the starting-point or anhypotheton on which this better mathematics based itself would appear to the common man to be not a mathematical but an ethical proposition.

XII

ANALOGY

In an earlier chapter we have seen that there is an incoherence between Plato's epistemology and his methodology. His belief in categorically certain knowledge conflicts with his hypothetical method and demands a Cartesian method or an Aristotelian apodictic starting from infallible intuitions. Only once, in the Divided Line, does he try to make his hypothetical method yield the certainty required by his theory of knowledge.

The present chapter will be devoted to exhibiting another incoherence, that between the hypothetical method recommended in the middle dialogues and the method actually practised there. (1) Very little use is actually made of the hypothetical method in these works. (2) What they rely on, in order to persuade us and apparently also in order to intuit the truth, is analogy and imagery. (3) In contrast to the selfconscious discussions of hypothetical method, which is not much used in the dialogue, analogy and imagery, which are frequent, receive very little discussion. Moreover—a further accenting of the incoherence—what is said about them is mostly against them. (4) Especially is this so if we may relate to images (εἰκόνες) what Plato says about imitation (μίμησις), for he is nearly always unfavourable to imitation upon the whole.

§ I. PLATO'S USE OF HYPOTHETICAL METHOD

To what extent is the hypothetical method actually practised in the middle dialogues?

In the *Meno*, where the hypothetical method is described for the first time, Socrates at once proceeds to practise it. He uses it as a way of getting some sort of answer to the question whether virtue can be taught without having previously determined what is the definition of virtue. He hypothesizes a definition or partial definition of virtue.

In the *Phaedo* the essence of the hypothetical method is put to use more thoroughly than in any other dialogue. The hypothesis is the theory of Forms; and this, laid down on several occasions in the dialogue, is found each time to lead without selfcontradiction to the conclusion that soul is immortal.

A further element in the hypothetical method, according to the *Phaedo*, is that, while you draw out the consequences of your hypothesis in the direction you desire, you should watch whether any contradiction arises, either between the consequences and the hypothesis from which they spring, or among the consequences themselves. If this happens, you must start again with another hypothesis. This possibility is never realized in the *Phaedo* with regard to the main movements of the dialogue. The theory of Forms remains uncontradicted throughout. The possibility is realized, however, with regard to the minor hypothesis that the soul is the harmony of the body; this is found to lead to contradictions and abandoned.

Still another element in hypothetical method, according to the *Phaedo*, is the prescription what you are to do if anyone attacks your hypothesis itself. You are first to complete your deductions from your hypothesis according to the regular procedure, just as if the hypothesis were not being attacked. Thereafter, provided that no contradiction has appeared in the course of the deduction, you are to defend your hypothesis by making it the conclusion of a second piece of hypothetical method, in which it is deduced from a second and higher hypothesis. If the second hypothesis is also attacked, you do the same with that, deducing it from a third, until you come to 'something adequate'.When we search the dialogues for some example of this procedure, the conclusion seems to be that neither in the *Phaedo* nor anywhere else is there any movement of thought which Plato is at all likely to have considered a case of this. He does not illustrate this extension of the method.

There is comparatively little of any kind of deduction in the *Republic*, hypothetical or otherwise, after Book I. Plato there offers well marked arguments to prove that the soul has three parts, that justice is doing one's own business, that justice brings more happiness than injustice, that imitative poetry is harmful, that soul is immortal. He has other less formal arguments to other conclusions. But upon the whole the *Republic* devotes a far smaller fraction of its length than does the *Phaedo* to explicit deductions. If we examine the few that there are, to see whether they are offered in a hypothetical spirit, we find that this is rarely so. The argument that the soul has three parts starts from a law of non-contradiction explicitly said to be hypothetical (437A). The argument against poetry and painting starts by 'positing' the theory of Forms (596A). But other arguments in the *Republic*, even when sufficiently formal to be called deductions, have two features very alien to the hypothetical method. In the first place, they have the dogmatic air of implying that the argument is final for all persons. In the second place, they do not 'confess their premisses', that is, they do not point to their premisses as unargued and questionable propositions on whose truth all the rest depends. It is essential to the hypothetical method described in the *Phaedo* to 'confess one's premisses'.

A special feature of the method described in the *Republic* is the upward path to an 'unhypothesized beginning'. We have concluded that this would be an intuition supervening upon a long labour of elenchus. Is this procedure ever exemplified in the dialogues? Upon the whole, it seems clear that the dialogues never offer any particular proposition as an 'unhypothesized beginning'. They might, however, show us a part of the long labour of elenchus without showing it crowned with success; do they do this? On the contrary, elenchus, though still recommended in the middle and late dialogues, is rarely practised there. Plato is now too busy with direct construction. He does not now attempt to construct by destroying, although his own method bids him to. There are, however, two dialogues in which we may perhaps see, if we choose, a section of the chain of elenchus leading to the intuition of a 'beginning'. The *Parmenides*, though extremely hard to interpret, has a strong appearance of being mainly composed of elenchus; and above all the *Theaetetus* is so elenctic that it has been mistaken for an early dialogue.

Upon the whole, the hypothetical method recommended in the middle dialogues is little exemplified there or elsewhere in Plato. There is plenty of isolated 'positing' and 'hypothesizing', but little of the conscious and methodical use of hypothesizing suggested in the *Meno* and *Phaedo*.

§ 2. PLATO'S USE OF ANALOGY AND IMAGERY

What the middle dialogues really rely upon, in order to persuade us and apparently also in order to intuit the truth, is analogy and imagery. Analogy is extremely frequent in the dialogues of Plato. 'As this, so that' is his refrain. Its absence is noticeable in the arguments of Euthydemus and his brother, a type of thinking which Plato depicts without sympathy and feels to be wholly alien to his own. It disappears to some extent in the later work; but the early and middle dialogues are full of it. The middle dialogues and the *Gorgias* are peculiar in making some of their most serious points by its means alone. Induction is here sometimes no longer a subordinate element in a syllogism. It becomes, in the form of analogy, the essence of the argument; any deductive elements are subordinate to it; and the argument often seems much more truly persuasive than where deduction is the governing factor.

The two most analogical dialogues of all are perhaps the *Republic* and the *Gorgias*. The *Republic* includes the analogy between the guards of the ideal city and the dog. This is introduced simultaneously with the first decision to have guards (375); it serves to show that it is possible to find men who are at once fierce to enemies and gentle to friends; it also introduces the idea that these guards must be philosophers. Later, when the military and the philosophic functions have been assigned to different persons, the soldier is said to be to the philosopher as the dog to the shepherd (440D). The same analogy serves to enforce the proposal that the women of the guards are to be treated just like the men (451D) and that breeding shall be only or mostly from the best individuals (459B).

Even more important to the *Republic* is the great analogy between the city and the man. Introduced merely as a likely way of suggesting hypotheses about the individual, it gradually comes to profess not merely to suggest such hypotheses but also to prove them true, and in the process it produces a wealth of political philosophy.

The third great analogy in the *Republic*, which works hand in hand with the second, is the equation: health/body = justice/soul. This is Plato's only evidence that injustice is mental disorder. It is also his main evidence for the main conclusion of the dialogue, that justice is better than injustice; and Socrates works it out in full and vivid detail (444C–445B, and the account of the tyrannical man).

This third analogy is even more prominent in the *Gorgias*,

where its function is in general the same. It is here used first (464–5) in a classification of the arts concerning body and soul in order to define the nature of rhetoric. Next (477–9) it proves that if you have done wrong it is better for you to suffer punishment than to escape; here it gives rise to the subordinate analogy between the physician and the judge. Next (504), returning to the first idea, it proves that the business of the good rhetorician is to make the citizens just. Next (517–18) it explains the frequency and plausibility of the false view that the business of rhetoric is to make the citizens comfortable. Next (521) it is developed into a vivid fantasy of a physician accused by a cook and judged by children, in order to illustrate Socrates' position in Athens. Lastly (524), with the addition of the idea that the body clothes or veils the soul, it is made into another vivid fantasy to enforce the doctrine of reward and punishment after death.

A very large number of the Platonic analogies, perhaps more than half, contain the joint notion of techne–episteme, which is in English the tetrad knowledge–science–art–technics. Thus the *Cratylus* explains language by supposing that there is an art or technique of wordmaking and then comparing it to the art of painting. It also draws an elaborate analogy between words and the tools of common trades, especially between words and the weaver's shuttle. Socrates frequently makes analogies between common trades and activities that are not usually considered trades at all. The most striking form of this is the assumption that virtue is a techne. But of all the ways in which the techne–episteme conception enters into Plato's analogical thinking the two most important are these: (1) Ideas/knowledge = sensibles/opinion; and (2) ruler/people = pilot/ship's company = physician/patients. The first of these is the major chord of all Plato's theoretical philosophy; and the second is the major chord of all his politics until the *Laws*. The first is the cause of his absolute distinction between knowledge and opinion. The second is probably not the cause, but certainly the most persuasive argument, for his insistence that the people should give unlimited and unquestioning obedience to the rulers. In the *Republic* it appears most prominently in the figure of the Ship (488). The *Statesman* makes use of the physician's behaviour to prove that a good ruler should not be bound by any laws. And when Plato at last renounced dictatorship, and decided that the ruler should persuade as well as command, he corrected his former analogy by declaring that only slave-doctors give unexplained orders like a tyrant; the free doctor of free men must teach and convince his patient (*Laws* 720). So much for the prevalence of analogy in the dialogues.

Analogy is the kind of epagoge that passes from case to case without mentioning the universal. The less evident the universal, the more likely we are to call it analogy and not epagoge. For, even when the universal is not stated, it may be more or less evident. It may be more or less given in the form of the cases. Consider these two forms of argument: (1) since this X is Y, that X is Y, (2) since this X is Y, that P is Q. Neither argument states the universal; but the second does not even imply it, whereas the first implies that it is 'All X is Y'.

Analogy seems to be essentially an argument from a single case to a single case. However many cases are available, the argument, if it is an analogy, chooses only one of them, or at any rate treats all that it takes as being for the purpose of the argument a single case. It is essentially not perfect epagoge; for that ascends to the universal. It is essentially not probable epagoge from a plurality of cases either; for it professes to be intuitive in character, to see into one thing by an insight obtained on another.

But it is a peculiar kind of intuition that analogy offers us, a sort of seeing and not seeing at the same time. One case cannot really give us insight into another unless it gives us insight into the universal covering both; and yet analogy refuses to mention the universal. Thus it takes and does not take the universal; cf. ὅταν τὸ καθόλου μὴ ὀνόματι ληφθῇ ἀλλὰ παραβολῇ, *S.E.* 17, 176ᵃ33.

Characteristic of analogy as opposed to epagoge is also the elaboration of the premiss and the corresponding elaboration of the conclusion. Platonic analogy infers from the premiss-case not one fact about the conclusion-case but many. It discovers various aspects and elements in the latter corresponding to those in the former. Thus a characteristic analogy is likely to be longer even than a characteristic epagoge, not because it cites more cases, for it cites often only one, but because it goes into that case in detail and finds a corresponding detail in the case inferred. In *Cratylus* 387–90, for example, though more than one premiss-case is actually used, yet in principle the whole string of propositions there obtained about wordmaking can be got out of the predominant premiss-case, which is the art of weaving.

Analogy as a sort of intuition slides imperceptibly into analogy as illustration or explanation. It then assumes either the form of an example or that of an image. By an 'example' is here meant a case brought forward in order to illustrate not an explicit universal but another case, the universal remaining more or less tacit. Such a procedure does, however, easily slide into what we more commonly mean by 'example', the explanation of a universal by citing one of its cases or species.

In an ordinary example the premiss-case is supposed to have some identity with the conclusion-case. Although no universal is mentioned, we vaguely suppose that one is present and identical in the two cases. Somewhat different from this is the hypothetical or impossible example, such as the statue that perfectly resembles a man inside as well as without. Here we still think that the same universal would inform both cases if there were two cases; but in reality there is only one. It is possible to go a step farther and offer as an illustration a case which both is unreal and also, in some hardly definable sense, contains no universal also contained by the illustrand. Plato's Cave is an unreality; and even if it were real it would not actually embody the universal it is meant to illustrate; and yet it really does illustrate something. How this can be is not easy to see; it is not easy, in other words, to define the sense in which such a case contains no universal also contained by the illustrand. But we feel that it is so.

Illustrations of this sort have a paramount claim to the name εἰκών or image, sometimes translated simile or parable. An image brings the proposition forward with great vividness, and vividness is persuasive. Its disadvantage is that as a whole it is something that cannot happen, a fairy tale. An analogue, on the other hand, sacrifices the vividness of the image for the sake of possibility or actuality. In his imagery, which abounds in the middle dialogues, Plato attains his most poetic passages, as the Cave, and his most whimsical passages, as when he explains the flux-theory as an extrapolation of the giddiness caused by much turning about in the search for truth (*Cra.* 411). The *Cratylus* is perhaps the dialogue where on the whole his fancy is most detached, most nonsensical, and most free; but it is more delightful in some others. Among his more famous images are the waxen tablet and the aviary in the *Theaetetus*, the image of the soul in the *Phaedrus*, and the Cave in the *Republic*.

§ 3. PLATO'S DISCUSSIONS OF ANALOGY AND IMAGERY

The hypothetical method is less used in the dialogues than it is abstractly discussed. Analogy and imagery, on the other hand, are much used but very little discussed.

The word ἀναλογία, according to Ast, occurs once in the *Republic*, once in the *Statesman*, thrice in the *Timaeus*, and once in the *Epinomis*. In all these places it is mathematical in meaning and refers to what we call mathematical proportion; the *Republic*-passage is a reference to the mathematical proportions of the Divided Line (534A). The *Statesman*-passage is an isolated explicit reference to geometrical analogy by way of a joke (257B). The *Timaeus*-passages are uses of the conception of mathematical proportion in the construction of the physical world. The adjective ἀνάλογον and the phrases ἀνὰ λόγον and ἀνὰ τὸν αὐτὸν λόγον occur in much the same places and have the same mathematical meaning (*Rp.* VI 509D; *Ti.* 32B, 37A, 56C). Neither the phrases nor the adjective nor the noun seem to be extended outside mathematics until Aristotle. In Plato they all mean the same as his phrase 'geometrical equality' (*Grg.* 508A).

Plato's word ἀναλογία therefore does not mean to him exactly what is meant by 'analogy' in this chapter. We may note in passing, however, that it means something closely related, and something that indicates a rule of method. For Plato believes that 'analogies' or 'geometrical equalities' are frequent in reality and basic to its structure, and this Pythagorean conviction indicates one simple but important rule of method: 'look for proportions in reality, for they are there and you will find them.' He never explicitly states such a rule, but he does say that 'geometrical equality has great power both among gods and among men' (*Grg.* 508A), he does find important proportionalities both in the structure of knowledge in its relation to reality (the Divided Line) and in the elements of the physical world (*Ti.* 31–32), and he does say that 'the finest of bonds is that which makes itself and the things it binds as much *one* as possible, and this is most finely achieved by proportion' (ἀναλογία, *Ti.* 31C). The form in which I have stated the rule of method nascent here, 'look for proportions in reality, for they are there and you will find them', leaps to mind when we put this passage of the *Timaeus* alongside the following sentence from the *Philebus* (16D): 'We ought always to assume and search for *one* form concerning everything on each occasion, for we shall find it there.'

To return to analogy in the sense intended in this chapter, there seems to be no word in Plato that conveys a concept close to this. (The nearest are εἰκών and παράδειγμα, of which the correct translations are usually something like 'image' and 'example'.) There are, however, certain passages that offer something approaching discussions of analogy. The first of these is the introduction to the great analogy between man and city in the *Republic*:

The inquiry we are attempting is not easy. It demands a sharp eye, in my opinion. I propose, therefore, since we are not clever people, to conduct the inquiry in this way. If some not very sharpsighted persons were told to read small letters from a distance, and then someone noticed that the same letters occurred elsewhere, in a larger size on a larger ground, it would seem a piece of good luck, I imagine, to read the large letters first and then examine the small to see whether they were the same.—Certainly, said Adimantus; but what, Socrates, can you see of this nature in the inquiry about justice?—I will tell you, I said. We say, I suppose, that there is a justice of one man and also a justice of a whole city?—Certainly, said he.—And a city is bigger than one man?—Bigger, said he.—Perhaps then justice would be more abundant and easier to detect in the bigger object. If you will, therefore, let us search for the nature of it in cities first; and then we will examine it in the same way in the individual, looking for the likeness of the greater in the form of the less. (*Rp.* II 368.)

When they have arrived at an account of the nature of justice and injustice in a city, Socrates speaks as follows:

Let us not speak quite positively yet; but if, when this form enters each individual man, we agree that it is justice there too, then we will admit the conclusion. We cannot do otherwise. And if not, we will examine something else. But now let us complete the inquiry we began in the belief that, if we tried first to see justice in one of the greater things that possess it, we should detect its nature easier in the individual. We chose a city; and so we established the best one we could, because we were sure that in the good city there would be justice. Let us therefore transfer to the individual what we found there; and, if it is admitted, that will be good, but, if it seems to be something else in the individual, we will go back to the city and interrogate it; and perhaps, when we look at them side by side and rub them together, we shall make justice flash out as from firesticks; and when it is visible we will confirm it among ourselves. (*Rp.* IV 434D–435A.)

To what extent have we here a discussion of analogy? On the one hand, the passage contains no abstract words such as 'analogy'; it does not give any explicit account of analogy as such in words framed for the purpose of dealing with analogy. On the other hand, it is something quite different from merely presenting a particular analogy without in any way drawing attention to its analogical character. It is intermediate between the presentation of a universal as such and the presentation of one of its cases without any reference to its universal nature. In other words, it presents the nature of analogy to us in an analogical manner. For it is itself an analogy: big letters/small letters = city/man. And, as we saw, the nature of analogy is to suggest the presence of a universal without saying what it is. This passage, then, suggests by means of an analogy that there is an analogy between the city and the man; but it does not say what the analogy is, nor even call it an analogy. It merely suggests the universal nature of analogy by juxtaposing two cases thereof, big letters = small letters, and city = man. (For each of these is an analogy by itself, and could be expanded into the full form, e.g. government/city = reason/man.)

Socrates does not say that he offers the analogy between city and man as a means of *proving* something about man. Though not very definite, he implies rather that it will merely *suggest* something about man, and that any proof of the hypothesis thus suggested will have to be a separate undertaking. The passage regards analogy as a method of discovery and not also as a method of proof or argument. It therefore provides no justification of Plato's use of analogies, including this very one between city and man, as a means of argument and persuasion. This, however, is not to say that such a justification is impossible.

The city which Socrates uses, as a means of suggesting propositions about the human soul, is not actual but constructed by himself. This seems a defect, from the point of view of the analogical procedure. To get ideas by analogy about the actual human soul, it seems that he ought to look at actual cities. In particular, to answer his two main questions, 'What constitutes a just man?' and 'Is a just man necessarily happier than an unjust one?', he ought to select actual cities commonly reputed just, and try to see how they differ from actual unjust cities and whether they are happier. No doubt he might beg the question in deciding which actual cities were just; but he begs it far more definitively in constructing his own. 'We established the best one we could, because we were sure that in the good city there would be justice' (434E). How could he decide what was a good city without assuming an account of justice? What he will get out of his analogy, therefore, seems to be whatever he himself put in. Similarly he begs his other question, whether justice always makes for happiness, when he deliberately constructs his city so as to be as happy as possible (420B).

Another passage containing something like a discussion of analogy is the account of example or παράδειγμα in the *Statesman* (277–9). The word 'example' has here, as often in Plato, the sense of a case used to illustrate a coordinate case, rather than a case used to illustrate its universal. The city of the *Republic* is, in this language, an example, a case of justice used to throw light on another case of justice. The *Statesman* gives us an abstract account of this process of 'throwing light'. 'It is hard', we there read, 'to make any of the more important things clear without using an example. For each one of us knows everything in a dream as it were, and at the same time is ignorant of everything with his waking mind.' (This is the only hint here of the doctrine of recollection, 277D3.) That is the defect of human knowledge. To explain how we overcome this defect by the use of examples, let us take an example of an example! Children beginning to read name the letters correctly when they see them in the shortest and easiest syllables, and yet fail to recognize them in other syllables. The way to overcome this is:

To lead them first to the cases where they judged these same letters rightly, and then to put them beside those not yet recognized and show the same likeness and nature existing in both contexts, until you have displayed the cases that were judged correctly laid alongside all those that were not recognized, and, being displayed and thus becoming examples, they cause the child to call every letter in every syllable both other, as being other than the rest, and the same, as being always the same as itself.—Absolutely.—So this much is sufficiently established, that an example occurs when that which is the same in another separate thing, and which is rightly conceived, is brought into comparison, and so effects one true opinion about each of two things which are thus regarded in one view?—It seems so.—Should we wonder then if the same thing naturally happens to our soul about the letters of all things, so that sometimes in some things it stands firm about each one by the help of truth, but at other times and in other things is carried away about them all, judging some of them rightly here and there amongst the combinations, and then failing to recognize the very same ones when they are transferred into the long hard syllables of things? (278A–D. The translation is partly taken from Campbell.)

This is the passage where Plato for the first and last time uses the verb *epagein* of leading a man on to knowledge; and Prantl calls it a 'miserable trace of Aristotelian *epagoge*' (*Gesch. der Logik* I 80).

We have here a definition of 'example', and a description of what it is in the nature of our cognitive faculties that makes example a useful thing. So far, this is an acceptable justification of Plato's use of analogy, since what he means by 'paradigm' here is what is meant in this chapter by analogy, namely, getting insight into a case by means of a coordinate case; but what it primarily justifies is the use of examples in teaching, not in suggesting new propositions to oneself or in proving such propositions. It is stated in terms of the man seeking to enlighten another, not of the man seeking to enlighten himself. To what extent can it justify the use of analogy in invention and proof as well as in teaching?

We might reply that it can do so because it implies that example works by producing a new insight or intuition. By calling the learner's attention to something he already knows, the teacher causes him to know something more. Demonstration, of course, also works by calling our attention to something we already know (the premisses); but there the new knowledge is entailed by the old, whereas in example it is not. In example, to modernize the image in the *Republic*, the juxtaposition of the two propositions causes the spark of knowledge to leap across from the old to the new, not because the old entails the new, but because of 'the same likeness and nature' dwelling in both of them, that is, in our language, because they are coordinate cases of the same universal, although that universal is not explicitly mentioned. This is what is in Plato's mind when he uses not ἀποδεικνύναι 'to demonstrate', but ἐνδεικνύναι 'to reveal' (277D, 278B). Now, such being the nature of example, we can, so to speak, teach ourselves with it as well as others. We can ourselves in our own minds put cases into which we already have insight alongside of cases still opaque to us, and increase our knowledge in that way; and Plato presumably believed this, since he makes the Eleatic stranger, after describing example, propose that the company now proceed to' use it in solving their problem.

There is a difficulty, however, in this attempt to make Plato's account of example justify his use of analogy in discovery and proof. It is true enough that Plato here conceives example as a means of inducing an intuition, though without at all sharply formulating the concept of intuition; but how can the selfteacher by this method choose the right case to serve as an example? The teacher of others can choose an example suited to enlighten his learners because he already sees 'the same likeness and nature' both in the illustration and in the illustrand; but how can the selfteacher find a case that really illustrates unless he already understands the illustrand? He seems reduced to blind trial and error, putting anything whatever alongside the thing to be explained and observing whether a spark passes; and this might continue indefinitely without success.

This difficulty is a species of the puzzle in the *Meno*: 'Inquiry is impossible; for if we already know the thing we cannot inquire after it, and if we do not already know it we can neither know what we are looking for nor know when we have found it.' The *Meno* answers the puzzle with the assertion that in some sense we already know everything, as evidence for which Socrates professes to elicit a geometrical truth from a person without education. The *Statesman* refers to this point so briefly as to escape notice on a first reading (277D3); but it makes firmly the complementary point that we often know a thing in one way and do not know it in another. The two together release us from the puzzle; when we search we can direct ourselves and know when we have succeeded because we already know everything; yet we need to search because, while we already know all things in one sense, in other senses we do not know them yet.

In order to enjoy the benefit of Plato's solution, we do not have to assert with him that every man already knows all things. If we only assert that every man already knows in some ways certain things that he does not yet know in other ways, we have escaped this particular difficulty about learning in general and the use of the example in selfteaching. Our preexistent knowledge of X, although vague, is enough to guide us reasonably well in the choice of examples; then the example guides us back to a more precise knowledge of the X that is both the beginning and the end of our search.

The prior knowledge of X is not infallible as a guide to the right example. It does not assure but merely suggests that the justice of a city will illustrate the justice of a man. Hence, when we have seen the nature of our example, we must not take it for granted that this is the nature of our X as well; we must turn back to that X and look for this nature therein. If we do not actually see it there, nothing is accomplished. Plato makes this point by faint implication when putting forward the justice of the city to illustrate the justice of a man (*Rp.* II 368D7, 369A); he makes it more strongly when he has discovered what justice is in a city (434), and he then refuses to conclude directly that it is the same in a man, but offers independent reasons therefor. He thus uses the example as a way of suggesting an hypothesis but not as a way of proving it. When he comes to the forms of injustice, however, he infers the nature of the man from that of the city by assuming the validity of the analogy (cf. 577C and other places in VIII–IX).

These indistinct and partial statements seem to be the nearest Plato comes to giving justifications for his use of analogy. On the other side, there are passages implying, equally partially and indistinctly, that analogy is an inferior or at least a risky tool. In the first place, we often find passages expressing a consciousness that a certain man has assumed two things to be alike when they are not, passages which are therefore in some sense rejections of proposed analogies. 'Perhaps', says Socrates, 'it is somehow unlike what I am likening it to' (*Phd.* 99E). 'I somehow think', says Meno (*Men.* 73A), 'that this is no longer like these others.' 'As if this were like that', says Thrasymachus (*Rp.* I 337C). 'But', says Critias, 'you are on the wrong track. This kind of knowledge is not like the others, nor are they like each other. But you proceed as if they were alike' (*Chrm.* 165E). And a little later (166B), when Socrates has offered another analogy: 'That is what I was saying Socrates. Your inquiry has now arrived at the very point in which temperance differs from all the kinds of knowledge; but you are looking for some likeness between it and the others.' Perhaps we may paraphrase οὔ μοι δοκεῖ τοῦτο ἔτι by 'that is going too far'

(*Cra.* 429B). 'I am afraid you are joining flax and not-flax, as they say' (*Euthd.* 298C). 'If we must follow our previous statements' (*Rp.* I 332D; cf. *Cra.* 430DE). *Cratylus* 432AB also entails the consciousness that two things, namely quality and quantity, might be assumed to be alike in a respect in which they are not. Socrates criticizes Meno's likening him to an electric ray: 'I am like the electric ray if it benumbs others because it is numb itself; but otherwise not', &c., *Meno* 80C. Elsewhere he points out a difference between the physician and the judge which invalidates a suggested analogy between them; 'you have taken up an unlike thing with the same logos' (*Rp.* III 408D).

There are also passages in which a more abstract suspicion of analogy appears. In the *Sophist* the question arises whether elenchus is the same as sophistry. Theaetetus urges that they are very like each other. 'So is a wolf like a dog', replies the stranger, 'and yet one is very gentle and the other very fierce. A safe man will always be on his guard most of all about likenesses (τὰς ὁμοιότητας). They are a very slippery tribe' (231A). Here something near the notion of analogy appears under the name of ὁμοιότητες.

Another word, by means of which Plato often comes near to expressing an unfavourable judgement on analogy, is εἰκώς. This word combines the notions of probability and resemblance, a combination which is apparently more than an historical accident, since the English word 'like' does the same. One thing is 'like' another if it resembles it; but a 'likely' tale is a probable one. Whereas, however, the word 'like' does not often convey both these ideas at once, the word εἰκώς frequently did so. A statement was *probable*, to the Greeks, because it *resembled* reality or the truth. Τὸ εἰκός was 'a probable inference from a resemblance'. The word was very unstable in valuation; it was often put forward for approval, but often also for disapproval. When it is regarded as something acceptable, it is usually not explicitly contrasted with anything else; there is only the implicit suggestion that some other propositions are not so 'likely' as this one. When, however, it is disapproved, there is usually an indication of what should be put in its place. A certain 'likely proposition' is said to have 'more plausibility than truth' (*Euthd.* 305E). Τὸ εἰκός is opposed to 'demonstration and necessity' in the *Theaetetus*; and we are told that geometers always use the latter and never the former (162E). It is again opposed to demonstration in the

Phaedo (92D), where Simmias says he obtained a certain proposition 'without demonstration through a certain specious probability' (ἄνευ ἀποδείξεως μετὰ εἰκότος τινὸς καὶ εὐπρεπείας) ; but
'arguments which make their "demonstrations" through probabilities are charlatans; and if you do not watch them they deceive
you nicely, both in geometry and in everything else'. In such
unfavourable passages two implications are usually present : first,
that an obscure and unscientific guess is commonly based on some
resemblance, and, second, that an inference based on resemblance
is risky. In this passage of the *Phaedo* Plato is evidently thinking that
reasoning through τὸ εἰκός is a dangerous method of proof, in fact
scarcely 'proof' at all, and that it is far inferior to the hypothetical
method expounded in that dialogue. (The passage was translated,
and discussed from another point of view, above, pp. 138–9.)

The *Phaedrus* is ambiguous about inferences through resemblance, but on the whole seems to condemn them. It brings τὸ
εἰκός into close connexion with synthesis and division, two activities which Plato considers of the highest value, and proper to the
dialectician himself (273DE). But the nature of this connexion
remains vague; and on the other hand Socrates certainly puts the
argument from resemblance in an odious light when he says that
the way to deceive is to pass from a thing to its opposite through a
series of graded likenesses, and hence successful deception requires
an accurate knowledge of the likeness and unlikeness of things
(262).

Such are the passages in which Plato displays something near
an abstract consciousness of analogical argument and offers an
evaluation thereof. They are only scattered hints, in which the
idea is a chrysalis rather than a butterfly; and hence it is not surprising that they seem contradictory or at least incoherent. The
proposal to look first at the large letters in the *Republic*, and the
discussion of 'example' in the *Statesman*, supported in a vague way
by the ambiguous *Phaedrus*, suggest that analogical argument is a
valuable instrument; but the opposite is suggested by a majority
of the passages in which the notion of analogy more definitely
appears, under the form of τὸ ὅμοιον or τὸ εἰκός. There is no
harmonization of these conflicting judgements, such as an attempt
to state when analogy is good and when it is bad; and the prevailing opinion, which runs against analogy, seems to condemn
Plato's own predilection for analogies in his dialogues.

§ 4. PLATO ON IMAGES AND IMITATION

This incoherence between Plato's use of analogy and imagery and his remarks about them becomes much greater if we may take as applying to images (εἰκόνες) what he says about imitation (μίμησις), an assumption that will be made in what follows.

Very little can be found in Plato's writings by way of explicit commendation of images and imitation. Most of what there is occurs in the *Cratylus*. The speakers in this dialogue assume that there is such a thing as correctness in imagery, hard though it may be to discover (εἰκόνος ὀρθότης 432C); and if so there must be legitimate occasions for its use. Furthermore, they urge that a likeness or image is a much better way of 'revealing' a thing than any conventional symbol which does not resemble it (435C giving judicial assent to 434A). Lastly, Socrates seems to be quite serious when he says that there can be an imitation that does not reproduce outward form and colour but goes to the essence of the thing, and that this is in fact the way in which words imitate reality (423).

Even in the *Cratylus*, however, which is the most favourable of all the dialogues to imagery, the final impression conveyed is the opposite. The question, which of the opinions expressed were endorsed by Plato himself, is more difficult than usual to determine in the *Cratylus*, because Socrates there distributes his arguments more evenly than usual on both sides of every question. Hence favourable views of imagery in this dialogue would be outweighed by the more probably Platonic statements against it in the *Republic* and the *Sophist*. But the *Cratylus* itself argues impressively that no image can be perfectly like its original, inside as well as out; for, if it were, it would not be an image but a replica or double (432B). This implies clearly enough the view, explicitly stated in other dialogues, that imitations are as such inferior. Furthermore, Plato places at the end of the dialogue, where if anywhere we may expect to find his own opinion, the emphatic and deliberate statements that realities must be learned not through their images but through themselves, and, if they are akin, through each other; and that, even if we can learn things from the words that are their images, it is much better to learn the realities from themselves and the images from the realities (438-9).

The *Republic* contains only a single commendation of imitation as such: the statement that we may allow ourselves to imitate the good man in his better moments (396CD). It contains, on the other side, two long passages elaborately condemning imitative poetry as such. In the first (392–8) Socrates distinguishes imitative poetry, such as drama, from narrative poetry, such as the first few lines of the *Iliad*, in order to reject all imitation except precisely that of the good man in his good moments. In the second and more argumentative passage (595–607), he seeks for a definition of imitation as such; and he finds that imitation is the manufacture of an object having the third grade of reality. (Socrates regards 595C–597E as a definition of imitation as such. The passage begins with the usual Socratic request for definition, 'Could you tell me just what imitation as a whole *is*?', and it ends with indications that the definition has been achieved: 'Very well then, said I; so the manufacturer of the offspring that is third from nature is he whom you call an imitator?—Certainly, said he. . . . So we have reached an agreement about the imitator.') In the *Republic*, then, Plato explicitly states that an image belongs to an inferior grade of reality.

In the *Sophist* again the general impression is that imitation is bad as such. The discussions of imitation in that dialogue occur in the course of defining the sophist. Plato's whole treatment of the sophist is contemptuous, and the notion of imitation shares in the contempt. Imitation is mere play (234B). It is introduced with the figure of a painter deceiving foolish infants into the belief that he is capable of creating anything in heaven and earth (233DE, 234B). The image or εἴδωλον is defined as 'another one such as the true one and likened thereto' (240A), which implies that the image itself is not 'true'; that which is a semblance of the reality is 'really unreal'.

These references accurately embody the general spirit of Plato's discussion of imitation and images in the *Sophist*. Only two details can be appealed to on the other side. Of these the first is the distinction of the image that only apparently reproduces the forms and colours of its archetype from that which really does so (235–6). The sophist falls in the former class; and surely the latter class, we might argue, is a kind of imitation that Plato considered good. But such an argument would be mistaken. Plato considers the latter to be, at best, only less bad than the former. Contrary to

Cornford's suggestion (*Plato's Theory of Knowledge* 198), by 'icastic' imitation Plato does not mean duplication or the making of a replica, so that there would be nothing to choose between copy and original, like a man making a plaster cast of a plaster cast. He has not withdrawn the statement in the *Cratylus* that an image perfectly like its original would not be an image at all. He is thinking only of correspondence in outward form and colour (235DE). He offers 'icastic' as a species of imitation or μιμητική; and he describes imitation in a way that excludes duplication (233D–234E). He is merely distinguishing, say, the statue whose proportions are identical with those of a man, from the statue whose proportions are different from those of a man because it is intended to give the impression of a man when seen from thirty feet below.

The other detail in the *Sophist*, to which one might appeal as evidence that Plato thought that imitation can sometimes be good, is his distinction between the imitator who really knows what he is imitating and him who does not (267). It would be easy to develop this into a distinction between good and bad imitation, to describe the nature and purpose of a good imitation, and so on; but the fact remains that Plato never does so. He uses the distinction here only to condemn the sophist for not knowing what he is imitating. He never develops it into a correction of his prevailing doctrine that images as such are bad.

Besides these explicit statements about the nature and value of imagery, Plato's whole theoretical philosophy is largely a condemnation of images and a struggle to get away from them. Man, he holds, has the misfortune to be so circumstanced that he inevitably begins life by taking shams for realities. The world revealed by the senses, which engrosses all of us at first, is only a half-real *image* of true being; and wisdom lies in the progressive substitution of the pure for the adulterated, looking forward to the day when 'we shall know through ourselves all that is pure' (*Phd.* 67AB). In accordance with this view he urges us to abandon the senses and seek knowledge by the soul alone; his insistence that the best knowledge makes no use whatever of sensibles, even as images of the real, is itself a condemnation of images (e.g. *Rp.* 510–11).

On the face of it, then, there is an inconsistency between Plato's principles and his practice about images. According to what he says about them, he ought never to use them; yet his works are full of them.

The explanation of this inconsistency is not that Plato failed to realize his own use of imagery; for he frequently refers to his figures as figures or εἰκόνες. 'Let us return to those *images* to which it is always necessary to liken kingly rulers: the noble pilot, and the physician who is worth many other men' (*Plts.* 297E). In the *Phaedo* the comparisons of the soul to a tuning and to a coat are both called images (87B). As to the *Republic*, it is quite likely that an examination of that dialogue would justify the universal statement that all of its major images are explicitly called images by the speakers. At any rate the following are so called: the comparison of the guards to dogs (375D); the Sun (509A); the Cave (517B, cf. ἀπεικάσον 514A); the supposititious child brought up in much wealth (538C); and, when Socrates introduces the image of the Ship, Adimantus takes the occasion to laugh at him for his frequent use of images (487E). Thus a dialogue which emphatically condemns imitation (595C–597E), and demands a form of cognition that uses no images at all (510–11, cf. εἰκόνες 510E), is itself copiously splashed with elaborate images explicitly called 'images' by the speakers.

There is no passage in Plato's works which fairly explains or even describes this incoherence. Probably it never struck him nearly so sharply and forcibly as it is here stated. The most we can say is that two ideas expressed in the dialogues suggest lines along which he might have chosen to remove the incoherence if he had thought of it. One of these is the assertion in the *Phaedrus* that a wise man would write philosophy down only as a form of *play*, or as a reminder to those who know. It follows that the dialogues are either amusements or memoranda; and it would be possible to justify their use of images on that ground. Or Plato might have adapted to this purpose the distinction, common enough in the dialogues, between teaching and discovering, διδάσκειν and εὑρίσκειν. He might have said that the image, though bad as a means of discovery, is good as a means of teaching. Much in the same way as the example (*Plts.* 278), it gives the pupil insights that he would not otherwise attain. It is therefore in place in the dialogues because Socrates, though he pretends to be making discoveries, is really communicating previous discoveries to others. This explanation would accord well with the passages where Plato represents sensible appearances as leading us to the realities they imperfectly imitate, such as the doctrine of recollection in the *Phaedo*, and the account of the lover's progress from visible to invisible beauties in the *Symposium*, and the *Republic*'s remarks on the kind of perception that sets us wondering (523–4).

Let us summarize the major incoherences in Plato's method and methodology in the middle dialogues. (1) The demand for absolute certain knowledge seems inconsistent with the recommendation of a hypothetical method that can be only approximative. (A deliberate attempt is made to overcome this in the Divided Line.) (2) The recommendation of a hypothetical method seems inconsistent with the fact that the methods mostly employed in the middle dialogues are analogy and imagery. (3) Plato's doctrine that dialectic does not use the senses seems inconsistent with his frequent use of imagery, and to some extent inconsistent with the use of analogy. (4) Plato's employment of analogy is hardly supported by his own views on analogy. (5) Plato's use of images is condemned by his own views on images and imitation.

Such inconsistencies are probably very common in persons who discuss method. They take away little or nothing from the interest of Plato's hypothetical method or the charm of his imagery; but they invite us to consider more carefully than has yet been done what sort of grounds justify a person in recommending a given method. We tend to assume that a successful man must know the causes of his success; but the spectacle which we have just contemplated suggests that a man might discover important new truths and yet be widely mistaken about the method by which he did so.

XIII

HYPOTHESIS IN THE *PARMENIDES*

PLATO went on using the word 'hypothesis' in his writings to the end of his life; but the *Parmenides* is the last dialogue in which he used it in the course of giving advice about the right method of thinking, and therefore the last dialogue I shall examine in this book.

The *Parmenides* is the most doubtful of all Plato's dialogues to interpret. Widely different explanations of it have been given, and no general agreement yet exists. My view of the contribution which the dialogue makes to the theory of dialectic depends on my view of its general nature. I must therefore give a long justification of my 'gymnastic' interpretation of the dialogue in general, before discussing its contribution to the theory of dialectic in particular. I shall discuss and recommend the following propositions. (1) The arguments in the first part of the *Parmenides* are directed against the existence of Forms, not of sensibles. (2) The theory of Forms discussed in the first part is that of Plato's own middle dialogues. (3) Plato regarded these arguments as neither fatal nor negligible, but serious difficulties requiring serious attention. (4) Plato never answered these arguments in his dialogues. (5) The second part of the *Parmenides* contains no statement of doctrine, either directly or indirectly. (6) The second part of this dialogue contains no statement of method, either directly or indirectly. (7) Both parts of the dialogue are intended to provide Plato's pupils with practice in dialectic and in the detection of errors in reasoning. (8) Cornford's interpretation of the dialogue combines this view with another view; but the two are really incompatible.

§ 1. THE FIRST PART IS AGAINST FORMS

It is a traditional view that in the first part of the *Parmenides* Plato represents Parmenides as bringing objections against the theory of Forms there stated by Socrates, objections which tend to make us believe that there are no such Forms. Burnet dissented from this opinion, and held that Plato here represents Parmenides

as agreeing that there are Forms but objecting to Socrates' view
that besides Forms there are things. The arguments, he wrote in
Greek Philosophy (I 254), 'are not directed against the reality of the
intelligible, but against that of the sensible'. Two years later A. E.
Taylor declared that these words express the point 'with perfect
exactness in the terminology of a later generation' (*Philosophical
Studies* 42). He stated that 'the object of the argumentation is not
to throw a doubt on the existence of Forms, but to urge the need
for a plain and explicit account of the *relation* which Socrates
commonly called that of *participation*, by which a thing is connected with what he calls the Form of that thing'. 'Parmenides
and Zeno nowhere raise any difficulty about the existence of such
Forms as the proper objects of knowledge' (41). In 1934 Taylor
restated this view in the following words:

> [Parmenides] does not, for a moment, quarrel with the young
> Socrates for believing in the 'separate and intelligible forms'; on the
> contrary, he expressly declares that without such objects there can be
> no philosophy and no science, for there is nothing else that can be
> really known (135BC). What he does criticize in Socrates is that he is
> trying to ascribe at least a 'phenomenal' reality to the sensible world
> and its contents by maintaining that they somehow 'participate' in
> the reality of the intelligible forms. All his criticisms aim at showing
> that Socrates can give no coherent explanation of this relation of the
> sensible to the intelligible, because all possible explanations are
> inconsistent with the strict *unity* of the 'form'. It is the ascription
> of any reality whatsoever to the *sensible* which he feels to be inconsistent
> with any kind of monism; the error of Socrates is precisely that he
> is determined to ascribe at least a derivative and secondary reality to
> the things of sense, which he ought to regard as a mere illusion.
> (*Plato's Parmenides* 13.)

Arguments showing serious difficulties in the notion of participation, that is, in the view that sensibles somehow share in Forms,
could be used to discredit the existence of Forms by anyone who
assumed the existence of sensibles. But they could also be used to
discredit the existence of sensibles by anyone who assumed the
existence of Forms. Burnet put this by saying that an argument
like the 'third man' is double-edged. The question is, therefore,
which edge Plato represents Parmenides as using in the dialogue.

Burnet's reason for his view was that the arguments in the first
part of the *Parmenides* are Eleatic in origin, and an Eleatic would

deny reality to the sensible and not to the intelligible. As evidence for this Eleatic origin he urged (1) that Plato puts the arguments into the mouth of the founder of Eleaticism, (2) that we know from the *Theaetetus* that Plato was busy with Euclid of Megara about the time he wrote the *Parmenides*, and (3) that there is good independent evidence that the 'third man' was invented by Bryson the Megaric. We must also reckon, as part of Burnet's case for this doctrine, his other doctrine that the latter part of the dialogue is primarily a refutation of the Megarics' first principle.

Taylor dissociates himself from the point about the 'third man'. A detailed and learned study has brought him to the conclusion that there appears to be no independent evidence that this argument was invented by a Megarian. The rest of Burnet's argument he accepts; and he adds that Plato makes Parmenides expressly declare that without the Forms 'there can be philosophy and no science, for there is nothing else that can be really known'.

We may omit Burnet's point about Euclid as too slight to have any effect, and his point about the 'third man' because it is abandoned by Taylor. We are then left with three distinct lines of argument for the view that Parmenides is represented as throwing doubt on the sensibles and not on the Forms. The first line includes all the considerations that may arise out of the facts that Plato put these arguments into the mouth of Parmenides and Parmenides believed sensibles to be illusions. The second includes all the force that this view gains from making a unity out of the dialogue by connexion with the view that the second part also concerns Eleatics. The third is the appeal to the passage where Plato makes Parmenides declare that, if you deny that there are Forms, you will have nowhere to turn your mind and so will completely destroy the power of dialectic. This appears to be the total of Burnet's and Taylor's evidence in the three works quoted. At first those works give the impression of containing a multitude of arguments; but this is because the mere unreasoned statement of the doctrine itself has the air of being an argument when it recurs after one of those fine passages of analysis and comment in which these writings abound.

I shall not deal in this section with the second argument, namely, that, by interpreting the first part of the dialogue as an Eleatic argument against the sensibles, we make the dialogue a unity, because the second part of it also concerns the Eleatics. In

Q

later sections I shall show that the second part of the *Parmenides* is not concerned with Eleatics. Therefore no unity is effected by finding Eleatic doctrines in the first part, and this argument falls to the ground. In this section I shall first examine the two other arguments of Burnet and Taylor and then offer positive reasons for the traditional view.

The argument from the fact that these objections are put into the mouth of Parmenides is difficult to estimate, because there seems to be no close parallel in the dialogues. There is no other first-class thinker whom Plato ever represents as speaking in his own person except Socrates, and Plato's relations to Socrates were importantly different from his relations to Parmenides. But two things may be said. (1) In the first place, there seems to be a large probability that this argument stands and falls together with the principle that Plato never makes Socrates utter doctrine which he did not in fact hold. This 'Principle of Historicity' will not be discussed here but dogmatically assumed to be false; and from that assumption we may infer with considerable confidence that Plato's giving these objections to Parmenides is no evidence of their being directed against the sensibles. (2) In the second place, Plato's picture of Parmenides is on any theory hopelessly unhistorical in two major points. It represents him as seriously reaching that absurd conclusion with which the dialogue ends, and the real Parmenides certainly never did any such thing. Worse still, in the very passage to which Taylor appeals for his interpretation, it unmistakably represents him as a pluralist, as believing in a plurality of Forms.

But, Socrates, said Parmenides, if on the other hand a man will not allow that there are *Forms* of things, in view of all that we have just said and similar considerations, and will not distinguish a Form *for each thing*, he will have nowhere to turn his mind, since he does not admit the eternal and identical existence of an Idea *of each thing*, and so he will completely destroy the power of dialectic. (135BC.)

(The same pluralism is probably implied also in Parmenides' rebuke to Socrates for not allowing Forms of hair or mud or dirt (130E); but Taylor follows Burnet in taking this as ironical, and it could be so interpreted if other considerations demanded.) For these reasons the fact that the objections are ascribed to Parmenides is no evidence for their being directed against the sensibles.

Let us now examine the particular passage to which Taylor appeals, and which has just been translated in another connexion. It is the second part of a dilemma, which as a whole is to this effect: 'If a man declares that there are Forms, he runs into very great perplexities, which tempt him to declare that there are no Forms after all, or if there are man cannot know them; yet, if he denies that there are Forms, he will have nowhere to turn his mind, and so will completely destroy the power of dialectic.' This dilemma is Parmenides' last word on the Forms in the dialogue. Now here Parmenides unmistakably represents the first alternative as a summary of the previous objections, and thus he quite definitely says that what the objections tend to prove is that 'these [Forms] do not exist, and if they did exist it is quite necessary that they should be unknown to human nature' (135A). The whole statement of the first alternative may be translated as follows:

These, Socrates, and many others in addition to these, are the inevitable consequences if there are these Ideas of things and a man insists on distinguishing some Form itself for each thing. So that the hearer becomes puzzled and argues that they do not exist, and that even if they did exist very much indeed it is quite necessary that they should be unknown to human nature; and in saying this he seems to have a real point, and, as we just said, he is amazingly hard to persuade to the contrary. (134E–135A.)

Thus an examination of the context of the passage to which Taylor appeals shows, not merely that the passage does not support his view, but actually that it is a first-class positive argument for the traditional view.

Of all the considerations offered by Burnet and Taylor for their view, only one is an appeal to the actual text of the *Parmenides* to see what Parmenides himself is there made to say he is doing and what his hearers are made to regard him as doing. This surely is an anomaly. When the question is what Plato represents Parmenides as proving by his arguments, the first thing to do is surely to look to the text to see whether Parmenides is made to say what he thinks he is proving, and if so what it is. Yet Taylor, after appealing to a single passage, devotes himself to a different matter, namely a philosophical examination of the arguments to show how they *might* be turned against the sensibles. He has made it clear that the arguments about participation might be so used; but, if we turn to the text to see how Parmenides and Socrates thought they *were* being used, we find abundant positive evidence that they were being used to throw doubt on the existence of the Forms.

To begin with, what novelty does Socrates regard himself as introducing in his original statement? The doctrine that sensibles exist and participate in Forms, it being already assumed by the company that Forms exist? Clearly not. What the company already assumes is that sensibles exist; and Socrates' novelty is that Forms exist and are participated in by sensibles. His first words are: 'Don't you think that there is some Form of likeness itself by itself, and something opposite thereto which is unlike; and that in these, which are two, you and I and the other things, which we call many, participate?' (129A). Here Socrates assumes the existence of you and me and the many, and urges that Forms also exist and that the many participate therein.

It was still open, however, for Parmenides to rejoin thus: 'Yes, Socrates, you are quite right in believing that there are Forms, and I agree with you. Where you go wrong is not in asserting the existence of Forms, but in assuming the existence of sensibles also, which you say participate in the Forms. I will now show you that participation is an impossibility, from which it will follow that sensibles do not exist.' Parmenides might have taken this line. But does he? After one sentence of praise he says this: 'And tell me, you yourself have made the distinction you mention, on the one hand certain Forms themselves, on the other the participators therein?' (130B). By itself, this sentence only tells us that the novelty lay in making the distinction, and does not say which of the distincts, if either, was newer than the other; but the next sentence is explicit. 'And does there seem to you to be some likeness itself distinct from the likeness we possess, and one and many and all that you heard Zeno speaking of just now?' Here, plainly, the novelty is likeness itself, and the likeness we possess is assumed. Parmenides at once explores just what Forms Socrates believes in, not what sensibles he believes in. He asks whether Socrates believes in a Form of man distinct from us and all who are such as we; he does not ask whether Socrates believes in us and all who are such as we, distinct from the Form of man. He asks whether there is a Form of hair distinct from the hair we handle, not whether we handle hair distinct from the Form of hair.

Later on Parmenides speaks as follows: 'I think the reason why you think each single Form to exist is of this sort. Whenever there seem to you to be many things that are large, there perhaps seems to you to be one and the same Idea as you look at them all, and so you hold the large to be one' (132A). This cannot be offered as evidence for the traditional view, because it is capable of various interpretations; but to make a complete statement of the traditional view we must say that according to it this passage implies that what Socrates is asserting, and what Parmenides is offering grounds for denying, is that Forms exist; and it also implies (though Plato would perhaps not have agreed to this on reflection) that if there were no many (that is, no sensibles) there would be no reason for believing in the Forms.

Parmenides introduces his last argument with these words:

So do you see, Socrates, how great the difficulty is if one distinguishes Forms as existing themselves by themselves?—Yes, indeed.—Then let me tell you that you practically have not yet *touched* on the immensity of the difficulty, if you intend to be always distinguishing and positing one Form for each set of things. (133AB.)

Surely this language quite clearly and quite certainly entails that Socrates is not defending and Parmenides not denying the reality of sensibles. We may be uncertain just what version of the theory of Forms is in question; but we cannot doubt that it is a theory of *Forms* and not a theory of sensibles.

After the last argument Parmenides poses his dilemma, and we have already seen that here, too, his language quite sincerely and irrevocably implies that he has been giving reasons for believing that there are no Forms. He now says, or clearly hints, that in spite of those reasons there must *be* Forms. But still they were reasons against there being Forms; his present assertion is in spite of, and not in accordance with, his previous arguments. We may, therefore, confidently accept the traditional view that Parmenides is objecting to the existence of Forms.

§ 2. THE FIRST PART IS AGAINST PLATO'S OWN FORMS

The next proposition to be maintained is that the theory of Forms discussed in the first part of the *Parmenides* is identical with the theory of Forms set out in Plato's middle dialogues, especially the *Phaedo* and the *Republic*. This needs no defence at the present time (for it is, as far as I know, generally accepted), but only a little explanation. It does not mean that every proposition asserted in the middle dialogues as part of the theory of Ideas is reasserted here. On the contrary, the few doctrines given here are very far from exhausting those expositions. There is nothing of what the *Republic* says about the Idea of the Good, or about the relation of the Ideas to the distinction between knowledge and opinion. There is nothing of the *Symposium*'s stages in the ascent to the Idea of Beauty. There is nothing of the *Phaedo*'s doctrine of recollection, although on the whole the *Phaedo* corresponds most closely to the account in the *Parmenides*. Socrates in the *Parmenides* gives only enough of the theory for his immediate purpose, which is to point out that not all things are liable to Zeno's contradictions. When we say that what he asserts is the theory of Ideas found in Plato's middle dialogues, we mean that he gives enough for us to recognize a central core of identity, and that the author, in composing the piece, intended this identity and did not intend to depict a theory distinct from that of the middle dialogues. If we add to this a denial of the Principle of Historicity and an assertion that the theory of Ideas in the middle dialogues was Plato's own belief at the time when he wrote them, we must conclude that in the *Parmenides* Plato presents objections to a theory that he himself had held at a previous time and perhaps still held.

§ 3. PLATO THOUGHT THE ARGUMENTS SERIOUS

Our third proposition is that Plato reckoned these objections to his doctrine of Ideas as neither fatal nor negligible, but serious difficulties requiring serious attention. That he did not think them fatal to any and every form of the doctrine seems evident at once. The dilemma with which Parmenides concludes his discussion of Socrates' theory hints clearly enough that there somehow must be Ideas after all. The *Timaeus* reaffirms the theory much later. External evidence, and especially the writings of Aristotle, make it certain that Plato went on believing in some form of the doctrine to the end of his life. Therefore he did not think these objections fatal.

There is, indeed, one way out of this conclusion, and that is to say that Plato was a sceptic. If he held that human reason is essentially selfcontradictory, he might have judged the objections fatal and gone on holding the theory nevertheless. And the view that he was a sceptic is not without plausibility, as the history of the Academy shows. Jackson thought that Plato was convinced by the final argument that Ideas really are unknowable. Some degree of scepticism is attributed to Plato by any Neo-Platonic interpretation, especially if it makes him hold that the conclusion of the second part of the *Parmenides* is true. Extremes meet; and Shorey, who was as far as possible from the Neo-Platonic interpretation, also made Plato a sceptic, though he would not have admitted it, when he wrote that 'any philosopher who cannot or will not accept the alternative of pure positivism or thoroughgoing materialism must disregard or evade these difficulties as Plato did' (*What Plato Said* 289). In the present discussion, however, I shall, like Taylor in *Plato's Parmenides*, assume without argument that this view is mistaken and that Plato was no sceptic. Adding to this assumption the strong evidence that Plato continued believing in Ideas to the end of his life, we must conclude that he judged the objections in the *Parmenides* less than fatal.

The second part of the present proposition, to which we may now turn, is that, on the other hand, Plato did not consider these objections contemptible. The evidence for this is as follows.

1. They are presented with considerable gravity. They are put into the mouth of a thinker for whom Plato professes a deep admiration; and this thinker insists on their seriousness (131E, 133AB), ending by saying that in view of them it needs a very good natural endowment to follow, and a still more amazing endowment to invent, a proof that there really are Ideas (135AB).

2. The *Philebus* (15BC) mentions the problems whether there are certain henads, and whether they become plural and split up among the indefinity of gignomena 'or are one and the same at the same time in one and many things, as wholes separated from themselves, which would seem most impossible'. The context makes it certain that these henads are the Ideas, so that Plato is here restating both the general problem of the first part of the *Parmenides*, namely, whether there are Ideas, and the special problem of the first objection, namely, how things can participate in the Idea without dividing it from itself. The context explicitly tells us that these are serious problems, unlike some other problems about the one and the many. And one sentence in particular confirms not merely our present contention that Plato thought these objections serious but also our former contention that he did not think them fatal; it is to the effect that these problems

'cause utter difficulty if you make the wrong admissions, and convenience if you make the right'.

3. Parmenides' critique shows that Socrates' theory is not yet formed on two important questions, namely, (a) what Ideas there are, or to which collections of things an Idea corresponds; and (b) what is the nature of the participation in the Idea by the many. Now there is no satisfactory answer to either of these questions anywhere in Plato's writings. Interpreters have found hints of answers, and passages which logically imply a certain answer; but it is never indubitable that Plato saw and intended the implication or the hint. Aristotle's discussion suggests that neither problem ever received a definitive solution. Surely, therefore, Plato must have regarded these objections as serious, since they point to two gaps which he was never able to fill.

4. The foregoing arguments are independent of our estimate of the true value of Parmenides' objections. They retain the same amount of force, even if we hold that the objections are in truth negligible. But if anyone believes that these objections really are philosophically profound, and that Plato was far too good a thinker to have overlooked their profundity, this will constitute for him a fourth reason for holding that Plato considered them serious difficulties.

The conclusion at which we thus arrive—that Plato thought he was stating serious objections to the theory of Ideas in the first part of the *Parmenides*—refutes the parody-view of the *Parmenides*, which is that the first part of the dialogue presents fallacious arguments made according to a bad logic by some opponents of Plato, and the second part refutes them indirectly by showing in an extremely forcible way that their logic will prove anything about anything. We may confirm this by examining two statements of the parody-theory, namely, those of Taylor and Professor Cherniss.

It is difficult to make out how serious Plato thought the objections according to Taylor. Mr. Hardie speaks of Taylor's view that they are 'more or less transparent sophistries' (W. F. R. Hardie, *A Study in Plato* 97). This interpretation certainly seems, as we have said, to follow from Taylor's general view of the dialogue. Furthermore, Taylor said that the second regress-argument is a 'manifest subreption' (*P.'s Prm.* 26); and that in it the premisses of Parmenides are 'an ingenious perversion' of the assertions of

Socrates (*Philos. St.* 89); while the first regress-argument depends
on an ambiguity which it is only reasonable to suppose Plato was
aware of, since in the *Sophist* he saw and explained the ambiguity
as far as it affected the possibility of significant denial (ibid. 51).

Yet the opposite view occurs in Taylor's writings also. Whereas
in 1916 he held that Plato saw the fallacy in the first regress-
argument, in 1934 he wrote that 'whether Plato was alive to this
confusion is more than we can say', and spoke of 'a series of at least
apparently formidable objections' (*P.'s Prm.* 10, 21). And this was
not simply a change of view since 1916, for in 1916, too, he quite
distinctly implied that Plato meant us to regard them as 'grave
objections' (*Philos. St.* 90). In both years, moreover, he confined
his unfavourable critique to the two regress-arguments. He did
not even assert, much less argue, that there was any fallacy in
Parmenides' first argument—that the many cannot participate
in the Idea without dividing it from itself—or in his last—that we
cannot know the Ideas. This silence seems to suggest that in his
view those two arguments are at least not quite disreputable and
were not so regarded by Plato. Most remarkable of all, perhaps,
is the fact that in both years Taylor praised Parmenides' 'refutation of idealism' in the highest terms, characterizing it as extremely neat and quite fatal. This argument is not an objection to
any standing part of Socrates' theory; but that does not make it
any the less incongruous to insert a first-class argument into the
middle of a series the rest of which were going to be shown by
indirection to be worthless. What reaction could Plato expect
from his readers to such a procedure? If they recognized the
perfection of this particular argument, they would have to reject
Plato's insinuation of the worthlessness of Parmenides' arguments
in general, and so the main purpose of the dialogue, as Taylor
expounds it, would be defeated. If, on the contrary, they accepted
the implication that Parmenides' arguments were worthless, they
would condemn the 'refutation of idealism' along with the rest,
and so Plato's beautiful argument would be regarded as proved
to be fallacious by Plato himself.

These considerations make it very difficult to determine just
what Taylor's view is about Plato's estimate of the quality of the
objections. That, however, is not our question here; and fortunately these considerations do show quite clearly that, if Taylor
did maintain that Plato reckoned the objections worthless, he can

be refuted out of his own writings. Furthermore, we may dissent from the view that the two fallacies which he has exposed seemed negligible to Plato. The mistake in the first regress-argument is acutely described by Taylor as the assumption that a character can be predicated of itself. The discovery that this assumption is false is by no means a small advance in philosophy. It is taken for true by Socrates and Protagoras in the *Protagoras* (330C).

Is there such a thing as justice or not? I think there is. What do you think?—I think so too, he said.—What then? If someone asked you and me, 'Protagoras and Socrates, tell me, this thing you just mentioned, justice, is it itself just or unjust?', I should answer him that it is just. And how would you vote? The same as I or different?—The same, he said.—Then justice is such as to be just, I should say in reply to the inquirer; and you would too?—Yes, he said.—If he then asked us, 'Do you also hold that there is such a thing as holiness?', we should say yes, I think.—Yes, said he.—'And do you say that this too is some thing?' We should say yes, shouldn't we?—He agreed to this too.— 'Do you say that this thing itself is such as to be unholy or such as to be holy?' I should be annoyed at the question, I said; and I should say 'Hush, man; how could anything else be holy if holiness itself is not holy?' What about you? Wouldn't you answer so?—Certainly, he said.

Taylor finds the fallacy in the second regress-argument to be that 'Parmenides is . . . allowing himself to substitute the *symmetrical* relation "is like", "resembles", for the asymmetrical relation "is a likeness of"' (*P.'s Prm.* 26). Far from being a 'manifest subreption', this is surely a confusion into which we are all liable to fall.

The fact is that what Taylor does in his 1916 article is to point out two fallacies with great acuteness and very careful argument, and then to assume without any argument at all that Plato must not merely have seen the fallacies as clearly as Taylor did but also have thought them unlikely to puzzle any decent thinker. We tend to assume that the careful argument has somehow established the second point as well as the existence of the fallacies; but in reality the pains Taylor has to take to reveal the fallacies are a probable argument that Plato thought them serious puzzles.

When we turn to Professor Cherniss's form of the parody-theory, we find the same difficulty in determining whether he thinks that Plato considered the objections serious. Once again there is the general impression that he means that Plato considered them worthless, but once again there are one or two special statements which seem to demand the contrary. Professor Cherniss writes as follows:

Of these objections the first is a quibble made plausible by shifting from Socrates' analogy of 'the all-pervading day' to the essentially different analogy of a sail-cloth; and at the bottom of the objection lies the thesis that *Being* is indivisible. This argument is developed abstractly by the tacit predication of material qualities to abstract Ideas (e.g. any *part* of the *Idea* of equality would be *smaller* than the Idea itself and yet, by the theory, the object which has this part smaller than equality will thereby be rendered equal to something). The Ideas are, then, said to be open to the objection of an infinite regress, an objection which depends upon debasing the Idea to the level of material objects and is due primarily to a juggling of the verb 'to be'. It amounts to saying that the statement 'Smallness is smallness' is equivalent to the judgement 'An Idea exists which has the predicate small.' The same objection of an infinite regression is brought against the device of 'imitation of the Ideas by objects', and it is based upon the same fallacious degradation of the Ideas to the level of phenomena. Upon this follows a dissertation of the impossibility of any communion between the world of Ideas and that of Phenomena. This difficulty Plato always recognized and the complete solution of it has never been found. (*American Journal of Philology* LIII 135-6.)

Here a long passage, seeming to tend to the conclusion that Plato thought all the arguments worthless, is unexpectedly terminated by the statement that he thought the last of them serious and never solved it. So that we can say of Professor Cherniss, as we said of Taylor, that, *if* his theory entails that Plato considered these objections contemptible, then he can be refuted out of his own writings; and we can put to him the same difficulty as before, namely, that, by including a good argument among the bad, Plato would be destroying the force either of his parody or of his good argument. We may also urge—and this is again parallel to something we have urged about Taylor—that the fallacies Professor Cherniss finds in these objections are not, as a matter of fact, contemptible. What he well calls the 'degradation of the Ideas to the level of phenomena' is certainly present in these arguments. (It is, in fact, most crudely present in the argument he considers the best, for Parmenides' last objection reifies the Ideas by equating the Idea of knowledge with God's knowledge, by equating the relation between the Ideas of relatives with that between the relatives themselves, and by making the Idea of knowledge itself know things.) But such reification, such treatment of the universal as if it were another particular, is not a childish error. While it is easy to say that the universal is not another particular, it is not easy but impossible always to avoid treating it as if it were, always to grasp it in its peculiarity. Fresh modes of the illusion are always arising as logic advances. Nor is it the fact that even now we understand perfectly the ambiguities of the verb 'to be', so that if any argument depends on those ambiguities it must be deliberate 'juggling'. We are certain that it is ambiguous; but we shall probably never exhaust the account of how it is so, nor neutralize its power to mislead us. The truth is not exactly that the objections set out in the first part of the *Parmenides* are profound, nor that some of them have never been completely solved, but that they are difficulties which in the nature of language and thought must perpetually be rearising and reovercome.

Furthermore, surely it is the duty of all holders of the parody-theory to show in some detail what is the logical error exposed in the second part of the dialogue, and how this same error lies at the root of the arguments in the first part. We have ground for complaint against both Taylor and Professor Cherniss in this matter; for the errors they discover in the second part are not the same as those they discover in the first. Taylor tells us that in the second part

the apparently single thesis really includes two assumptions, and . . . the two are incompatible. . . . Parmenides says 'what is, is one', and in saying this he assumes two things about 'what is', (*a*) that it *is*, or is real, and (*b*) that it is a *unit*, and these two positions are incompatible. (*P.'s Prm.* 31–32.)

What is there here that we also find in the first part? Neither is there anything nor does Taylor try to show that there is anything.

Professor Cherniss describes the fallacy in the second part thus: 'This result is accomplished by a systematic abuse of εἶναι, the meaning being swung from the copulative to the existential and stress being put now on the exclusive and again on the extended meaning of the word' (op. cit. 126). He explains in a note that the copulative sense is used in Hypotheses 1, 4, 6, 8, and the existential sense in the other four. Now it is true that he tells us that there is a juggling of the verb 'to be' in the first part also. But (1) he does not explain what sort of juggling it is, nor show that out of the many ambiguities of this word Plato picks the same one to play with in the second part as he played with in the first. (2) The main fallacy that he finds in the first part has nothing to do with the verb 'to be'. It is 'the degradation of the Ideas to the level of phenomena'. This—the main fallacy of the first part—has, as far as he tells us, no counterpart in the second. How, then, can the second expose the logic of the first? There is no need for us to examine whether the holders of the parody-view analyse the fallacies correctly, as long as they themselves do not find the same fallacies in the two parts. For you do not expose one fallacy by giving an example of another.

The conclusion at which we thus arrive is that two important supporters of the parody-theory give us no good ground for abandoning our third proposition, namely, that Plato considered the objections in the first part serious but not fatal.

§ 4. PLATO NEVER ANSWERED THE ARGUMENTS

Our next proposition is that Plato never answered these serious objections in his dialogues. Now there are only two places in which readers have thought they found the answers. One is the *Sophist*'s doctrine of the communion of kinds, and the other is the second part of the *Parmenides* itself. The view that they are answered in the *Sophist* is very attractive. Socrates in his original statement of the theory of Ideas seems quite clearly to deny that they communicate with each other (*Prm.* 129E); and the *Sophist* represents the doctrine of communion as an answer to Parmenides, and Parmenides is the introducer of the objections here. Unfortunately, however, none of these objections really assumes that the Ideas do not communicate or loses its force when we make the opposite assumption. The first argument is that Socrates cannot decide which sets of Manies have a corresponding Idea: how does communion help this? The second argument is that many things cannot participate in one Idea without dividing it from itself: how does communion help this? The fourth argument is that participation cannot be imitation because that would involve an infinity of Ideas corresponding to each set to which any Idea corresponded: how does communion help this? The fifth argument is that we can never know the Ideas because we have our being toward ourselves and they have theirs toward themselves; far from denying, this argument seems to assert some sort of communion among the Ideas.

In the third argument Taylor finds a mistake exposed in the *Sophist*. The argument is that, if there must be a one wherever there is a many, then, by necessary reapplications of the same principle, there will be an infinity of ones wherever there is a many. Taylor points out that this assumes the falsehood that bigness is big, and its generalization that all universals are predicable of themselves. He then suggests that what tempts us to make this false assumption is 'the linguistic fact that we commonly use the same word "is" to symbolize both predication and identity'; but Plato saw and explained this ambiguity in the *Sophist*, 'so far as it affects the possibility of significant denial' (*Philos. St.* 50–51). Against this it must be urged that the *Sophist* does not reveal the fact that 'is' may mean either predication or identity, but at most the fact that 'is' may mean either existence or identity, which is a different ambiguity of this multisignificant word, and not one that helps to refute the third argument against the Ideas. Moreover, what leads us to the false assumption that universals are predicable of themselves is not the fact that 'is' may mean either predication or identity. Socrates does not think that 'justice is just' because he confuses it with the proposition that 'justice is justice', but because he assumes that it must be either just or unjust, because he is not keeping in mind, or has never realized, that there are predicates and subjects that cannot be synthesized in any way, either affirmatively or negatively.

It appears, then, that the *Sophist*'s doctrine that the Ideas communicate with one another, while it does contradict a part of Socrates' original statement of the theory, does not at all invalidate any part of Parmenides' criticism, because on a review of each of his arguments in turn we find that none of them assumes that the Ideas do not communicate. It further appears that, as we find this to be the fact, so we find no reason to believe that Plato himself thought otherwise.

If, instead of asking whether these arguments assume non-communion, we ask whether the doctrine of communion clears up the difficulties they put, the answer is surely negative again. The doctrine of communion does not help us to know which sets of Manies have Ideas corresponding to them, or how the Idea can be participated in without being divided, or what participation is, or how men can know the Ideas; nor is there any reason for supposing that Plato thought it did.

The other form of the view that Plato does answer these objections somewhere in the dialogues—the view, namely, that he answers them in the second part of the *Parmenides* itself—cannot be squarely met now. We have already answered one species of it, namely, the parody-theory, to this extent, that two important supporters thereof fail to exhibit the same fallacies as occurring in the two parts of the dialogue, and therefore fail to show that the second part is in fact an answer to the first. Nor do they give reasons for supposing that, although the second part does not answer the first, Plato thought it did. Other species of the view that the second part answers the first will be met later on.

But why set down objections if you are not going to set down their answers? Because it is a useful act to show men that they have something to learn and make them eager to learn it. This answer will appear in a more specialized and more convincing form when we come to say positively what really is Plato's general intention in this dialogue. But even in its present form it surely is, in view of the statement in the *Phaedrus* about committing serious thoughts to writing, quite satisfactory. That Plato never published an answer to these objections, in spite of believing them important, is not one of the mysteries of the *Parmenides*.

§ 5. THE SECOND PART DOES NOT STATE A DOCTRINE

Far more puzzling is the fact, to which I now turn, that Parmenides, after his objections to the Ideas, gives detailed instructions about method, which he apparently intends quite seriously and regards as important, and that by way of explaining this method he adds an example of it, which example seems to be perfectly absurd. Since the example is absurd, are we to understand that after all he is not serious about the method? Or should we take it the other way round, and say that, since he is serious about the method, he must have somehow intended the example to seem sensible? Or can we in any way combine into a rational whole our two first impressions (1) that he is really recommending the method, and (2) that he thinks the example ridiculous?

Let us bear in mind the following division. An example of reasoning may (1) illustrate how you ought to reason, (2) illustrate how you ought not to reason, (3) serve to prove some doctrine, or (4) serve to disprove some doctrine by showing that it leads to consequences which are not so. Or perhaps it may do more than one of these things, or a fifth.

The second and fourth alternatives are incompatible. A chain of reasoning cannot be both an example of bad reasoning and also a satisfactory reduction to absurdity of some proposition, for if the reasoning is bad the proposition has not been really shown to lead to an absurdity. It is perfectly reasonable to say to a man: 'Your own principles lead to absurdities by your own methods of reasoning.' And if this is established, we then know that *either* the man's principles are false *or* his methods of reasoning are fallacious. But we do not and cannot know, from such a demonstration, that *both* the man's principles are false *and* his methods of reasoning are fallacious. For, if his principles are false, the absurdity of the conclusions may be due merely to the falsehood of the principles, and the reasoning may be valid; while, if the reasoning is fallacious, the absurdity of the conclusions may be due merely to the invalidity of the reasoning, and the principles may be true. From these facts it follows quite rigorously that, if Plato thought his example proved both that somebody's premises were false and also that his reasoning was fallacious, Plato was mistaken. Burnet said that, 'so far as the arguments are sophistical—and one or two of them must certainly have been known by Plato to be so—that is probably quite deliberate' (*Gk. Ph.* I 263). He also said: 'The Megaric doctrine is refuted. If we postulate a One which is only one (as the Megarics did), we can say nothing whatever about it. Or if (as the Megarics also did) we identify One with Being, we shall have to predicate of it all sorts of incompatible predicates' (ibid. 272). Since these statements together imply that Plato thought he was showing that the Megarics were wrong both in their premises and in their reasoning, they attribute to him a mistake in logic. Taylor seems quite explicitly to attribute such logic to Plato:

> It should follow that the real purpose of these perplexing 'antinomies' is to expose the contradictions in which we are entangled if we commit ourselves to the premises of certain other philosophers who are the unnamed objects of Plato's criticism, and we are also permitted to suspect that the *methods* of these philosophers as well as their premises are intended to be satirized; in fact, that the *logic* which leads to the 'antinomies' is the logic of the victims rather than of their critic. (*P.'s Prm.* 8–9. His italics.)

We may begin by eliminating the third alternative. Plato is not directly stating a doctrine in the second part of the *Parmenides*. This follows both from his not being a sceptic and from the symmetry of the eight movements and from their indiscriminateness.

1. If Plato was not a sceptic and if the conclusion of the second part of the *Parmenides* is utterly sceptical and absurd, then Plato is not giving us a positive doctrine in this passage. This argument was powerfully stated by Taylor (*P.'s Prm.* 8); and little need be added to his statement here. The premiss, that Plato was not a sceptic, is an unargued postulate in this discussion. As to the other premiss, that the conclusion of the second part of the *Parmenides* is utterly sceptical and absurd, it hardly needs recommendation because it has rarely if ever been denied. Since Plato makes Parmenides and Aristotle declare that the conclusion of the first movement cannot be true (142A), it seems very unlikely that he believed the conjunctive statement of all the conclusions with which the whole illustration ends. The reason why he does not repeat this denial at the end of each of the subsequent movements is probably that, since the second movement completely contradicts the first in every particular, he thinks it now quite obvious without comment that the conclusions of these movements cannot be true. This argument by itself seems fatal to every attempt to find a positive doctrine in the second part of the *Parmenides*.

2. The second part of the *Parmenides* has an extremely symmetrical and unified character, which is perfectly obvious and obviously intentional. Parmenides is here made to draw the consequences of just two hypotheses, namely 'if there is a one' and its contradictory 'if there is no one'. The two movements thus obtained are subdivided into four by considering in each case the consequences to 'the one itself' and the consequences to 'the others'. The four movements thus obtained are subdivided into eight by taking separately the affirmative and the negative consequences in each case. Thus Plato finally has eight movements as follows.

If there is a one.
1. Negative consequences to the one.
2. Affirmative consequences to the one.
3. Affirmative consequences to the others.
4. Negative consequences to the others.

If there is no one.

5. Affirmative consequences to the one.
6. Negative consequences to the one.
7. Affirmative consequences to the others.
8. Negative consequences to the others.

(The second of these movements, which is far the longest, has a short appendix which is introduced rather as if it were a new movement (155E4); and this has led some interpreters to say that the second part of the *Parmenides* consists of nine movements, not eight.) Thus not merely does Plato present the whole eight movements as constituting one single example of the method, but he balances them against one another by three different interlacing principles, according as the hypothesis is affirmative or negative, as its results are affirmative or negative, and as we consider its results to the one or to the others. There is only enough disproportion to prevent the symmetry from becoming insipid and dragging. At the end of the fourth movement, though there is some doubt about the text, he appears to sum up the conclusions of all four as if they were to be taken as one. Anyhow it is certain that at the end of the last movement he states all the results together in one compound proposition. In view of this thoroughly unified symmetry Plato cannot have meant us to pick out some of these movements as giving his doctrine and to reject the rest; and no claim to find positive doctrine in this illustration of method has much right to a hearing until it is ready to say how we are to understand *all* the movements. But, if we look at the interpreters who have actually thought they saw a positive doctrine in the second part of the *Parmenides*, we discover, as far as I have read them, that none of them except Cornford finds a positive doctrine in each of the movements. They all either say, or suggest by silence, that only in some of them is Plato giving us his doctrine. For example, Jackson found that Plato gives us his own views in movements 2 and 3; but in the others he develops the consequences of four other views (*JP*, vol. xi, summarized on p. 324); Mr. Hardie finds a positive doctrine in the first two movements and is silent about the rest. From one point of view these interpreters are wise in their procedure, for it seems impossible to imagine how Plato could have been conveying positive doctrine in all eight movements or even in any three of them. Yet surely the symmetry of these movements, and the equality with which they are all presented, compel us to find a positive doctrine in all of them if we find it in any. This argument also seems to be conclusive by itself.

3. Taylor pointed to the indiscriminateness of the conclusions drawn from the hypotheses, indiscriminate assertion in four of the movements and indiscriminate denial in the other four. The movements with affirmative results attribute all possible predicates to their subjects, whether those subjects exist or not; the movements with negative results deny all possible predicates of their subjects. Every one of the eight includes in principle all possible predicates. It is surely inconceivable that Plato meant us to find a positive doctrine here. This argument also seems to be conclusive by itself.

Let us examine in detail one particular claim to find positive doctrine in this illustration, that of Mr. Hardie. He first tells us (W. F. R. Hardie, *A Study in Plato* 101) that the original hypothesis is raised in two forms, (1) if it is one (εἰ ἕν ἐστιν), and (2) if one *is* (ἕν εἰ ἔστιν), the difference between them being made explicit at the beginning of the second statement of the hypothesis (142C). A dozen pages later he states the doctrine thus:

Both the One which is one and the One which exists have a real reference. The former, which is not a whole of parts and is 'beyond' all predicates (cf. Proclus *in Rem Pub.* i. 285), refers to the One which is identified (by Plato, as we shall see) with the Good. To it may be applied the words of Bradley when he speaks of his Absolute as being 'too rich not too poor for division of its elements'. On the other hand, the second hypothesis refers to what is one in a lower or derivative sense; the unity of the object of scientific intelligence, and even of opinion, a one-many which 'communicates' with other forms and is participated in by things. This unity is not the unity of the supremely real but of that which, in the language of Neoplatonism, 'emanates' from the One. Mind and its objects 'proceed' from the One, just as, in Plato's simile, the seeing eye and the seen colour depend upon the transcendent source of all illumination. Thus, for this view, the hypotheses of the *Parmenides* offer a condensed statement of the logical basis of the metaphysics which the *Republic* conveys by the well-known simile of the sun.

What does Mr. Hardie do about the three powerful arguments mentioned above against his type of view? About the argument from the fact that Plato was not a sceptic, taken as a whole, he does nothing at all; and this may give us some confidence in rejecting his view. He does, however, consider one sentence which supports this general argument, namely, that at the end of the first movement when Parmenides suggests and Aristotle agrees that these things cannot be so. He writes as follows:

As the answers are throughout dictated by the questions, it can hardly be argued that not 'Parmenides' but 'the youngest present' rejects as 'impossible' the conclusions of the first hypothesis. But the passage is not unnatural on the transcendentalist view, if we remember the double purpose which the view attributes to the hypotheses. It is impossible to accept the first hypothesis, without the further qualification supplied by the second, as what is true about 'that which is one'. To rest in it without attempting to 'view the matter otherwise' would be to adopt a position hard to distinguish from that of the 'beginners and late learners' in the *Sophist* (251ᵇ). It would render all predicates and thought impossible; but predication and thought are facts and these facts require, for their interpretation, the logic of intercommunicating forms. Thus the first hypothesis is not true in general of what is one, but only of one One. (Op. cit. 116.)

This seems a very weak defence. Surely the plain sense of Plato's statement is that the consequences drawn in the first movement are not and cannot be true. Surely any other reading of the passage *is* 'unnatural' and could be justified only if required by a theory of the *Parmenides* for which there was strong independent evidence. But Mr. Hardie's theory of this part of the *Parmenides* does *not* possess strong independent evidence, as I hope to show; and, as I hope I have shown, it *does* possess grave disadvantages.

Mr. Hardie does even less about the symmetry-argument than about the scepticism-argument. He does not notice it at all; and he appears to give us no hint how we are to understand the last six movements. (He does, in the passage quoted on p. 243, speak of 'the hypotheses of the *Parmenides*' as if he had told us how to understand them all; but he has not. Perhaps the words 'first two' háve fallen out here.) Nor does he take any notice of the argument from the indiscriminateness of all the movements.

Thus we see that Mr. Hardie by no means meets any one of these three arguments for holding that Plato is not offering us a doctrine in the second part of the *Parmenides*. But, apart from meeting objections, what positive evidence has he for his view? It seems to fall into three groups. First comes the supposed differ-

ence in meaning between the hypotheses of the first two movements. Second comes what can be inferred from the passage on
method which constitutes an introduction to the eight movements. Third come the superessentiality of the Good in the
Republic and any other evidence for Neo-Platonic views in Plato.

1. Mr. Hardie finds a confirmation of his views in the fact that,
as he says, 'the original hypothesis is raised in two forms: (1) if it
is one (εἰ ἕν ἐστιν), and (2) if one is (ἓν εἰ ἔστιν)' (op. cit. 101–2).
The difference, he says, is made explicit at the beginning of the
second statement of the hypothesis. Parmenides there says that
'we are asking now what must follow' from the hypothesis not
that the one is one, but that the one *is* (142C). And 'if the one
is' is explained as meaning 'if the one participates in Being'
(οὐσίας μετέχει). Mr. Hardie thinks that this implies that the first
movement refers to a one beyond being.

Presumably Mr. Hardie does not infer this distinction from the
difference of the first two hypotheses in word-order, from the fact
that in the statement of the first hypothesis εἰ precedes ἕν, whereas
in the statement of the second ἕν precedes εἰ. We are prevented
from supposing that Plato meant the word-order to signify any
difference by the fact that the second hypothesis is stated in both
orders, first as ἓν εἰ ἔστιν and then as εἰ ἓν ἔστιν (142B3, 142C3).
But, even if we overlooked this point, or supposed Plato to have
made a slip here, we should still be much at a loss to give any
significance to the word-order; for inspection reveals that (excluding the third statement of the second hypothesis in 142C3)
εἰ precedes ἕν in the first and fifth movements, and ἕν precedes εἰ
in all the others. It would be specially hard to give any meaning
to this because, whereas the first movement is negative in its
results, the fifth is affirmative.

However, it is not at all likely that Mr. Hardie thinks the word-
order significant. Does he perhaps rely to some extent on the
accentuation? The word ἐστι is in general paroxytone when it is
existential in meaning, and oxytone or without accent when it is
copulative. But when preceded by εἰ or by μή it is always paroxytone, whatever its meaning (M. W. Chandler, *Greek Accentuation*
(2nd ed.) 267). Now it is preceded by either εἰ or μή in every one
of the eight movements except in the first movement and in the
third statement of the hypothesis in the second movement (142C3).
A criterion which fails in three quarters of the cases does not seem

a good one to rely on; but the really fatal argument against any inference from accents is that Plato did not know of their existence and hence could not use them to convey his meaning. He wrote to be intelligible without them, and they only represent a later reader's interpretation of his meaning.

Since neither the word-order nor the accentuation can be significant, there remains only the context to determine whether Plato made any distinction of meaning in the hypotheses. Mr. Hardie finds that Plato explicitly makes such a distinction at the beginning of the second movement. Plato's words are these: νῦν δὲ οὐχ αὕτη ἐστὶν ἡ ὑπόθεσις, εἰ ἓν ἕν, τί χρή συμβαίνειν, ἀλλ' εἰ ἓν ἔστιν (142C). I venture to suggest that Mr. Hardie has misunderstood this passage. Why does he assume that the hypothesis which Plato expresses with the words εἰ ἓν ἕν is identical with the hypothesis of the first movement, which Plato called εἰ ἓν ἔστιν? Surely this hypothesis, εἰ ἓν ἕν, is mentioned only in this passage, being momentarily introduced in order to bring out by contrast something in the hypothesis that *is* being examined. It is not any one of the eight hypotheses from which consequences are inferred in the eight sections. If it were it would have contained, as they all do, the word ἐστιν. It follows that Mr. Hardie is mistaken in supposing that Plato is here telling us how the hypothesis of the first movement differs from that of the second. He is not talking about the first hypothesis at all, but elucidating the second by distinguishing it from a third mentioned only for this purpose. Mr. Hardie takes νῦν as meaning 'in the present movement'. That is, in general, a possible meaning; but in this particular context it must mean 'actually' or 'as things are', in contrast with the imaginary state of affairs suggested in the previous sentence.

Mr. Hardie does not appeal to any other passage as evidence for his view that Plato intends a difference between the hypotheses of the first two movements. The only argument that now remains in favour of it is the general impression, if any, that we receive from the two movements. But an inspection of these two movements does not reveal any such difference. Their symmetrical indiscriminateness seems to be crowned by a complete indifference of their hypotheses. Furthermore, the opening sentence of the second movement seems to imply that the hypothesis now to be discussed is the very same as that discussed in the first movement: 'Are you willing that we go back again to the hypothesis from the beginning, in case something different appears to us to be the truth when we go back?' (142B1).

2. His argument from the passage of transition between the two main parts of the dialogue is that this passage 'is calculated to lead us to expect that the second part of the dialogue will throw some real light on the difficulties which have been raised in the first' (op. cit. 100). It is so calculated; but stating a positive doctrine is not the only means of throwing light, and the passage itself implies that this is not the means Parmenides is going to adopt. He is going to help Socrates out of these perplexities, not by giving him a doctrine, but by teaching him a method and exercising him therein. When Socrates can handle the method skilfully he will be able to chop his own way out of the tangle. Parmenides is not chopping a path for him, but giving him an axe.

3. Mr. Hardie calls our attention to the facts that Plato identified the One with the Good, and said in the *Republic* that the Good is beyond Being. He points also to some other passages that might be Neo-Platonist. But he admits that they are 'inconclusive' and that the *Republic*'s implication that the Good is the supreme object of intelligence is not the Neo-Platonic doctrine that the Good can be known only by an immediate contact which transcends intelligence (op. cit. 118–19). We surely must allow that this evidence gives only a faint degree of probability. Even if the whole of Plotinus were actually to be read in some dialogue of Plato (excepting his professed interpretations of Plato), that still would not be good evidence that Plato's *Parmenides* referred to the One and its first emanation. The few resemblances that we actually have cannot stand against any good argument to the contrary; and that we have good arguments to the contrary has been shown. This completes my examination of Mr. Hardie's view.

I have eliminated the alternative that the second part of the *Parmenides* is a direct statement of doctrine. I can now eliminate more briefly the possibility of its being an indirect statement of doctrine, that is to say, of its proving some proposition by reducing its contradictory to absurdity. This follows from the fact that the illustration takes two contradictory hypotheses, 'if the one exists' and 'if the one does not exist', and reduces them both to absurdity. If the example had ended with the fourth movement, we might have thought that Plato was establishing indirectly the

proposition that the one does not exist. But he disproves that
proposition too.

§ 6. THE SECOND PART DOES NOT STATE A METHOD

The second part of the *Parmenides*, then, is not a statement of
doctrine, either directly or indirectly. Is it a direct or indirect
statement of method? There is one extremely good reason for
holding it to be a direct statement of method, a straightforward
example of a method that Plato recommends us to practise, and
this is that Plato makes Parmenides deliberately and seriously
introduce it as such. The transitional passage says, with every
appearance of earnestness, that Socrates' difficulties about the
Forms are due to his want of training. Parmenides prescribes for
him a training which he defines as Zeno's procedure with certain
modifications. He then gives the illustration.

The second part of the *Parmenides* certainly does illustrate
(whether well or badly may be a question) the procedure of
getting oneself into a better position to judge whether a proposition is true by ascertaining its consequences; and it also certainly
illustrates (whether well or badly may again be a question) the
procedure of ascertaining both its own consequences and those
of its contradictory. To this extent the illustration really does
illustrate what it is said to; and the theory that the second part
of the *Parmenides* is a direct statement of method is correct.

Yet there are also extremely grave difficulties in saying that the
second part of the *Parmenides* is a model of reasoning which Plato
meant us to copy. They are as follows:

1. The example seems bewildering and absurd. We can hardly
believe that it would really put Socrates in the way of escaping his
former bewilderment.

2. Even in the apparently serious introduction Parmenides once
refers to the example as 'play' (137B). An example held up for
imitation to all who profess the serious business of philosophy
does not seem naturally described as 'play'.

3. There seem to be some rather crass sophisms in the example,
which Plato apparently must have intended as such. Interpreters
differ greatly whether the movements are fallacious in the large
and radically; but most are agreed that there are one or two
apparently wilful sophisms of detail. For example, Plato surely
must have believed that there was something wrong with this:

The one will not be the same as itself.—Why not?—Because the nature of the one is, of course, not also the nature of the same.—How so?—Because a thing does not become one whenever it becomes the same as something else.—What then?—If it becomes the same as the many it must become many and not one.—True.—But if the one and the same are in no way different, whenever anything became the same it would always become one, and whenever one, the same.—Certainly.—If therefore the one is to be the same to itself, it will not be one to itself; and so being one it will not be one. But this is impossible; and so it is impossible for the one to be either other than an other or the same as itself. (139DE.)

Again, Plato surely believed that there was something wrong with this:

Since we found it different from the others, the others would surely be different from it.—Of course.—It would be just as different from the others as they from it, and neither more nor less?—Obviously.— If then neither more nor less, equally.—Yes.—Then in that it was of a nature different from the others and the others were of a nature different from it in the same way, in this way the one would be the same as the others and the others the same as the one. (147C.)

In the subsequent fuller statement of this fallacy Plato probably knew that he was crassly overlooking the possibility of ambiguity when he said: 'Whether you utter the same word once or many times, you must always mean the same thing.' He probably saw that this fallacy of division is a fallacy: 'If any thing were a part of many things among which was itself, it will of course be a part of itself, which is impossible, and of each one of the others, since it is a part of all' (157CD).

These are all very minor parts of the argument; but it is a strange procedure to introduce even a single rusted link into a chain on which you advise men to depend.

4. It seems very probable that Plato held the combined conclusion of the first four movements to be false, since it is clearly an absurd proposition, and he suggests that the conclusion of the first movement by itself is false. The hypothesis of these first four movements is 'if there is a one'. Therefore if Plato had thought the reasoning of these movements valid, he would have thought that he had disproved the hypothesis that there is a one. But now it also seems probable that Plato held the combined conclusion of the second set of four movements to be false, since this too is

clearly an absurd proposition, and essentially the same absurd proposition. But the hypothesis of the second four movements is 'if there is no one'. Therefore if Plato had thought the reasoning of those movements valid, he would have thought that he had disproved the hypothesis that there is no one. Thus he would have thought that the eight movements together disproved both the hypothesis that there is a one and the hypothesis that there is no one. But surely he thought that these two hypotheses are contradictories one of which must be true. Therefore he did not think all the reasoning valid.

5. We have adopted with reason the view that Plato believed the arguments in the first part of the *Parmenides* to be invalid, although by no means crassly so. We shall, therefore, be giving some unity to our interpretation if we also hold that he considered those of the second part invalid, though not always crassly so.

For these reasons it is necessary to eliminate the attractive idea that the second part is meant to be a model for our reasoning; and to hold the somewhat difficult view that, while the introduction does seem to promise us a model for our reasoning, while the example does illustrate the precept there given that we should examine the consequences of our hypotheses, while it does illustrate the other precept that we should examine also the consequences of their contradictories, it nevertheless did not seem to Plato valid reasoning. The nature of the introduction to the second part forces this conclusion on every interpreter who refuses to say that Plato thought the second part valid reasoning.

There is only one alternative left of the four we enumerated above, namely that this example is an indirect statement of method, a proof of the fallaciousness of a certain kind of reasoning by showing that it leads to all possible conclusions, whatever premises it starts from. On this hypothesis Plato must have thought the passage contained a fallacy other than those minor and crass examples previously mentioned. Let us, therefore, see what pervasive fallacies we can discover.

It is not at all easy to say what fallacies occur in the second part of the *Parmenides*, unless we content ourselves with very vague language. It would be true to say that practically every invalid inference here is made possible by an ambiguity. As in the *Euthydemus* and the *Sophist*, Plato here shows us vague and formal terms, such as 'one' and 'same' and 'other', being used abstractly and absolutely, without the definite references that alone can make them serviceable, and so permitting many strange and subtle ambiguities. His hypothesis itself is most remarkably vague. Among the conceivable translations into English are these: 'If everything is one', 'If it is one', 'If a one exists', 'If unity exists'. Translators find themselves obliged to give different renderings in different places. On reflection we may well be amazed that, given such a cryptic and ambiguous phrase, anyone should immediately infer consequences therefrom, and not rather ask himself what it means. This readiness to infer consequences from sentences which, because they take relative words absolutely and syntactical devices as names of things, are nearly empty of meaning and may be filled with whatever the momentary context suggests, is what people are condemning when they talk contemptuously of 'dialectic'.

So much may safely be said about the fallacies; but when we try to say precisely what these ambiguities are we step on to much more treacherous ground. It seems impossible to find any single ambiguity that makes possible the whole set of inferences. We have already seen that some links in the chains are quite special and isolated fallacies; and we may now add that this is particularly so in the movements that have affirmative conclusions. Plato seems to be able to base his negative inferences on a single error, notably the fourth and the eighth; but in the affirmative inferences he seems obliged to snatch at any and every fallacy in turn in order to reach the symmetrical conclusions he requires, especially in the fifth.

The syntactical forms 'X is Y' and 'X is not Y' may mean either identity and non-identity or attribution and non-attribution. 'The ruler of England in 1707 was Queen Anne' states an identity; but 'The ruler of England in 1707 was feminine' states an attribution. There are places in the second part of the *Parmenides* where it seems fairly probable that the conclusion is obtained by assuming the equivalence of non-identity and non-attribution, an assumption made easy by the fact that syntax does not always distinguish them. This is perhaps most likely in the fourth movement, which seems to be as a whole the argument that, since the others-than-the-one are not the one (non-identity), therefore they have no attributes that would entail their being in any way one (non-attribution). The whole of the first movement, moreover, gets its persuasiveness in part from the fact that unity is not identical with anything but unity. This tautology is represented by the ambiguity of language as the important discovery that nothing can be predicated of unity or the one. The same fallacy seems to occur in some of the affirmative movements too, though less pervasively. Thus in the second movement we read the phrase, 'The others-than-the-one neither are one nor share in it, since they are other' (149C), which is a neat example because here non-identity and non-attribution are stated side by side. Taylor finds this ambiguity in the first regress-argument in the first part of the dialogue (*Philos. St.* 50–51).

This is not to say that Plato himself never saw any difference between identity and attribution. On the contrary, he distinguished in the *Sophist* (245A) between being one (πάθος μὲν τοῦ ἑνὸς ἔχειν) and being unity (αὐτό γε τὸ ἓν αὐτὸ εἶναι); and in the *Parmenides* itself (158A) he says: 'Nothing but the one itself can be one. . . . But the whole and the part must *share in* the one.' It is to say that both in the *Parmenides* and in the *Sophist* (e.g. 244BC, 250) he sets before us arguments that fallaciously overlook this distinction, and that he himself was habitually entangled in at least one form of the fallacy in his theory of Ideas.

Another ambiguity seems to pervade the second part of the *Parmenides*, namely, the confusion between an adjective and a substantive considered as characterized by that adjective. This is most obvious in the two phrases 'the one' and 'the others'. Do these mean unity and otherness? If so, they are only two out of innumerable entities that may be discovered in the universe. Or do they mean, on the one hand, some substance which is called the one because it is characterized by the adjective unity and, on the other hand, everything else in the universe? If so, they together exhaust the universe. They mean sometimes the first and sometimes the second. They must mean the second, for example, at the beginning of the fourth movement, when Parmenides explicitly says that besides the one and the others there is nothing whatever. Yet if the one is some substance characterized by unity in the movements that deal solely with the one, we cannot tell any more about it than the fact, from which we start, that it is one. And it is clear that in the first movement, at any rate, Parmenides' inferences seem plausible because we take his one not as a substance that has unity but as the adjective unity. Every time he mentions the one we take his sentence in the way that makes it most probable; and we do not notice the ambiguity because of the subtlety and strangeness of the distinction between a thing that is characterized by unity and the unity that characterizes it.

Perhaps these two forms of ambiguity are ultimately identical. Anyhow, there seems to be a close connexion in the *Parmenides* between confusing an adjective with the substantive characterized thereby and confusing non-identity with non-attribution. Parmenides seems often to start from the truth that Xness is not Yness, infer that Xness is not Y, and infer, thence, that the thing that is X is not Y. In this process the first step uses the confusion between non-identity and non-attribution; and the second uses the confusion between the adjective and the substantive it characterizes.

What we call 'reification' is perhaps a third aspect of the same ambiguity. Plato's theory of Ideas makes universals into things, because it confuses them with perfect particulars. It fails to distinguish between circularity and the perfect circle, and so the idea becomes a thing as the perfect circle is a thing, the example or paradigm that all other circles should follow. This is to make an adjective into a substantive characterized by that adjective.

The term 'other' is obviously relative. It applies to everything relatively to something. It is, as Plato expresses it in the *Sophist*, one of those kinds that communicate with all other kinds. It is, in medieval language, a transcendental, an attribute that transcends all categories and belongs to everything there is. The term 'one' is also a transcendental. It is selfcontradictory to assume, of any conceivable object or objects, that it or they are in no way one. The hypothesis of the last four movements, that the one is not, is therefore selfcontradictory, if taken to mean that nothing is in any way one; and you can infer everything from it if you can infer anything. It may be that this is part of the explanation of those movements. It may be, also, that Parmenides obtains many of his conclusions by shifting from the transcendence of the adjectives one and other to the departmentalness of some vaguely substantival one and substantival others. It may be, again, that he uses an ambiguity by which one may mean either a transcendental adjective something like unifiedness or a departmental adjective something like 'without parts'. I have not, however, succeeded in isolating clear cases of these ambiguities anywhere in the argument.

An apparently quite distinct type of fallacy is the assumption that one of a set of adjectives must apply to a given subject, when in truth none applies; for example, that the one must be greater or less or equal, and that it must be in motion or at rest. This assumption made, it is possible to prove that one of the set applies by showing that the others do not. The fallacy is particularly bad when the argument by which we eliminate the other alternatives is an argument which, rightly understood, eliminates the whole set. If the only possible cases of P are p_1 and p_2, and we prove that X is not p_1 by an argument which really shows that X is not P, we have no right to conclude that X is p_2. This perhaps often occurs in the second part of the *Parmenides*; and there seems a clear case at 161C. Here considerations which really prove, if anything, that the one is neither equal nor unequal are used to prove that it is not equal and therefore unequal.

Moreover it is not equal to the others; for if it were equal, it would be; and it would be like them in virtue of its equality. But these are both impossible, if one is not.—Impossible.—And since it is not equal to the others, must not the others also be not equal to it?—They must. —And is not what is not equal unequal?—Yes.—And is not the unequal unequal to something unequal?—Of course.—So the one shares in inequality, with regard to which the others are unequal to it. (161CD.)

This review of the fallacies in the second part of the *Parmenides*, uncertain as it is, seems more probable than any attempt to point to one single pervasive fallacy. We need not insist upon its details, but only upon the general assertion that there is more than one major fallacy present. Even if, as suggested, the confusion between identity and attribution is not really distinct from that between the adjective and the substantive which it characterizes, a diversity of fallacies remains. For besides this there is the assumption that one of a set of adjectives must apply to a given subject when in truth none applies, and the treatment of transcendentals as departmentals, and various minor invalidities.

The conclusion that there is more than one major fallacy in the second part of the *Parmenides* renders improbable the suggestion that this passage is an indirect statement of method, a proof of the fallaciousness of a certain kind of reasoning by showing that it leads to all possible conclusions whatever premises it starts from.

For anyone who wished to defend one of these ways of reasoning could argue that the absurdity was due only to the other fallacies; and Plato would have weakened his case against one and all of them by introducing the others. We should hardly care to evade this conclusion by holding that Plato saw only one of the fallacies and thought the rest valid reasoning. Nor does it seem possible to make out that there is never more than one major fallacy in the same movement. But, before finally rejecting the view that this part of the *Parmenides* is meant to be an indirect statement of method, let us examine two attractive forms in which this view has been held.

First comes Professor Cherniss's belief that the passage contains throughout only one major fallacy. He writes as follows:

> This result is accomplished by a systematic abuse of εἶναι, the meaning being swung from the copulative to the existential and stress being put now on the exclusive and again on the extended meaning of the word.
>
> Εἶναι in the copulative sense in A1, 4, B2, 4, in the existential sense in A2, 3, B1, 3.
>
> There are other sources of fallacy which appear sporadically, e.g. the juggling of ἕτερον and ἄλλο in 164B ff. (*AJP* LIII 126.)

Professor Cherniss does not go into further detail about this fallacy. He does not, for example, take the first movement and show us just how it uses the copulative–existential ambiguity of 'is' to obtain its strange conclusion. The implication of the passage quoted seems to be that 'is' is used unambiguously in the copulative sense throughout the first movement, unambiguously in the existential sense throughout the second and third movements, unambiguously in the copulative sense throughout the fourth movement, and so on. In other words, that it is used unambiguously in the copulative sense throughout all the movements that reach negative results, and unambiguously in the existential sense throughout all those that reach affirmative results.

If we take this interpretation of Professor Cherniss's view, according to which there is no ambiguity within each movement itself but only when two movements are added together, it ought to follow that, apart from minor or unintentional fallacies, each movement by itself is valid and reaches true results; that only when we add together the results of the affirmative and the negative movements do we get a falsehood. But this consequence cannot be accepted; for each of the affirmative movements taken by itself leads, roughly speaking, to the conclusion that the one is (or the others are) everything; and each of the negative movements to the conclusion that the one is (or the others are) nothing. Each of these results by itself is absurd; and Plato must have thought so; and he says at the end of the first movement that he thinks that result absurd.

Leaving now this special interpretation of Professor Cherniss, which is likely to be wrong, let us turn to the general nature of his view, which is quite unmistakably that the fallacy in the second part of the *Parmenides* is first and foremost the ambiguity of the copulative and the existential senses of 'is'. It is very difficult to speak with any confidence about the nature of the invalidity of these arguments; but to the best of my judgement the fallacies are not this but such as I have described above. Professor Cherniss is right in finding an ambiguity of εἶναι here; but it is the confusion between the identifying and the attributive uses, not between the existential and the copulative. Furthermore, it is by no means the sole important fallacy here. And the fallacies here are by no means contemptible, but extremely difficult both to locate and to describe and to avoid.

The other special form which we may examine of the view that the second part of the *Parmenides* is an indirect statement of method is that which finds here an indirect statement of the doctrine of Communion put directly in the *Sophist*. It is attractive to suppose that this part of the *Parmenides* reaches its absurd results by a method which assumes that the doctrine of Communion is false; and then the *Sophist*, by establishing this doctrine, gives the reason for the fact already demonstrated as a fact by the *Parmenides*, that this method is unreliable. This supposition gives good sense to Parmenides' extraordinary 'jest' and neatly links the dialogue with one composed at a comparatively near date. It gains support from the fact that Socrates appears to deny Communion in his original statement of his theory of Ideas in the *Parmenides* (129DE):

If therefore anyone tries to show that such things are both one and many, stones and planks and the like, we shall say that he demonstrates something to be one and many, but not the one to be many or the many to be one, and that he is not saying anything astonishing, but what we should all admit. But if anyone first distinguishes apart by themselves those forms of which I was now speaking, such as likeness and unlikeness and multitude and the one and rest and motion and all such, and then shows that they are capable of mixing and separating among themselves, I should marvel extremely.

As further evidence for the supposition that the second part of the *Parmenides* is an indirect statement of the doctrine of Communion, we may note this fact. Plato says (*Sph.* 251) that his doctrine of Communion is (among other things) a refutation of the view that we can only say 'man is man' and cannot also say 'man is good'. Now why should anyone feel himself driven to the paradoxical view that you cannot say 'man is good (or bad or tall or white or anything else)' but only 'man is man'? Surely because he has failed to distinguish attribution from identification, and is therefore compelled to suppose that 'man is good' asserts the identity of two things, whereas in reality it asserts that one of two non-identical things characterizes the other. But this confusion between attribution and identification is the very fallacy which, according to our previous analysis, appears most pervasively in the second part of the *Parmenides*. Is it not probable, then, that this confusion is the subject of both dialogues? The *Parmenides* shows to what havoc the confusion leads; the *Sophist* shows just what the confusion is.

Perhaps someone might reply that the *Sophist's* doctrine of Communion is intended to clear up the puzzles about being and non-being developed in the *Sophist* itself (241–51), so that we have no reason for referring it to a previous work. But to this we could answer that the confusion between identification and attribution is probably the main source of the *Sophist's* difficulties also. For example, what the stranger represents as the limit of perplexity in 250 is apparently nothing but the argument that, since Reality is not identical with Motion or Rest, therefore Reality neither moves nor rests. Thus, both in the second part of the *Parmenides* and in the aporematic part of the *Sophist*, Plato would be playing with this ambiguity; and in the doctrine of Communion he would be sterilizing it for good and all.

Here is another argument in favour of the view that the second part of the *Parmenides* is an indirect statement of the doctrine of Communion. At the end of the discussion of Communion in the

Sophist there is a passage that reads like a criticism of the second part of the *Parmenides*.

If anyone disbelieves these oppositions, let him inquire and say something better than has now been said. Or if he thinks he has discovered something difficult, and takes pleasure in dragging an argument now to this side and now to that, he is being earnest about what is not worth much earnestness, according to our present arguments. For there is nothing clever or hard to discover in this. It is that that is both hard and fine.

What?

What was said before, to let these things go and be able to follow what is said and examine each detail, both when a man says that what is other is in some way the same and when that what is the same is other, in that mode and that respect in which he says either of them to be so. But to show that the same is other in some sort of way, and the other the same and the great small and the like unlike, and to enjoy thus constantly producing contradictions in discussion—this is no true examination, but the manifest immaturity of someone who has only just begun to grasp reality.

Quite.

Why, my dear man, this trying to separate everything from everything is completely boorish and unphilosophic and unbecoming in every way.

Of course.

Isolating each thing from all things is the most complete destruction of all discussion; for it is the interweaving of the forms with each other that gives us speech. (*Sph.* 259.)

This passage seems to fit very well the affirmative movements of the *Parmenides*, in which every predicate is indiscriminately affirmed of the subject, and the negative movements, in which every predicate is indiscriminately denied thereof. And we seem to be told that such activities involve a failure to respect the Communion of Kinds.

Yet the supposition that the second part of the *Parmenides* is an indirect statement of the *Sophist*'s doctrine of Communion, and the arguments that have been suggested in its favour, seem too vague to be convincing; and if we try to make them more precise they seem to break down. Here follow five arguments for the proposition that Plato did not regard the second part of the *Parmenides* as an illustration of what happens if you deny Communion.

1. We have seen reason to believe that there is more than one fallacy in this part of the *Parmenides*. If this is so, it is far from clear how the doctrine of Communion could dispose of the whole paradox. Surely it could dispose of only one, or of a related group. The rest would remain unsolved—an unsatisfactory state of affairs—unless we could find that Plato dealt with them elsewhere.

2. The doctrine of Communion is not merely the doctrine that Kinds 'communicate'. It is also the doctrine that Kinds do not 'communicate'. It is the denial of the two universal statements: (1) that every Kind communicates with every other Kind and (2) that no Kind communicates with any other Kind; and the assertion of their two contradictories: some pairs of Kinds communicate and others do not. If, therefore, the second part of the *Parmenides* contravenes this doctrine, it must do so by assuming either that no Kind communicates with any other Kind, or that every Kind communicates with every other Kind, or both. Now it will have to be both, for the results of the affirmative movements affirm certain cases of Communion, and the results of the negative movements deny certain cases thereof. On the theory, then, that the second part of the *Parmenides* is an indirect statement of the doctrine of Communion, we should have to say that the affirmative movements assume that every Kind communicates with every Kind and the negative movements assume that no Kind communicates with any Kind. If we do not say *at least one of these*, we shall not make the second part of the *Parmenides* contradict the doctrine; for the doctrine is precisely the compound assertion of the two contradictories of these two universal statements. And if we do not say *both of these*, we shall have no explanation either of all the affirmative or of all the negative movements. But when the theory that the second part of *Parmenides* is an indirect recommendation of the doctrine of Communion is thus made precise, it loses all the attraction it had in its vague form. We can find no evidence that the affirmative movements assume that *all* Kinds communicate; but, if fewer than all, the doctrine is not denied. And we can find no evidence that the negative movements assume that *no* Kinds communicate; but, if at least one pair is exempted from the assumption, the doctrine is not denied.

It might have been the case that a mistake was revealed in the

Parmenides, not by the *Sophist*'s general doctrine of Communion, but by one or more of the particular Communions which it establishes. Examination seems to show, however, that this is not the case either. The particular Communions which the *Sophist* establishes are, first, that Rest and Motion do not communicate with each other; and, second, that Being, Same, Other (and Not-being, if Plato regards that as distinct from Other), all communicate with everything. Here we note first that nothing is said about Unity or the One, although that seems the obvious Kind to discuss if you are going to expose a mistake in the *Parmenides*. Next we note that, since Motion and Rest are of very minor importance in the *Parmenides*, no doctrine about them in particular could clear up the errors of this dialogue. There remain Being, Same, Other (Not-being); and what we are told about them is that each of them communicates with every other Kind. Now about this information it can only be said that no one has yet shown *how* it reveals, either directly or indirectly, the fallacy in the *Parmenides*, and it may be doubted whether anyone ever will.

3. The doctrine of Communion is itself entangled in one of the major fallacies of the second part of the *Parmenides*, namely, the confusion between the adjective and the substantive characterized thereby. For let us ask whether by the proposition that 'X communicates with Y' Plato means that 'the adjective Xness is characterized by the adjective Yness' or that 'some or all substantives characterized by the adjective Xness are also characterized by the adjective Yness'. We are obliged to answer that he means both because he fails to distinguish them.

Here is the evidence that the Communion of X and Y sometimes means that a substantive characterized by Xness is also characterized by Yness.

A. The doctrine of Communion is represented as refuting the contention of certain 'late learners' that you must not say that 'man is good'. What sorts of proposition did these late learners think they were rejecting? Surely not the uncommon sort of proposition that attributes an adjective to an adjective, such as 'Manness is good'. Surely their delight and their absurdity came from their paradoxically denying the validity of all the most ordinary statements, such as 'Socrates is good'. The doctrine of Communion must therefore maintain that you can sometimes attribute an adjective to a substantive characterized by another adjective; otherwise it would be irrelevant as a reply to the 'late learners'.

B. The doctrine of Communion is represented as making possible certain physical doctrines:

And those who at one time put all things together and at another separate them, whether they put them together into one and separate an infinity out of one, or separate them into limited elements and put them together out of these, and whether they make this happen by turns or all the time—in any case they would be talking nonsense, if there is no mixing. (*Sph.* 252.)

If Plato is thinking of physical theories here, as he seems to be, his doctrine of Communion must include the proposition that sometimes *a substantive* characterized by Xness is also characterized by Yness; for propositions that were only about the characters of characters would not affect the proposition that physical things join and separate.

On the other hand, there are also two convincing evidences that in his notion of Communion Plato included such propositions as that 'Xness is Y'. (A) He describes it as holding between Kinds or γένη (e.g. 253B8), not between things or ὄντα. And γένη are apparently the same as εἴδη (254C2). (B) His proof that not everything communicates with everything is to appeal to Motion and Rest, a pair which he declares evidently do not communicate. Now he realized well enough, as his reference to spinning tops in the *Republic* shows, that a substantive somehow characterized by the adjective 'moving' may at the same time be somehow characterized by the adjective 'resting'. He is not denying this familiar fact. He is denying, as he explicitly says, that 'Motion itself' could rest (252D6). That is, he is denying that the adjective 'moving' could be characterized by the adjective 'resting'.

The above considerations make it clear that Plato's Communion includes both the case where an adjective is characterized by another adjective and the case where a substantive characterized by an adjective is also characterized by another adjective. It not merely includes them but confuses them. That it does so is another manifestation of the permanent failure of the theory of Ideas to distinguish between universals and perfect particulars. This is why Communion can include physical mixture, as it seems to do in 252B. If universals are treated as things, their mixture is the same as the mixture of things. In the absence of the concept of relation, all statements whatever appeared to Plato as either affirming or denying a Communion between at least two things. His Communion is thus an enormously ambiguous notion. It is supposed to be present whenever we can make any true statement that has a grammatically affirmative form; whereas, in fact, there is no one or two or three or even fifty kinds of relation or union or Communion one of which is meant by every affirmative statement.

So much for the argument that the doctrine of Communion is not the exposure of a fallacious method in the *Parmenides*, because it is itself vitiated by one of the major fallacies vitiating the *Parmenides*.

4. 'But', it might be said, 'even if the doctrine of Communion does suffer from one of the fallacies committed in the *Parmenides*, it may still detect and point out another of those fallacies; and we have seen reason above to believe that it does so.' Let us therefore examine that argument, which was to the general effect that the doctrine of Communion is the detection of the confusion between identity and predication, on which the second part of the *Parmenides* largely depends for its results. The answer to it is that only by a speculative interpretation can we obtain the statement that Plato regarded his doctrine of Communion as pointing to the distinction between identity and attribution. The suggestion made above was that the 'late learners' rejected 'man is good' because they confused this attribution with an assertion of identity. But it does not follow that Plato himself analysed their mistake in this manner. Plato certainly thought of his Communion as refuting the 'late learners'. But it does not follow that he thought the manner of refutation was to show that they confused attribution with identity. Nor is there anything in the text to show that he thought this. He does not regard this or any other of his doctrines as the detection of an ambiguity or a confusion, though interpreters have sometimes written as if he did. The nearest he comes to such a twentieth-century way of talking is the following:

> Therefore let no one say that we are presuming to assert the being of not-being represented as the opposite of being. We have long ago said good-bye to the question whether there is any opposite of being or not, either explicable or completely inexplicable. But as to our present account of not-being, let a man either refute it and convince us that we are wrong, or, so long as he cannot, let him say as we do that the

kinds mingle with each other; and that, since being and the other traverse all of them and each other, the other shares in being and *is* because of this sharing, while yet it *is not* that in which it shares, but, being other than being, is clearly necessarily not-being. (*Sph.* 258E–259A.)

This passage cannot rightly be called the assertion of an ambiguity; and this is the nearest Plato comes to describing his doctrine of Communion in this way. There is therefore no force in the argument which attempts to show that the second part of the *Parmenides* depicts the consequences of denying Communion by reference to the confusion between identity and attribution.

5. Certain persons delight in the paradox that you must not say that 'man is good', as Plato says; but certain others, who do not delight in it at all, nevertheless may feel themselves urged toward it by certain difficulties. They may be in the dilemma that, on the one hand, they feel sure you can say 'man is good', but, on the other hand, they do not see *how* you can, or they see something which appears to entail that you cannot. To such more responsible thinkers it is folly to say: 'But you obviously can say "man is good"; and, if you could not, all discourse whatever would be impossible, including the paradox that you cannot say "man is good".' For these thinkers already know that you can say that 'man is good', and that the supposition that you cannot immediately destroys all thought and speech. Their trouble is that, nevertheless, they seem to see a good reason for denying that you can say that 'man is good'. What they want is to be shown the fallacy in the argument which troubles them. They know it must be a fallacy; but they want to see that it is. Now for such thinkers Plato's exposition of his doctrine of Communion is no help whatever. For he merely points to the fact that we *must* be able to say 'man is good', because otherwise no thought or communication would be possible. He does not even notice any arguments to the contrary, much less show us where they go wrong. Nor does he do anything to elucidate the nature and presuppositions of this Communion which he asserts (unless you think it elucidated by his comparison of it to the arrangements of letters in significant words, *Sph.* 253). He does not tell us *what* it is, but only *that* it is. Having established its existence in one page (252) by this sure but unsatisfying method, he spends the rest of his discussion in ascertaining which pairs communicate in a small selected set of

kinds and applying the results to the notion of not-being. His procedure is thus rather like that of a scientist who should tell us that, in view of the evidence, we *must* say that this body passes from one place to another separated place without passing through the interval, but should leave it entirely to us to discover the fallacy in the arguments which seem to show that such a thing cannot happen.

These considerations show that if the doctrine of Communion were meant to be the key to the second part of the *Parmenides* it would be a very poor one. It would merely tell us that some things communicate and others do not, which we knew before, and would leave it to us to see our way through the fallacies of the eight movements by this feeble ray, which cannot be done.

In view of these five arguments we must reject the suggestion that the second part of the *Parmenides* is an indirect statement of the doctrine of Communion. This concludes our examination of two specially attractive forms of the view that this part of the *Parmenides* is an indirect statement of method.

§ 7. THE DIALOGUE PROVIDES MENTAL EXERCISE

We have now eliminated all four of the alternatives described above. It appears that the second part of the *Parmenides* is neither a direct nor an indirect statement either of doctrine or of method. (The only reservation we have had to make in this conclusion is that this passage does embody, though perhaps badly, two rules of method seriously recommended in the preceding part of the dialogue.)

The interpretation of the second part of the *Parmenides* now to be recommended rests mainly on the notion of exercise or γυ-μνασία, which Parmenides stresses in the transitional part of the dialogue and which he names five times (*Prm.* 135C, 135D twice, 136A, 136C). The second part of the *Parmenides* is an exercise or gymnastic. It does not in itself attain truth of any kind; but it sets the muscles of the mind in a better state to obtain truth hereafter. Even to follow these arguments is a strenuous undertaking; to attempt, as we must, to see what is wrong with them calls for the greatest acuteness and persistence.

This is also the spirit in which Plato puts forward the objections to the theory of Ideas in the first part. We have seen that he thought them serious but not fatal. He offers them here as an exercise in logic. They must be invalid, for the theory of Ideas must be true; but who can see *where* they are invalid? Thus not merely the second part but the whole of the *Parmenides* is an exercise in method. The dialogue is a unity. A short central passage urges the need for training in logic. On either side of it are disposed long argumentations which are excellent material for such a training. Their excellence lies in this, that, on the one hand, they are both extremely difficult to see through, while, on the other hand, they would both incite Plato's readers vehemently to try to see through them—the first set because they attack the principles of Plato's own philosophy, the second set because their conclusion is profoundly unsatisfying to any human mind. In neither part did Plato think the arguments certain, and in neither part did he think them silly. In both he thought them very real and very difficult difficulties, but superable.

The dialogue is addressed primarily to Plato's own supporters. It rebukes them for being shallow and cocksure in their adhesion, first, by showing them serious difficulties in their view, then, by urging that they need more dialectic, and, lastly, by showing the kind of tangle the dialectician must fight his way through. It is a manifesto for more dialectic and less enthusiasm. Grote, to whom this interpretation is due, says that the dialogue is 'intended to repress premature forwardness of affirmation, in a young philosophical aspirant', and that it is another way of doing what elenchus does and what Socrates in the *Apology* declares to be his business—combating unexamined belief and overconfident affirmation (George Grote, *Plato and the Other Companions of Socrates* (London, 1865), II, 263, 296–8). The *Parmenides* does for the young philosopher what the Socratic elenchus did for the common man. It is the elenchus of the philosopher, who thought himself beyond the need of elenchus.

What relevance have Parmenides and Zeno to this purpose? Why are they introduced? To make Socrates the bearer of this rebuke would not have done; for he had become identified in the early dialogues with that elenchus of the common man, and in the middle dialogues with that enthusiastic theory of Ideas, which were now tending to raise an unjustifiable pride in some of Plato's pupils. Socrates excluded, no more authoritative figure than Parmenides could be found. Plato very likely considered only Parmenides great enough and distant enough to be his critic.

And Parmenides' pupil, Zeno, had concentrated on the hard and patient task of reasoning as Plato wishes his followers to do.

The gymnastic intention of the *Parmenides* is the cause of the subtle slide that takes place in the discussion from one hypothesis to another. The speakers talk as if they were discussing from beginning to end one and the same hypothesis, namely that of the real Parmenides. Thus Socrates and Zeno in their conversation make it plain that they are talking about the well known theory of Parmenides; and Parmenides in his 'laborious game' says he will 'start from myself and my own hypothesis'. Yet in fact only the conversation between Socrates and Zeno deals with the theory of the real Parmenides. The feigned Parmenides, when he begins the dialectical exercise, is made without admitting it to shift to a subtly different theory. One gross evidence of this shift is that in the conversation between Socrates and Zeno ἕν is contrasted with πολλά, but in the dialectical exercise it is contrasted with τὰ ἄλλα. The phrase ' εἰ ἕν ἐστι ' can express the theory under discussion in both parts; but in the early part (128D1) it means 'if everything is one' or ' ἕν . . . εἶναι τὸ πᾶν ' (128B1), which is contrasted with the theory that things are many; whereas in the laborious game it means 'if there is a one' and is contrasted with the theory that there is no one. The word ' ἕν ' is a predicate in the earlier part but a subject in the later; and the word ' ἐστι ' is copulative in the former part but existential in the latter. The shift comes in 136AB, the first place where Parmenides himself is represented as mentioning an Eleatic discussion. Here the word ' πολλά ' still occurs, and memory of the former conversation inclines us to take ' εἰ πολλά ἐστι ' as meaning 'if things are many', while the context, with its talk of hypothesizing the existence or nonexistence of this and that, inclines us to take it as meaning 'if there is a many'. After this passage the word ' πολλά ' does not occur in any expression of the hypothesis under discussion or of its rival. Instead we find ' τὰ ἄλλα ' as the contrast to ' τὸ ἕν ', and ' ἕν εἰ μὴ ἔστι ' as the rival hypothesis. Thus the contrasted concepts are in the early passage ἕν and πολλά, but in the exercise ἕν and τὰ ἄλλα; and the contrasted hypotheses are in the early passage εἰ ἕν ἐστι and εἰ πολλά ἐστι, but in the exercise εἰ ἕν ἐστι and εἰ ἕν μὴ ἔστι.

One main purpose of this shift is to make a better dialectical exercise, to make the 'laborious game' more laborious. For four of the eight movements of the exercise are made by means of the idea of 'the others', that is, the others than the one. Without these 'others' the exercise would be only half as formidable. But on the real Parmenidean hypothesis, 'if everything is one', there are no 'others', and it is nonsense to talk about them. Furthermore, the new hypothesis is much more suitable for producing bewilderment than the old, because it is vaguer and less tied to facts. What is this 'one' that we are now talking about? In the original hypothesis it was the all, the universe. But now it is not, for besides it there are the 'others'. So what is it? And what are they? We are left without a clue, and yet with an uneasy feeling that we ought to know, and must not reveal our ignorance. And this is a good opportunity for a dialectical mystification.

It is not inconsistent with this 'gymnastic' theory of the *Parmenides* to hold that Plato regarded the dialogue, especially in its latter part, as amusing. But the smile is not that of parody; it is that which we reserve for some perfect but queer and inhuman achievement of the human spirit, for virtuosity divorced from significance and passion, for an amazing *tour de force*. The Academicians probably smiled at the second part of the *Parmenides* as the serious student of logic smiles at the perfection of the paradox of the class of all classes that are not members of themselves.

It is a defect of the gymnastic theory that it makes Parmenides seriously recommend a training in method, promise an example of that training, and then give, not exactly an example, but rather a material on which we may train ourselves. The second part of the dialogue is not really, as it professes to be, a case of the exercise that Parmenides recommends, but an argument by examining which we who read the dialogue may obtain that exercise. This seems to be, on the gymnastic theory, a real though slight incoherence and defect in Plato's composition. But there are only two ways out of it. One is to say that Parmenides' recommendations about method are not seriously meant; and the other is to say that the 'illustration' really is good reasoning. Both of these seem much worse; and the incoherence on the gymnastic theory is much less than on the 'parody' theory, according to which a serious recommendation about method is succeeded by an 'illustration' which is a parody of a vicious logic.

The *Parmenides* thus comes nearest of all Plato's works to being wholly methodological. The *Sophist*, the *Statesman*, the *Phaedrus*, its only rivals, have a much larger proportion of matter of another sort. In the *Parmenides* everything, including the important contributions to the theory of Ideas, directly serves the purpose of urging the practice of dialectic.

§ 8. CORNFORD'S INTERPRETATION COMBINES INCOMPATIBLES

Cornford's interpretation of the second part of the *Parmenides* (*Plato and Parmenides*) is a combination of two interpretations which he represents as harmonizing with each other, whereas they really conflict and weaken each other.

The first of these interpretations is as follows: The second part of the *Parmenides* is not parody or sophistry, but a serious and very subtle analysis. Nearly all the conclusions of all the hypotheses are true and important. What Plato here analyses is the logic of Parmenides, which he shows to be incorrect. The fifth movement, for example, 'is a brilliant refutation of the Eleatic dogma that nothing can be said about "what is not"' (*P. & P.* 230). The explanation of the first and second movements is as follows:

Hyp. I [shows] that from the notion of a bare unity which negates any kind of plurality, nothing can be deduced or evolved. Parmenides, who insisted on the absolute unity and indivisibility of his One, was logical in so far as he inferred the non-existence of anything else: there could be no 'Others', no plurality of real things, no world of sensible appearances. But he was not justified in ascribing to his One itself any further attributes. It could not even exist or be the object of any kind of knowledge. He did, however, regard it as existent and knowable, and he called it not only 'One' but 'One Being'. Hyp. II [starts] afresh from this notion of a One which has being, and [shows] that such a One, just because it is not absolutely one, unique and indivisible, can have some of the further attributes which Parmenides deduced, but equally well other attributes which he denied. It can have many parts or aspects or elements; and there can be 'Others', in a number of different senses. If we add (as Parmenides did) the attributes of spatial extension and shape, there is no reason why it should not have motion and all the kinds of change in time. In fact there is nothing to arrest our thought from proceeding all the way from the conception of a 'One Entity' to the existence in space and time of a multitude of physical bodies, capable of motion and of every kind of change, and perceptible by the senses. (203–4.)

The defects which the *Parmenides* reveals in the logic of Parmenides, according to Cornford, are mostly failures to detect ambiguity. Parmenides would never have reached his results if he had observed and separated the various senses of 'one' and 'exist', and so forth.

Cornford further holds that Plato, by thus refuting the logic of Parmenides, was able to restore that which Parmenides had destroyed, namely, the Pythagorean cosmology. The *Parmenides* lays the logical basis for the Pythagorean type of cosmology stated in the *Timaeus*. For example, the great-and-small or the Indefinite Dyad, which is the unlimited element in Plato's cosmology, is the subject of Movement VII and is also introduced in Movements III and IV (239).

So much for Cornford's first interpretation. It may be summed up as the view that the second part of the *Parmenides* removes Parmenides from the path of the physicist by convicting him of ambiguity, and lays the logical foundation for a Pythagorean physics; and it may be called the 'anti-Elea theory'.

Cornford would probably have preferred to adopt the anti-Elea theory by itself, without any additional hypothesis, if he judged it possible; but certain aspects of the second part of the dialogue make that impossible. One of these is that there is no explicit mention of ambiguity in the dialogue; and the other is that there appear to be many fallacies. The anti-Elea theory says that each movement of the second part of the *Parmenides* is a valid and important contribution to logic; Cornford therefore required some additional hypothesis to explain why these movements seem very fallacious. The anti-Elea theory also says that this dialogue points out ambiguities in the logic of Parmenides; therefore Cornford needed an additional hypothesis to explain why there is no mention of ambiguity in the dialogue.

The second hypothesis, which Cornford added to his first to meet these difficulties, is in general the same as Grote's. It is a form of the gymnastic theory, according to which the *Parmenides*, instead of describing and analysing sorts of fallacy, presents cases thereof and leaves the task of analysis to the reader.

The form which Cornford would have liked to give to the gymnastic theory, if he could, would be that each movement takes a different sense of 'one' or 'being' or some other word, but within each movement the same sense is preserved throughout. Thus we should be given an exercise in distinguishing the different senses in the different movements; and, when we had done that, we could discover in each movement, taking it in its proper sense, an important contribution to logic.

Even in this most favourable form of the gymnastic theory for him, the theory would still weaken Cornford's other interpretation of the second part of the *Parmenides*. For the purpose attributed to the dialogue by the one theory will not combine well with that attributed to it by the other. A piece of writing containing concealed ambiguities, just so far as it is well adapted to puzzle a student and make him search for fallacies, is ill adapted to reveal to him the precise fallacies in a thinker whose defects are not yet exposed. You cannot effectively say at the same time 'Here are the ambiguities' and 'Where are the ambiguities?'. It is too much to hope that a student will first be well puzzled by the arguments; then, after considerable exercise, discover and define the different senses used in the different movements; and then realize that Parmenides confused these senses and that the movements show what happens if we keep them separate. To make the world aware for the first time of hitherto unnoticed ambiguities, you must point to them as clearly as you can, not hide them in a puzzle. Cornford had to add the gymnastic theory, in order to square his anti-Elea theory with the text, but at the same time the gymnastic theory makes the anti-Elea theory less probable. The anti-Elea theory needs, and yet is injured by, the gymnastic theory.

But the text will not even allow Cornford to maintain the form of the gymnastic theory most suitable to him. He confesses with admirable candour that fallacies sometimes occur even within a single movement (*P. & P.* 115, 130). He also notes places where, in the course of a movement using a word in one sense, Plato resumes a previous sense (*P. & P.* 157, 170, 227).

The exercise in detecting fallacies thus becomes intertwined with the argument against Parmenides in so intimate a manner that surely no reader would ever get beyond the former. I venture to suggest that Cornford applies at every stage whichever of two disparate hypotheses suits his book just then. Whenever he can, he represents an argument as a 'brilliant refutation' of some Eleatic thesis, for that is what he would prefer to hold all the time; but, when his apologizing skill is defeated by some unusually gross fallacy, he applies the gymnastic interpretation and declares that Plato is here setting us a fallacy to detect. The result is an incredible hodge-podge. It is impossible to believe that Plato, desiring to publish a refutation of Parmenides' logic and the foundation of a better one, would have inserted fallacies here and there to puzzle the reader. He could not have helped seeing that the second purpose defeats the first.

This alternate application of different hypotheses explains Cornford's swinging from the highest praise of Plato's arguments to attributions of fallacy. We hear of 'astonishing lucidity', 'brilliant refutations', 'sound conclusions', 'fine and important distinctions'. Yet we also hear that Plato is content to draw a true conclusion from true premisses which do not entail it, and that he did not scruple to introduce a *non sequitur* here and there (*P. & P.* 130).

This alternation between different hypotheses also explains why Cornford sometimes seems to call the same argument now valid and now invalid. How can the fifth movement return to a previous sense of 'is' half-way through itself (*P. & P.* 227), and yet be 'as a whole' a brilliant refutation of an Eleatic dogma (*P. & P.* 230)? If the consequences deduced in Movements I and II 'do actually follow' (*P. & P.* 109), why does he thereafter point out fallacies in them (*P. & P.* 150–1, 157, 160–4)?

The same alternation between different hypotheses explains, thirdly, why Cornford sometimes seems to be making the peculiar suggestion that, just by pointing to a fallacy in the argument, he is showing us that Plato was *not* being fallacious! Thus, having told us of an argument that it introduces fresh assumptions, 'which obviously contradict those on which we have so far proceeded' (*P. & P.* 161), and that 'Plato's purpose [here] is to puzzle the reader by apparent contradictions and set him thinking out the difference between the various senses of "not one"' (*P. & P.* 163), he later tells us: 'We may claim that this curious section supports the view that Plato is not merely indulging in a parade of sophistical arguments. If that were all, he would hardly have been at the pains to construct so intricate a piece of reasoning' (*P. & P.* 164). Do you really turn a bad argument into a good one by pointing out that fresh assumptions have been introduced, which obviously contradict the previous ones? And how can a fallacy in the inference fail to vitiate the conclusion (*P. & P.* 224)?

Cornford muffled the clash of his anti-Elea theory with the

gymnastic theory by his misinterpretation of the deductive form of the movements. By the 'deductive form' he meant the fact that, within each movement, every single proposition except the first is represented as following from the first, either directly or indirectly, without the aid of any other premiss. The form in which the movements are cast suggests that the original hypothesis by itself necessitates every subsequent statement in that movement. In a modern phraseology, the speaker pretends that the number of the postulates in the postulate-set for each movement is one and one only.

This 'deductive form' is false, as everyone would nowadays agree. Cornford finds three ways in which it misrepresents the facts. In the first place, premisses additional to the original hypothesis are surreptitiously introduced from time to time. In the second place, Plato, in order to preserve this deductive form, often says 'A is B' or 'A must be B', when all he means, and all his argument justifies, is that there is no reason why A should not be B (*P. & P.* 115), e.g. 'we must understand the statement that "the One Entity, being limited, *will have* shape" as meaning that the attribute of extension *can*, without any illogicality, be added' (*P. & P.* 146). Cornford finds that the deductive form frequently 'embarrasses' Plato in this way, by compelling him to say that A is B when he means only that Parmenides has not proved that A is not B (e.g. *P. & P.* 150). Thirdly, he finds that this same deductive form makes Plato represent as demonstrations or inferences what are really definitions. This occurs especially at the beginning of a movement; there the first few propositions, though presented as consequences of the hypothesis, are really definitions of the sense to be given to the hypothesis in the coming movement (*P. & P.* 111). It occurs also in the middle of movements (*P. & P.* 172, 186).

Why did Plato adopt this misleading deductive form? I venture to suggest that Cornford gives a false answer; and that, when we see the true answer, the full incompatibility of the anti-Elea theory with the gymnastic theory becomes apparent.

Cornford's explanation of the deductive form is as follows:

By casting the whole into the form of a deduction, I understand Plato to indicate that there is no logical barrier such as Parmenides' goddess set up between the deductions of the first part of his poem and the mythical cosmogony of the second part. The existence of a mani-

fold and changing world in time is not an irrational or selfcontradictory illusion of mortals. Reasoning will carry us all the way from
Parmenides' own hypotheses of a One which has being to the notion
of the sensible body with contrary qualities. The Pythagorean evolution, starting from the Monad and ending with the sensible body, is
restored and justified. But this train of reasoning simply postulates the
addition of one attribute after another, in a logical order. It must not
be confused with an account of how a sensible world could actually
come into existence, by 'emanation' from a supreme One. There is no
hint of any moving cause. The production of a sensible world can be
explained only in the imagery of a creation myth such as we find in
the *Timaeus*. (*P. & P.* 204.)

This explanation provides Cornford with a measure of recon-
ciliation between his two interpretations of the second part of
Parmenides, the anti-Elea theory and the 'gymnastic' theory. Plato's
adoption of the deductive form appears, in the first place, as a
part of the anti-Elea theory: it is designed to indicate that, contrary to what Parmenides said, we can construct a logically im-
peccable account of the world our senses report. But it is a part
of the anti-Elea theory which leads on fairly well to the gymnastic
theory; for, having once adopted the deductive form, Plato was
compelled to use *non sequitur*'s, furtively introduced premisses, and
definitions disguised as demonstrations; and these are fallacies on
which the student must exercise his logical acumen. The deductive form therefore discharges, according to Cornford, two ser-
vices: first, it indicates that Parmenides' logic cannot hinder us
from rational cosmology, and, second, it enables Plato to set us
exercises in detecting fallacy while at the same time presenting
what is really a valid argument.

About this suggestion two points must be made; and the first is
that this deductive form would have been a ridiculously ineffec-
tive way of doing what Cornford says it was intended to do. For
let us consider. What we have in the text is eight movements, each
professing to be a rigid deductive system having only one initial
postulate. And what Plato expects us to infer from that scheme,
according to Cornford, is that there are no such logical obstacles
as Parmenides supposed to an empirical cosmology. Surely there
is not the faintest connexion between the premiss and the conclusion. Surely no single reader would ever grasp what Plato was
trying to convey.

The other point is that this deductive form is not something peculiar to the *Parmenides*. It is the form which Plato believed common to all deductions by the hypothetical method and to every elenchus. Plato's standing and unquestioned assumption was that an argument can and usually does proceed from one single postulate or hypothesis, without requiring any additional premiss. Plato in the *Parmenides* is not slyly but consciously insinuating premisses which he knows to be additional assumptions. He is genuinely failing to notice the extra premisses as such, just as he fails to notice them in his most serious arguments in other dialogues, just as in the last argument in the *Phaedo*, for example, he genuinely regards the theory of Ideas as the only premiss required to arrive at the conclusion that soul is immortal.

The deductive form of the movements in the *Parmenides* is not something which Plato sat loose to as Cornford supposes; it was his whole conception of deduction, and he never got beyond it. It follows that Plato was not so serenely above the fallacies and ambiguities and surreptitious premisses of those movements as Cornford declares. He knew there was something wrong; but he could not say what it was with any sureness and abstractness.

§ 9. TRANSLATION OF THE PASSAGES ON METHOD

So much for a general view of Plato's *Parmenides*. It will now be easy to survey in the right light the small part of it that explicitly discusses hypothetical method.

We are told in this work that Socrates asked Zeno 'to read again the first hypothesis of the first logos'; and when it had been read again he said: 'How do you mean this, Zeno? If things are many, then they must be both like and unlike; and that is impossible, for unlike things cannot be like and like things cannot be unlike? Is not that what you are saying?' (127DE). After further explanation of his interpretation of Zeno's book, Socrates is made to continue thus (*Prm.* 128):

I see, Parmenides, that Zeno wants to be your friend not merely in other ways but also in his book. For he has in a way written the same as you did, and yet he changes it so as to try to deceive us into thinking that he is saying something different. For you in your poems say that the all is one, and you provide excellent proofs; he on the other hand says it is not many, and he too proposes many and great proofs. So one of you says it is one, and the other says it is not many, and each says it so that he seems to have said something quite different from the other though he is really saying pretty much the same, and that is why you appear to be talking over the heads of the rest of us.

Yes, Socrates, said Zeno. Yet you have not entirely grasped the meaning of the book, although like the Laconian puppies you are running well and on the trail. In the first place you do not see that the book has not such a high opinion of itself as to be written with the intention which you ascribe to it, and to deceive men into thinking that it is doing something great. What you have mentioned is accidental; the essence of the book is to defend Parmenides' argument against those who try to make fun of it by saying that, if it is one, many consequences follow that are ridiculous and contrary to the argument itself. It is a reply to those who assert the many, and it gives them as good as they gave and better by showing that the consequences of their hypothesis, 'if it is many', would be even more ridiculous than those of its being one, if they were sufficiently explored. That was the sort of partisan spirit that led me to write it, I being a young man at the time. And then someone stole a copy, so that there was no question of deliberating whether it ought to be brought into the light or not. So what you fail to see, Socrates, is that it was written out of a young man's partisanship and not out of an old man's ambition.

Socrates then sets out a theory of Ideas and Parmenides criticizes it (*Prm.* 129–34). Then the conversation proceeds as follows:

These, Socrates, said Parmenides, and many others in addition to these, are the inevitable consequences if there are these Ideas of things and a man insists on distinguishing some Form itself for each thing. So that the hearer becomes puzzled and argues that they do not exist, and that even if they did exist very much indeed it is quite necessary that they should be unknown to human nature; and in saying this he seems to have a real point, and, as we just said, he is amazingly hard to persuade to the contrary. And it takes a very gifted man to be able to learn that there is some genus of each thing, and that there is an essence itself by itself. It takes a still more wonderful man to be able to discover it and teach it to another person who has adequately examined all these points.

I agree with you, Parmenides, said Socrates. What you say is very much to my mind.

But, Socrates, said Parmenides, if on the other hand a man will not allow that there are Forms of things, in view of all that we have just said and similar considerations, and will not distinguish a Form for each thing, he will have nowhere to turn his mind, since he does not admit the eternal and identical existence of an Idea of each thing, and so he will completely destroy the power of dialectic. Of this sort of thing you seem to me to be even more aware.

True, he said.

So what will you do about philosophy? Where will you turn if these things are unknown?

I do not think I see at present.

The reason is, Socrates, he said, that you are trying to define a certain fine and just and good and each of the Ideas too early, before you have been exercised. I noticed it yesterday as I was listening to you talking to Aristotle here. Now your keenness for discussions is a fine and holy thing, you can be sure of that; but train yourself and practise more on what most people think useless and call idle talking, while you are still young. Otherwise the truth will evade you.

What is this exercise, Parmenides, he said?

What you heard from Zeno, he said. Except that I admired you, in your talk with him too, for insisting on considering the confusion, not in visibles nor concerning them, but concerning the things that a man would grasp best by discussion, and that he would take to be Ideas.

Well, I do think, said he, that in that way it is easy to make things like and unlike or anything else.

And you are right, he said. But there is something more that you must do. Besides hypothesizing that a thing exists and then observing the consequences of the hypothesis, hypothesize also that this same thing does not exist, if you want to get more practice.

How do you mean, he said?

Well, he said, take the hypothesis Zeno hypothesized, if there is a many, and ask what must follow both to the many themselves with regard both to themselves and to the one, and to the one with regard both to itself and to the many; and then ask what will happen both to the one and to the many with regard both to themselves and to each other *if there is no many*. Or again, if you hypothesize that likeness exists or does not exist, ask what follows from each of these hypotheses both to the things hypothesized and to the others, with regard both to themselves and to each other. And the same with unlike and motion and rest and generation and destruction and being itself and notbeing. In a word, whatever you hypothesize as existing or not existing or having any other predicate, you ought to inquire the consequences to itself and to each one of the others, whichever you choose, and to the majority and to the lot in the same way; and the others with regard both to themselves and to whatever else you may choose, whether you hypothesize what you hypothesize as existing or as not existing, if you are going to complete your training and be sure of discerning the true.

That is a tremendous undertaking, Parmenides, he said; and I do not wholly understand it. Why don't you hypothesize something and go through the process, to make me understand better?

That is a big job, Socrates, said he, to put on a man of my age.

Well, Zeno, said Socrates, why don't you go through it for us?

He said that Zeno laughed and said: Let us ask Parmenides himself, Socrates. I am afraid it is not a light matter that he means. Don't you see what a job you are putting on him? If there were more of us it would not be right to ask him, for such things are not suitable to be said to a crowd, especially by a man of his age. For most people do not realize that without this circuitous and exhaustive wandering it is impossible to come upon the true and possess intelligence. I add my request to that of Socrates, Parmenides, as it is a long time since I have heard it through.

When Zeno had said this (Antiphon said that Pythodorus said), he himself and Aristotle and the others begged Parmenides to show them what he meant and not refuse their request. So Parmenides said: I must consent. But I feel like the horse in Ibycus, the old racehorse that was about to run again in a chariot race, and was trembling because it knew what was coming, to which Ibycus likened himself because, he said, he himself at an equally advanced age was being forced into love against his will. I find myself too remembering, and very frightened as to how at my age I can ever swim across such a vast sea of words. All the same I must oblige you, especially since as Zeno says we are among ourselves. Where shall we begin, then; and what shall we first hypothesize? May I, since we have decided to play this laborious game, start from myself and my own hypothesis, and ask what must follow if I make an hypothesis about the one itself, either that there is a one or that there is no one?

Certainly, said Zeno.

Who will reply to me, he asked? I think it should be the youngest. For he will make the least trouble, and be most likely to answer as he thinks. Also his answers will give me some rest.

I am ready to do that, Parmenides, said Aristotle; for when you say the youngest you say me. Ask and I will answer.

Very well, he said. If there is a one, then this one would not be many? (*Prm.* 134E—137C.)

§ 10. HYPOTHETICAL METHOD IN THE 'PARMENIDES'

Hypothetical method in the *Parmenides* includes, we see, positing an hypothesis and drawing its consequences. This was the essential element in the other three dialogues also, although in the *Meno* it was undeveloped and in the *Republic* it was assumed and passed over. It is here said to have been intensely practised by Zeno and Parmenides, whereas in the *Republic* and the *Phaedo* Socrates ascribed it to no one beyond himself, and in the *Meno* he tended to ascribe it to mathematicians.

Hypothetical method in the *Parmenides* obviously includes the same elenctic element as it did in the *Phaedo* and the *Republic*. That is to say, the practitioner always has in mind the possibility that the consequences of the hypothesis will turn out to include something selfcontradictory or contradictory to the hypothesis or otherwise intolerable, and if so this constitutes an elenchus of the hypothesis, which must then be replaced by another one. The two hypotheses whose consequences Parmenides develops in the dialogue, namely 'if there is a one' and 'if there is no one', both lead to what seem both to us and to the imagined company intolerable selfcontradictions. Zeno is made to say that in his book he developed the consequences of the hypothesis 'if it is many' and showed them to be very ridiculous; and that he intended this as a refutation of the hypothesis.

In the *Phaedo* and the *Republic* Plato's conception seemed to be that, if the hypothesis gave rise to contradictions, it was thereby refuted and that was the end of it, but, if it did not do so, that constituted negative support of the hypothesis, and the question then arose whether it could be given any further more positive support. The *Phaedo* contemplated deducing it from some 'higher' hypothesis, 'until you came to something adequate'. The *Republic* said that you might possibly reach 'an unhypothesized beginning', and spoke of this event in language slightly suggesting Aristotle's subsequent doctrine of intuition. Is this idea present in the *Parmenides* too?

When we ask whether the upward path of the *Republic* reappears at all in the *Parmenides*, the answer seems to be that there is almost no trace of it, and that there are two new features of hypothetical method in the *Parmenides* which seem hostile to the upward path of the *Republic*.

There is almost no trace in the *Parmenides* of the upward path of the *Republic*. The words 'unhypothesized' and 'beginning' do not occur. The metaphor of 'upward' does not occur. Parmenides speaks of 'the truth' (135D) and of being 'sure of discerning the true' (136C) and of 'coming upon the true and possessing intelligence' (νοῦς 136E). And these three phrases are all there is in the methodological passage of the *Parmenides* to remind us of the highest possibility of dialectic according to the Divided Line. In spite of the word ' νοῦς ', recalling Aristotle's word for intuition and the ' νόησις ' of dialectic in the *Republic*, we must say that there is nothing here of the *Republic*'s upward path. Furthermore, these three little expressions are incidental in a discussion whose general tendencies, to which we will now turn, seem positively hostile to the spirit of the Divided Line.

There are in the *Parmenides* two new features of hypothetical method which seem hostile to the upward path of the *Republic*. One of these is that hypothetical method is here presented first and foremost as a mental gymnastic. Plato here likens the dialectician drawing consequences from hypotheses to the athlete training his body. The athlete training his body is not actually competing in public games or fighting a battle; he is only making himself more capable of doing so. The dancer working at the bar is not actually dancing, but only making herself more capable of dancing in future. This is overwhelmingly the way in which hypothetical method is regarded here. He emphasizes the need for a laborious thoroughness, a pursuit of the consequences down every by-way and round every turning, a 'circuitous and exhaustive wandering', a 'tremendous undertaking'. Thus the *Parmenides* has a tendency towards Aristotle's devaluation of dialectic; for Aristotle lowered dialectic from first to second place as an intellectual method, and in his manual of the art, namely his *Topics*, he regarded it as primarily a gymnastic, secondly a tool of controversy, and only thirdly a tool of philosophic science (101^a27).

The other new feature of hypothetical method in the *Parmenides*, which seems hostile to the conception of it in the *Republic*, is the prescription that we should draw the consequences in every case not merely of the hypothesis but also of its contradictory. The dialogue seems to expect that both sets of consequences will include inconsistencies. Parmenides deduces selfcontradictions both from 'if there is a one' and from 'if there is no one'. Zeno, in deducing ridiculous consequences from 'if it is many', does not deny that Parmenides' rival theory 'if it is one' also leads to ridiculous consequences; he only says that the former are more ridiculous.

What should our next step be, after we have deduced inconsistencies from each of two contradictory hypotheses? Although any reader of the *Parmenides* who adopts the present interpretation of it will feel this question strongly demanding an answer, the dialogue neither expresses the question nor clearly implies an answer. It merely says that we must draw the consequences of both contradictories if we are 'to come upon the true and possess intelligence'. Yet does anyone, who follows Plato's Parmenides through his drawing of the consequences both of 'if there is a one' and of 'if there is no one', feel inclined at the end of the last movement to say, 'Now I have come upon the true and possess intelligence'? We seem obliged to answer no. The puzzle is slightly less in the case of the hypotheses that 'it is one' and 'it is many'; for here Zeno is made to say that the consequences of the latter are more ridiculous than those of the former. This seems to imply that our next step is to adopt that one of two conflicting hypotheses whose consequences are less distasteful. Of two alternatives, we must adopt the one that leads to fewer absurdities, though both of them will lead to some. There is not the faintest hint of how anything better could be done. The procedure reminds one of Aristotle's remark on dialectic: 'For the sake of knowledge and philosophical wisdom it is no mean instrument to be able to survey and to have surveyed the consequences of either hypothesis; for it then remains to choose one of them correctly' (*Topics* VIII 14, 163ᵇ9–12).

The methodological aspect of the *Parmenides* thus seems to be, like its other aspects, bewildering, sceptical, and depressing. As the great theory of Ideas is here no longer the eminently reasonable doctrine it was in the *Phaedo* and the *Republic*, so the great method of hypothesis is severely lamed by the discovery that an hypothesis and its contradictory may *both* lead to absurdities. It is no longer sufficient to establish a proposition merely by deducing a falsehood from its contradictory.

Cornford felt that, if this were Plato's view, he 'should have burnt his books and relapsed into unbroken silence' (*Mind*, 1942, p. 387). Yet some persons do not need so high an estimate of the powers of human reason as others do in order to avoid apathy and despair; and Plato may have been able to face this situation with equanimity. However, we hear no more of hypothetical method after the *Parmenides*; and the renewed enthusiasm of the *Phaedrus* and the *Sophist* is based on the new method of 'division'.

INDEX

The entries under 'Aristotle' and 'Plato' do not include all references to their writings, but only those in which some light is thrown on the passage referred to.

Abstraction, level of in P., 2, 27–29, 45 f., 52, 211, 216 ff.
Adam, James, 2–3, 151, 180, 192.
Alexander of Aphrodisias, 22.
Allan, D. J., 29.
Analogy, 42, 45, 202–17, 222; the word, 209.
Analysis, 179; in geometry, 121, 166; for analysis = διαίρεσις see Division.
Ἀνατίθεμαι, 95, 116, 117.
Anaximander, 140.
Anhypotheton, 156 ff., 204, 278.
Antilogic, 85, 140 f.
Approximation, 108, 152, 157.
Archer-Hind, 30, 100, 137.
Argument, 20–21, 38.
Aristotle, 3, 16, 20 f., 29, 101 ff., 118 ff., 181, 209, 230, 232; on epagoge, 33–37, 41, 45 f., 46–48, 175; on dialectic, 20 f., 46–48, 72, 88, 90 ff., 279, 280; on the syllogism, 21, 175; on the hypothetical syllogism, 118 ff.; on intuition, 146, 175, 279; on question-and-answer, 84.
— passages discussed or translated:
Analytica Priora, 21; I 1: 118 ff.; II 23, 24: 33, 35 f.
Analytica Posteriora, 175; I 1: 45; I 2: 101 ff.; I 10: 102; I 18: 46; II 13: 47; II 19: 37, 46, 175.
Eth. Nic., I 4: 175; VI 6: 175.
Metaphysics, A 6: 90; M 4: 41, 46–48, 90.
Sophist, 91 f.
Soph. El., 16, 22, 29; 165ᵇ27: 37; 169ᵃ37 ff.: 84; 172ᵃ15: 84; 176ᵃ33: 207.
Topics, 19, 21, 22, 37, 72, 88, 279; I 1: 21; I 2: 175, 279; I 8: 37; I 12: 20 f., 33; VIII 14: 280.
Art or τέχνη, 62 f., 74.
Ast, Friedrich, 68, 97, 209.
Axiomatization, 132 f., 168 f.

Beginning (ἀρχή), 140 f., 158 ff., 175 f., 198, 200, 278.

Bergson, 5.
Burnet, John, 67, 68, 89 f., 98 f., 111 ff., 141, 155, 177, 223 ff., 240.

Campbell, Lewis, 73, 213.
'Case', 33 ff., 42, 207.
Certainty, 72 f., 146, 156, 157 f., 169, 172, 176, 178.
Chandler, M. W., 245.
Cherniss, Harold, vii, 117, 118, 234 ff., 255 f.
Conjecture (εἰκασία), 149, 151, 180 ff., esp. 190 ff., 197.
Contradiction, in the consequences of an hypothesis, 26–32, 106 f., 129–33, 170 f., 173, 275, 278–80.
Conviction (πίστις), 149, 151, 180 ff., 193–6.
Cornell University Press, v.
Cornford, F. M., vii, 1, 68, 103, 105, 166, 220, 242, 268 ff., 280.
Creationism, vi, 28–29.
Cross, R. C., vii.

Deduction, 105, 109, 133, 140 f., 168 f., 272–4; see also Syllogism.
Definition, v, 14, 24, 46–48, 49 ff., 100–2, 137.
Descartes, 73, 109 f., 141, 146, 179.
Dialectic, 20 f., 52 f., 61–92, 149, 150 ff., 156–79, 251, 265, 268, 276; achieves certainty, 72 f., 156 ff., 172, 176; history of, v, 47–48, 52–53, 70, 88–92, 265–8; relation to division, 52, 70, 280; relation to elenchus, 19, 83 f., 86, 135 f., 139 f., 170 f., 176, 265; relation to eristic, 84 ff.; relation to essence, 52, 70; relation to hypothetical method, 53, 70, 156 ff., 280; relation to mathematics, 74, 75 f., 166 ff., 197 ff.; relation to sense and reason, 75–77, 163 f., 178; scope of, 69, 71, 74 f., 197–201; value of, 69 f., 72, 84 ff., 279, 280; the word, 69 f., 77, 85, 90 f.
Dialogues, 122; three periods of, v;

early ds., v, 7–60 *passim*, esp. 18–19, 61 f.; middle ds., 19, 61 f., 69, 89, 202–5, 229 f.; late ds., 18–19, 29, 69, 84, 89, 280.

Διάνοια, *see* Thought.

Diogenes Laertius: passages discussed: II 106: 87; VIII 57: 91; IX 25: 91; IX 52: 87; IX 55: 87.

Direct and indirect, 23.

Division, v, 52, 70, 89, 162–5, 280.

Εἰκασία, *see* Conjecture.

Εἰκός, 216 f.

Elenchus, 7–32, 274; definition of, 7; aim of, 10–19; effects of, 9–17; history of, v, 18 f., 61 f., 83–84, 204; logic of, 20–48, 112 f., 131–3, 170 f.; personal character of, 15–17, 26; relation to definition, 24, 48; relation to dialectic, 19, 83 f., 86, 135 f., 139 f., 170 f., 176, 265; relation to hypothetical method, 135 f., 139 f., 170 f.; P.'s discussions of, 10–15; the word, 7, 9, 13, 15.

Empedocles, 91 f.

Enumeration, complete, 36 f., 43.

Epagoge, 33 ff., 175, 207, 213; defined, 33; cf. 42; frequency of, 41–45; P.'s consciousness of, 45 f., 213; relation to analogy, 207; relation to definition, 46–48; relation to syllogism, 20, 38 ff.; the word, 45 f.

Eristic, 70, 84 ff.

Essence, 49–60, 61, 70.

Euclid, 102, 109, 132, 168.

Evolutionism, vi, 31.

Example, 33, 208, 212 ff.

Farquharson, A. S. L., 120 f.

Ferguson, A. S., 180, 183, 189.

Forms or Ideas, 2 f., 50–60, 61, 70 f., 134, 195, 197–201, 223 ff., 252, 253.

Friedländer, Paul, vii, 117.

Good, 142 ff., 147, 153, 159 f., 166, 169, 170 f., 174, 176, 184, 185 ff., 196, 230, 247.

Goodrich, W. J., 30.

Grote, George, 265.

Hardie, W. F. R., 3, 103, 105, 131 f., 180, 191, 232, 242, 243 ff.

Hilbert, 168.

Hinks, D. A. G., 92.

Hutton, James, vii.

Hypothesis, the notion, 30–31, 93 ff.; origin of the notion, 89, 99 f.; the word, 68, 95 f., 98 f., 111; relation to definition, 100 ff., 137; premiss or conclusion?, 110 ff., 134 ff.; how tested, 110 f., 133–41.

Hypothetical method, 53, 105–13, 274, 277 ff.; employment of in the dialogues, 202 ff.; history of, v, 70, 122, 176, 177, 178, 277 f., 280; originality of, 177 f.; relation to dialectic, 70, 154, 179; relation to elenchus, 139 f., 170 f., 176, 278; relation to intuition, 109, 146, 172 ff., 179; relation to sense, 110; a second-best, 110, 145, 146; value of, 178 f.
— syllogism, 23–26, 45, 92, 118 f.

Ideas, P.'s theory of, *see* Forms.

Images, 42, 154 f., 181, 191, 208, 218 ff.

Imitation, 218 ff.

Induction, *see* Epagoge.

Intelligence (νόησις), 149, 151 f., 155, 175, 180 ff., 193–6, 198–201, 278 f.

Interpretation, 1–6, 27–29, 192.

Intuition, 35–38, 43, 65, 109, 172 ff., 178 f., 207, 213 f., 278 f.

Irony, Socratic, 8–9, 18.

Isocrates, 88.

Jackson, Henry, 30, 155, 231, 242.

Jowett, Benjamin, 35, 186.

Knowledge: distinct from opinion, 17, 146, 194, 206; is possible, 146, 174, 176, 179; achieved by dialectic, 72 ff., 156 ff., 172 ff.; not achieved by mathematics, 153, 157; how related to elenchus, 8, 11–15, 17; how related to hypothetical method, 107–9, 139 f., 146 f., 172 ff.; is virtue, 14 f., 206; in the Platonic analogies, 206 f.; like is known by like, 194 f., 198, 199 f.

Lee, H. D. P., 91, 102.

Liddell and Scott, 67, 68 *bis*, 95, 98, 156, 191.

Like-by-like, 194 f., 198, 199 f.

Logic: has a history, vi, 2–6, 27 ff., 31,

36; not distinguished from ontology by P., 71 f.; twentieth-century l., 168 f.
Logos, 8, 31, 35, 52, 55–56, 58, 124, 135, 139 f., 153 f., 170 f.
Lutoslawski, Wincenty, 174.

Maier, Heinrich, 141, 163, 164.
'Mathematicals', 2–3, 181, 192, 197.
Mathematics: and dialectic, 74, 75 f., 166 ff., 197 ff.; and hypothetical method, 99 f., 141, 152 ff., 177 f.; its hypotheses, 103 ff.; dogmatic, 152 ff., 157; its method, 112; two marks of, 154 f.; uses images, 76, 154 ff., 195; object of, 181, 192, 194 f., 197–201; history of, 100, 152, 166, 177; twentieth-century m., 156, 168 f.; for geometrical analysis see Analysis.
Megarians, 87 f., 225.
Μετατίθεμαι, 95, 106.
Method or μέθοδος: the notion, 61–69, 73; the word, 67–69; grounds of, 178, 222; m. and intuition, 65; P.'s actual method, 202 ff.
Midwifery, 83 f.
Milhaud, Gaston, 167.
Moore, G. E., 60.
Morrow, Glenn R., vii.
Murphy, N. R., 131, 189.

Negative instance, 24, 35, 37, 45.
Nettleship, R. L., 81, 83.
Νόησις, see Intelligence.

Opinion, 17, 146, 181, 189, 192, 196, 206.
Ὁρμηθέντα, 129, 131.

Parmenides, 67, 226, 265 f., 278.
Patterson, Woodford, vi.
Philosophy, 71, 74.
Πίστις, see Conviction.
Plato: passages discussed or translated:
Apology, 49.
    21–23: 10, 13 f.
    27: 26, 34.
Charmides, 24, 49.
    159–60; 37.
    159: 60.
    160: 21, 96.
    161: 79.
    165: 8.

167–9: 39.
167 D: 35.
170: 25.
172: 97.
174: 44.
Cratylus, 204, 208, 218.
    387–90: 39, 207.
    390: 69, 74, 77.
    393: 35.
    398: 78.
    423: 218.
    424: 64.
    425: 66, 69.
    426: 64.
    432: 38, 218.
    434: 218.
    435: 218.
    436: 131 f., 147.
    438–9: 218.
Crito, 8, 49.
    46: 107 f.
    49: 78, 159.
    50: 79.
Definitions, 96, 99.
Euthydemus, 24, 26, 85, 87, 205.
    271–2: 85.
    275: 78.
    279: 43.
    281 D: 35.
    288 E: 44.
    290: 74.
    292 E: 44.
    294, 298: 15.
    305: 216.
    307: 86 f.
Euthyphro, 24, 49.
    5: 58.
    6: 54.
    7: 44.
    10: 34.
    11: 98 f.
Gorgias, 15, 16, 24, 26, 29, 41, 49, 82, 205 f.
    449 ff.: 53.
    449: 82.
    453 ff.: 53.
    453: 55, 81.
    454: 94.
    457: 29.
    460: 26, 35.
    461: 26, 82.
    462: 9.
    467: 35.

Plato: (cont.)
471: 15.
474–9: 16.
474–5: 36, 43.
476: 35.
477: 44.
485: 77.
487: 29.
488 f.: 26.
490: 41.
495–6: 40.
496: 35.
498: 9, 26.
501: 43.
503–5: 40.
506–7: 78.
513: 17.
Hippias Major, 49.
284: 33.
Hippias Minor, 39, 43, 49.
365: 79.
373: 43.
Ion, 21–22, 49.
539: 21 f.
Laches, 10, 24, 41, 49.
183: 36.
185: 35.
188: 18.
189 f.: 42.
190: 60.
193: 26, 41, 44, 78.
196: 26.
Laws, 69.
720: 206 f.
Letters:
II 314: 68.
VII 341: 80, 174.
342–3: 52.
344: 19, 81, 174.
Lysis, 24, 25, 41, 45, 49, 51.
Meno, v, 9, 24, 37, 41, 51, 53, 70,
114 ff., 202, 214.
71–77: 50.
71: 9, 55, 79.
72–73: 56 f.
74–75: 54.
74: 55, 56.
75: 9, 69, 85.
80: 9–10.
82: 26.
83: 78.
84: 11.
86–87: 99, 114 ff., 152.

86: 152.
87–88: 40.
87: 53, 76.
88: 37, 43.
89: 117 f.
98: 8.
Parmenides, 1, 32, 70, 142, 204, 223 ff.
128: 31, 266, 274 f.
129: 228, 237, 256 f.
130: 226, 228.
131: 231.
132: 229.
133: 229, 231.
135–7: 239, 248, 264 f., 275 ff.
135: 71, 226 f., 231, 278 f.
136: 32, 97, 100, 266, 278 f.
137: 78.
139: 249.
142: 243, 244, 245, 246.
147: 249.
149: 252.
157: 249.
158: 252.
161: 254.
Phaedo, 70, 89, 123 ff., 146, 169 ff.,
176, 202 f., 230.
67: 220.
75: 78.
78: 64, 78.
85: 139 f., 145.
90: 69, 85.
92: 90, 99, 138 f., 217.
94: 142.
96: 71.
97: 65, 68.
99–101: 125 ff., 170 ff.
99: 17, 76, 110, 142 f.
100: 70, 100, 126 ff., 170.
101: 26, 30, 65, 85, 98, 118, 129 ff.,
171.
102 ff.: 274.
107: 168.
Phaedrus, v, 51, 62, 69–70, 217, 267 f.
249: 163.
260: 51 f.
261: 85, 87.
262: 217.
263–4: 64, 65.
265 f.: 162–5.
269–73: 69.
269: 75.
272–4: 66.
273: 217.

Plato: (cont.)
275–7: 79–80.
277: 79.
Philebus, 70.
15: 84, 231.
16–18: 69.
16: 69, 75, 209 f.
17: 85.
42: 97.
58: 69.
59: 74.
61E: 71.
Protagoras, 24, 41, 49, 82.
312: 35, 42, 53.
329: 80.
330: 234.
332–3: 22.
332: 7, 34.
334: 9.
336: 9.
339: 96.
347: 80, 110 f.
348: 81.
361: 96
Republic: 2–4, 70, 71, 89 f., 146 ff.,
203 f., 205 f., 219, 221.
I: 7, 24, 40, 41, 44, 49, 60, 93,
230.
I 332: 42.
334: 94.
335: 94.
336–7: 10.
341: 10.
346: 98.
348–9: 9.
348: 81.
353: 35.
II 368: 63, 64, 210 ff., 215.
375–6: 71.
376: 63.
380: 29.
III 392–8: 219.
IV 420: 212.
432: 67.
434: 210 ff.
435: 66, 69, 210 ff.
436: 3, 107.
437: 96, 107, 111 f., 171.
V 454: 85, 86.
457: 29.
475–6: 75.
475: 71.
477: 72, 146.

VI 486: 71.
487: 42.
488: 189, 206.
504: 66.
509: 4.
510–11: 2–4, 68, 69, 72, 74, 76,
112, 147 ff., 180 ff.
510: 103 ff., 148, 154, 200.
511: 98 f., 138, 153, 156 ff.,
160 ff., 198 ff.
VII 514–16: 149 f., 159, 173 f.,
180 ff., 189, 196, 208.
517: 180 ff., esp. 185 ff.
518: 46.
521: 185.
531: 68, 75.
532: 62, 90, 183 ff.
533: 66, 69, 70, 75, 147, 150 f.,
153, 160 f.
534: 52, 55, 70, 74, 77, 151,
164, 170 f., 193 f.
535: 151 f.
538–9: 84.
538: 176.
VIII–IX: 215.
X 595–7: 56, 219.
Sophist, 2, 67, 69–70, 72, 93, 219 f.,
237 ff., 267 f.
216: 87.
218: 68.
225: 87.
227: 68, 69, 75.
229: 66.
230: 12–14, 18.
231: 216.
233: 219 f.
234: 219 f.
235: 72, 219 f.
239–40: 52.
240: 219.
242: 66.
243: 68.
244: 252.
245: 72, 252.
246: 97.
250: 252, 257.
251–9: 256 ff.
252: 261, 263.
253: 164, 261, 263.
254: 261.
258: 262 f.
259: 258, 262 f.
263: 83.

Plato: (cont.)
267: 220.
Statesman, 65–7, 69–70, 206, 267 f.
259: 63.
260: 79.
265: 67.
266: 67, 68.
277: 68, 78, 212.
278: 46, 212, 221.
279: 63, 212.
283–7: 65 f.
286: 68.
297: 221.
Symposium, 41, 43, 174, 230.
210–11: 162, 174.
216; 18.
Theaetetus, 146, 204.
146: 50.
149–51: 83 f.
154: 78.
155: 29 f.
162: 216.
164: 86, 87.
165: 77.
171: 79.
183: 68.
187: 79, 81.
189: 83.
200–1: 81.
201–10: 55 f.
201: 58.
209: 55.
Timaeus, 74, 230.
31: 209.
51: 146.
Plotinus, 4, 247.
Posit (τίθημι), 93 f., 96.
Prantl, Carl, 213.
Primary answer, 7, 49.
Proclus, 164, 243.
Protagoras, 87 f., 141.
Προτίθεμαι, 94, 112.
Provisionality, 107 f., 109 f., 152, 157 f., 161.

Question and answer, 75–84.

Reason, 75–77.

Rodier, G., 163, 165.
Ross, Sir David, v, vii, 46 f., 102.
Russell, Bertrand, 132, 168 f.

Schaefer, Stanley, v.
Sense, 46, 75–77, 110, 143, 145, 148 ff., 154–6, 163 f., 175, 220 ff.
Shorey, Paul, 1, 82, 119, 158, 172, 231.
Sidgwick, Henry, 63, 88, 103.
Simplicius, 140.
Socrates, 7, 10, 13, 14, 16 f., 29, 41, 46–48, 71, 83 f., 89–91, 177.
Solmsen, Friedrich, 103.
Stenzel, Julius, 29, 168.
Stewart, J. A., 47.
Stocks, J. L., 193.
Συγχωρεῖν, 97.
Suidas, 68.
Syllogism, 175; defined 21; direct and indirect, 22 ff.; hypothetical, 24 f., 118 ff.; relation to definition, 48; relation to epagoge, 38 ff.; the word, 21; relation to elenchus, 20 ff., 38 ff., 46 ff.
Synthesis, v, 162–5.

Taylor, A. E., 89 f., 91, 103 ff., 141, 224 ff., 231, 232 ff., 238, 240, 241, 243, 252.
Thesis, 22, 25, 94.
Thompson, E. S., 78, 99.
Thought (διάνοια), 149, 151, 155 f., 157, 180 ff., 190–201.
Thought, history of, vi, 4–6, 27–29, 31, 192.
Τίθεμαι, 93–96.
Transcendentals, 253 f.

Ὑποτίθεμαι, 94–98.

What-is-X? question, 49–60.
Whitehead, A. N., 132, 168 f.
Wild, John, vi.

Zeller, Eduard, 163.
Zeno of Elea, 31, 47, 87 f., 91 f., 265 f., 278.

PRINTED IN GREAT BRITAIN
AT THE UNIVERSITY PRESS, OXFORD
BY VIVIAN RIDLER
PRINTER TO THE UNIVERSITY

ANCIENT
PHILOSOPHY

1. Otto Apelt. *Platonis Sophista. Recensuit, Prolegomenis et Commentariis Instruxit*

2. Grace Hadley Billings. *The Art of Transition in Plato*

3. Thomas H. Billings. *The Platonism of Philo Judaeus*

4. Ingram Bywater. *Aristotle on the Art of Poetry. A Revised Text with Critical Introduction and Commentary.*

5. Lewis Campbell. *The Theaetetus of Plato. A Revised Text and English Notes.* Second Edition

6. Henri Carteron. *La notion de force dans le système d'Aristote*

7. Harold Cherniss. *The Riddle of the Early Academy*

8. Ingemar Düring. *Aristotle's De Partibus Animalium. Critical and Literary Commentaries*

9. Ingemar Düring. *Aristotle's Chemical Treatise. Meterologica, Book IV. With an introduction and commentary*

10. Ingemar Düring. *Die Harmonienlehre des Klaudios Ptolemaios* bound with
Ingemar Düring. *Porphyrios Kommentar zur Harmonienlehre des Ptolemaios*

11. Ingemar Düring. *Ptolemaios und Porphyrios über die Musik*

12. Wilmer Cave France. *The Emperor Julian's Relation to the New Sophistic and Neo-Platonism: with a study of his style*

13. John Gibb and William Montgomery. *The Confessions of Augustine.* Second Edition

14. Carlo Giussani. *T. Lucreti Cari De Rerum Natura Libri Sex. Revisione del testo, commento e studi introduttivi*

15. Sir Thomas Heath. *Mathematics in Aristotle*

16. William A. Heidel. *Selected Papers.* Edited with an introduction by Leonardo Tarán

17. Roger Miller Jones. *The Platonism of Plutarch and Selected Papers.* Edited with an introduction by Leonardo Tarán

18. Hal Koch. *Pronoia und Paideusis. Studien über Origenes und sein Verhältnis zum Platonismus*

19. Clara Elizabeth Millerd. *On the Interpretation of Empedocles*

20. Constantin Ritter. *Bibliographies on Plato* ("Berichte . . . über Platon erschienenen Arbeiten")

21. Léon Robin. *Pyrrhon et le scepticisme grec*

22. Richard Robinson. *Plato's Earlier Dialectic.* Second Edition

23. W.D. Ross. *Aristotle's Prior and Posterior Analytics. A Revised Text with Introduction and Commentary*

24. Paul Shorey. *Selected Papers.* Edited with an introduction by Leonardo Tarán

25. Paul Shorey. *The Unity of Plato's Thought*

26. G. Stallbaum. *Platonis Opera Omnia.* (This set is published here in fourteen volumes and includes Stallbaum's commentary on Plato's *Parmenides*.)

27. E. Seymer Thompson. *The Meno of Plato, edited with Introduction, Notes, and Excursuses*

28. Eliza Gregory Wilkins. *"Know Thyself" in Greek and Latin Literature*

29. John Cook Wilson. *On the Interpretation of Plato's Timaeus. Critical studies with reference to a recent edition*
    bound with
    John Cook Wilson. *"On the Platonist Doctrine of the ἀσύμβλητοι ἀριθμοί"*

30. Martinus Wohlrab. *Platonis Theaetetus. Recensuit, Prolegomenis et Commentariis Instruxit. Editio Altera et Emendatior*